二语自由主动词汇发展 "停滞现象" 的实证研究

岳颖莱　著

吉林大学出版社

·长　春·

图书在版编目(CIP)数据

二语自由主动词汇发展"停滞现象"的实证研究 /
岳颖莱著. —长春:吉林大学出版社,2020.1

ISBN 978-7-5692-6073-1

Ⅰ.①二… Ⅱ.①岳… Ⅲ.①第二语言-词汇-研究
Ⅳ.①H003

中国版本图书馆 CIP 数据核字(2020)第 020986 号

书　　名　二语自由主动词汇发展"停滞现象"的实证研究
　　　　　　ERYU ZIYOU ZHUDONG CIHUI FAZHAN "TINGZHI XIANXIANG"
　　　　　　DE SHIZHENG YANJIU

作　　者　岳颖莱　著
策划编辑　孟亚黎
责任编辑　周　鑫
责任校对　殷丽爽
装帧设计　崔　蕾
出版发行　吉林大学出版社
社　　址　长春市人民大街 4059 号
邮政编码　130021
发行电话　0431-89580028/29/21
网　　址　http://www.jlup.com.cn
电子邮箱　jdcbs@jlu.edu.cn
印　　刷　三河市铭浩彩色印装有限公司
开　　本　787mm×1092mm　1/16
印　　张　19.25
字　　数　249 千字
版　　次　2021 年 3 月　第 1 版
印　　次　2021 年 3 月　第 1 次
书　　号　ISBN 978-7-5692-6073-1
定　　价　92.00 元

Abstract

Free active vocabulary (FAV) refers to words that can be used voluntarily by people (Laufer & Paribakht, 1998). FAV is of great significance in second language (L2) study. However, FAV seems to be difficult to be acquired. Even advanced L2 learners' vocabulary use in speaking and writing tends to be limited. As early as in 1991, Laufer (1991) found that there is a "threshold" in L2 free active vocabulary development. He found that during learners' study process, FAV fails to increase constantly with the growth of L2 proficiency. Observing this phenomenon, Laufer (1991) put forward the "Threshold Hypothesis", proposing that L2 FAV would stagnate in L2 learning.

The aim of this research was twofold: first, to have a deeper understanding of FAV developmental process; second, if FAV experiences stagnation, to find possible reasons for the stagnation and possible ways to tackle the problem. To achieve this research aim, four sub-studies were conducted, which involved both quantitative and qualitative methods.

The first quantitative sub-study is a 12-month longitudinal research. Twenty-seven randomly selected third-year university students, whose major was English, were observed for 12 months. In the first and twelfth months, a composition of about 200 words was collected; meanwhile, tests for free active vocabulary, passive vocabulary (PV) and controlled active vocabulary (CAV) were conducted. Then all scores of the tests were put into the Statistical Package for the Social Sciences (SPSS) to be analysed. The purpose of this part of study was to obtain details on FAV development, and to explore the relationship between L2 learners' free active vocabulary knowledge and other types of vocabulary knowledge.

The second quantitative sub-study is a word association research exploring the cognitive mechanism in FAV development. First, a group of frequently produced words and seldom produced words were selected. Then word association tests were conducted to explore the lexical networks of the two kinds of vocabulary in the participants' mental lexicon. Their responses to the stimulus words were classified into different categories, and the number of responses in each category was counted. Then the results were put into SPSS to be analysed. The purpose of the sub-study was to compare the lexical networks of the two types of vocabulary, which may shed some light on the lexical construction procedure in FAV development.

The first qualitative sub-study is the interview. It aimed to investigate whether students and teachers attached importance to FAV development, and whether effective teaching and learning strategies were adopted to promote FAV growth. Possible reasons for FAV stagnation were investigated as well.

The second qualitative sub-study is the documentary analysis. The course structure in the period of the 12-month longitudinal sub-study was examined. The English units taken during the period were analysed. *The College English Syllabus for English Majors* in China was examined as well. The purpose of the documentary analysis was to detect possible factors in course design that may affect FAV development.

To achieve a more comprehensive picture of FAV development, two additional sub-studies were conducted, with one being quantitative and the other being qualitative. The first one was a 36-month longitudinal study, and the second one was a documentary analysis of courses. In the 36-month longitudinal sub-study, 40 English-major university students were tracked from the end of Year One to the end of Year Four. In the first month, the twelfth month, the twenty-fourth month, and the thirty-sixth month, tests for FAV, PV and CAV were conducted. Then all scores of the tests were put into SPSS to be analysed. This sub-study attempted to obtain a more comprehensive picture on FAV development. In the documentary analysis of courses, the course structures that participants took during the 36-month longitudinal sub-study period were collected and investigated.

Results of the sub-studies led to several findings. First, it was found that the FAV threshold phenomenon existed when L2 learners reached upper-intermediate to advanced L2 proficiency level. Four features were captured in the threshold phenomenon. The first feature is that the threshold phenomenon occurs early, as it occurs at the end of Year Two of the participants' university study; the second feature is that the threshold phenomenon is long-lasting; the third feature is that the threshold phenomenon is "stubborn", as it does not grow with the growth of PV and CAV; the fourth feature is that the FAV threshold tends to occur widely, as it occurs at most of the word frequency levels.

Second, it was found that both PV and CAV kept growing when L2 learners reached upper-intermediate to advanced proficiency level; FAV was not significantly correlated with PV and CAV in this stage, and the gap between PV and FAV, and between CAV and FAV became larger.

Third, there are three tendencies in lexical network construction when a word is developing into FAV. The first tendency is that the word's lexical network tends to be semantised. The second tendency is that some types of nodes tend to increase in the process, while other types of nodes tend to decrease; and they change at different speeds. The third tendency is that the connections of the lexical network tend to get stronger and tighter. In summary, the lexical network tends to develop in a way that the word becomes easier to be accessed, activated, and retrieved.

Fourth, it was found that there were possible factors for FAV stagnation in both teaching and learning. In teaching, the first factor is that teachers seem not to have given adequate attention to FAV in classroom instruction. The second factor is that little effort has been made to facilitate students in FAV development. The third factor is that there are inadequate units for output training in the curriculum. In learning, there are several possible factors for FAV stagnation as well. The first factor is that students' effort to improve FAV may not be enough, as the strategies they adopted were rather limited; sometimes the effort was not persistent, as it was given up later. The second factor is that there is insufficient intentional learning in FAV study.

Fifth, some effective teaching and learning strategies were detected from the research. The learning strategies include sentence making with the target word, note-taking on the target word, putting down example sentences, collecting synonyms, etc. The effective teaching strategies include providing synonyms of the target word, negotiating word meanings, analysing the word's contexts, encouraging students to make sentences with the word, and raising students' attention to the word. In general, the research aim was fulfilled.

Table of Contents

Chapter 1   Introduction

1.1   Research Motivation

Free active vocabulary (FAV) refers to the words that can be used voluntarily by people (Laufer & Paribakht, 1998). FAV is of great significance in second language (L2) study. To some extent, it determines the quality of speaking and writing (Astika, 1993; Coady, Magoto, Hubbard, Graney & Mokhtari, 1993; Engber, 1995; Laufer, 1994; Yamamoto, 2011). However, it seems that FAV is difficult to be acquired, as even advanced English as a second language (ESL) learners' vocabulary use in speaking and writing tends to be limited. The weakness in FAV usage is reflected in the teaching experience of the researcher. In her eight-year ESL teaching career, the researcher found that her English-major students, including those senior students who had been studying English as a second language for over ten years, were confined to the most common, unnuanced words in writing. For example, when students needed to express "laugh repeatedly in a quiet but uncontrollable way", few of them could think of the word "giggle"; instead, most of them would use the word "laugh" or "smile", even if they knew that in this way the nuanced meaning would be lost. For another example, when they wanted to say that a tiger is stepping impatiently in cage, few of them could think of the verb "pace". A more common, basic word "walk" was usually used as a substitute, even if they knew "walk" may not be the most accurate and appropriate word in this case.

This researcher's personal experience is consistent with the finding of Jullian (2000) that although upper-intermediate to advanced L2 learners can communicate with correct grammar, they usually overuse core words. The overuse of general core words in speaking and writing not only results in a poor and child-like discourse, but also makes them unable to describe different moods and connotations with specific semantic loads (Jullian, 2000). Also, L2 learners' experience reflects this problem as well. Yu (2011) conducted a survey among 88 English-major students who were in the second year of university study. The survey shows that 87.3% of them felt that their FAV was too limited, which made them unable to express what they wanted to express (Yu, 2011).

In addition to personal experiences, some empirical studies also show that L2 learners' FAV is far from adequate, as there is a big gap between native speakers' (NSs) and L2 learners' FAV size. Cobb (2003) found that in NSs' expository texts, 70% of the words fell into the first 1,000 frequency zone; in NSs' oral conversational texts, 80% of the words fell into this zone. By contrast, as high as 90% of words used by advanced ESL learners in expository and argumentative writings were from the first 1,000 frequency zone. Cobb (2003) therefore proposed the Overuse Hypothesis that even advanced L2 learners tend to overuse general, unnuanced words. Laufer (1994) found there is a big gap between NSs and L2 learners in FAV usage as well. Laufer (1994) compared words used by a group of 18-year-old NSs, who had not entered college yet, and a group of first-year English-major university students in Israel. He found that in

NSs' argumentative writing on general topics, 25% to 28% lexical items fell into the beyond-2,000 word frequency range; by contrast, the percentage of Israeli students was only half of the NSs. The salient gap between NSs and L2 learners of various proficiency levels in FAV usage demonstrates that L2 learners' FAV size is far from being adequate. The limitedness of FAV becomes a factor that hinders the improvement of L2 learners' writing and speaking quality.

1.2   Research Background

1.2.1   Threshold Phenomenon in Free Active Vocabulary Acquisition

As early as in 1991, Laufer (1991) found that there is a "threshold" in L2 FAV development. He found that during learners' study process, FAV fails to increase constantly with the growth of L2 proficiency; its growth stops after developing to a certain level. Observing this phenomenon, Laufer (1991) put forward the "Threshold Hypothesis", proposing that L2 FAV would stagnate in L2 learning. After Laufer's research, a great deal of studies (e. g. Gu & Li, 2013; Huang, 2012; Laufer, 1994; Lu, 2008; Tan, 2006; X. Wu & Chen, 2000; G. Zhang, Han & Zhu, 2005; Y. Zhao, 2011) proved the existence of the "threshold", or as Cobb (2003) called it, the "ceiling effect". Meanwhile, as is stated in Section 1.1, there is a big gap between NSs' and L2 learners' FAV size. If the "threshold" problem cannot be solved, the efficiency of L2 learners' language study will be seriously affected.

1.2.2 Weaknesses of Past Research

Although the threshold phenomenon in L2 FAV acquisition has drawn increasing attention, relevant research is far from thorough.

First, numerous studies have proved the existence of "threshold", yet most of them did not pay specific attention to the details of the threshold. For instance, when the phenomenon occurs, does it occur at all frequency levels? Or does it occur at some of the frequency levels? What is the Lexical Frequency Profile (LFP) like when the threshold occurs?

Second, previous studies have tried to detect reasons for the emergence of threshold, but conclusions are usually unilateral. Ineffective teaching and learning strategies are always blamed for the failure of FAV's constant growth (Cui & Wang, 2006; Gu & Li, 2013; Lu, 2008; Tan, 2006; G. Zhang et al., 2005); lacking of motivation is blamed as well (Yang, 2007). It seems that cognitive causes have seldom been investigated. In addition, those factors being blamed are only speculations, not backed up by empirical studies. Little attention has been paid to learners' cognitive mechanism, which may help uncover the root causes for FAV stagnation. Meara (1990) pointed out that exploring the cognitive process in learners' vocabulary acquisition is an important part in L2 vocabulary acquisition study. The fact that L2 learners may recognise a word well but may never be able to automatically use that word indicates that the cognitive process in vocabulary acquisition may be more complicated than what people thought. However, how lexical networks affect words' retrieval and activation is still, to a great extent, elusive to people.

Third, relevant studies are primarily cross-sectional (e. g. Cui & Wang, 2006; Gu & Li, 2013; Huang, 2012; Laufer, 1998; Liu, 2001; Lu, 2008; Tan , 2006, 2007; Wen, 2006; G. Zhang et al. , 2005). Due to the large quantity of time and energy needed in a longitudinal study, most relevant research adopted cross-sectional study instead of longitudinal study to explore the developmental pattern of FAV. In addition, few studies have adopted long-time longitudinal study and track the development of different types of vocabulary knowledge simultaneously. Such studies are needed as they can help researchers obtain more accurate information on FAV development.

Fourth, literature review shows that almost no research has investigated the courses students took and checked whether some factors in course design may affect FAV progress. As English is a foreign language in China, class instruction is one of the major sources from which students obtain English training. Therefore, the course design is a significant part in L2 learning and should not be overlooked in relevant research.

Efforts were made in the present research to overcome the four weaknesses stated above. A 12-month longitudinal sub-study was conducted to track L2 learners' free active vocabulary development. Additionally, the development of passive vocabulary (PV) and controlled active vocabulary (CAV) was also tracked so that the relationships between FAV and PV as well as between FAV and CAV could be investigated. The lexical network and the units undertaken by the participants were also examined. In addition, to achieve a more comprehensive picture of the FAV development process, a longer longitudinal sub-study, which last for 36 months, was conducted. Results of the two longitudinal sub-studies were compared. Another additional sub-study was the documentary analysis, in which the courses the participating students took in the 36-month longitudinal sub-study period were collected and analysed. Results of the two documentary analysis sub-studies were compared. Details about these additional sub-studies will be introduced in Chapter 10.

1.3 Research Objectives and Research Questions

1.3.1 Research Objective One and Corresponding Research Questions

The first research objective of this study is to investigate the developmental process of FAV when L2 learners reach the upper-intermediate to advanced L2 proficiency level. The following questions are asked in relation to the research objective:

• What is the development pattern of FAV when L2 learners reach upper-intermediate to advanced proficiency level?

• If the threshold phenomenon occurs in the FAV development, what are the features of the threshold phenomenon?

1.3.2 Research Objective Two and Corresponding Research Questions

The second research objective is to investigate the relationship between FAV and PV, and the relationship between FAV and CAV. There are four research questions associated with this research objective:

• What is the developmental process of PV when L2 learners reach upper-intermediate to advanced L2 proficiency level?

- What is the relationship between FAV and PV?
- What is the developmental process of CAV when L2 learners reach upper-intermediate to advanced L2 proficiency level?
- What is the relationship between FAV and CAV?

1.3.3   Research Objective Three and Corresponding Research Questions

The third research objective is to explore how lexical network is constructed in the process of FAV development. Based on the research objective, one research question is proposed:

- What are the differences (if any) of the mental lexicon organisation between frequently produced words and seldom produced words?

1.3.4   Research Objective Four and Corresponding Research Questions

The fourth research objective is to find possible factors in learning and teaching that may affect FAV development. Based on the research objective, two questions are designed:

- What are the possible factors in teaching that affect FAV development?
- What are the possible factors in learning that affect FAV development?

1.3.5   Research Objective Five and Corresponding Research Questions

If the threshold phenomenon is detected in the longitudinal

sub-study, a fifth research objective and corresponding research questions will be proposed. The fifth research objective is to find effective ways to tackle the FAV threshold phenomenon. The research question is:

- What are the effective strategies (if any) to tackle FAV threshold phenomenon?

1. 4　Participants

The participants of the study were English-major students at a public university in China. All the participants experienced standard education in China (primary school, junior high, senior high, and university). These students were at the end of Year Three when the research was conducted. With English being their major, they were considered to have a high level of motivation to study the language. The students' ages were mostly 21 to 22. It was believed that the subjects were suitable for this study, since being English-major students in the third year at the university, they had been studying English for at least nine years (six years in middle school before entering college), and had done a number of discipline-related units. The courses that the participants took were designed according to *The Syllabus of English Courses for College English Majors* by the Chinese Ministry of Education. The syllabus requires that in the four years' study, English-major students should receive 2,000 to 2,200 academic hours' discipline-related instruction. Also, according to the syllabus, by the end of the third-year study, the English-major students should reach the Sixth Proficiency Level. The syllabus provides a detailed description on the Six Proficiency Level. In speaking, learners should be able to pronounce English words correctly, and they should be able to speak English naturally and fluently; they should be able to introduce China's well-known and historic sceneries fluently and correctly, and introduce China's policies and conditions fluently as well; they should be able to express their views systematically, coherently, and in an in-depth way. In vocabulary size, they should be able to recognise 7,000 to 9,000 English words. In listening, they should be able to understand the news report from the channels of English-speaking countries; they should be able to have a dictation of recordings that speak 150 words per minute, and the error rate should be lower than 6%. In reading, students should be able to read the politics articles as difficult as articles in magazines of *The Times* and *The New York Times*; they should be able to read the original English literature as difficult as *The Great Gatsby*, and they should be able to read the biographies as difficult as *The Rise and Fall of the Third Reich*. In addition to understanding the works, they should be able to analyse the views of the author, the structure, the genre and styles of the works. The reading speed should reach 140 to 180 words per minute, and the under-standing rate should be no less than 75%. Within 5 minutes, they should be able to read an article of 1,300 words, and after reading they should be able to tell the gist of the article. In writing, students are required to be able to write summaries of stories, book reports, course papers, and formal letters. The language they use in writing should be correct and appropriate, and the writing should reflect in-depth thinking. According to the syllabus, the writing speed should be 250 to 300 words per minute. Meanwhile, students are required to be familiar with the use of all sorts of encyclopedia, including the Encyclopedia Britannica and the Encyclopedia

Americana. The syllabus requires that students should be able to independently seek answers for questions in language and in other world knowledge. At the end of the fourth-year study, the proficiency level required by the syllabus is even higher. Based on the requirement of the syllabus, it is postulated that the participants in this research are representative of upper-intermediate to advanced ESL students in China.

1.5 Research Methods

The study was conducted by means of a mixed approach, involving both quantitative and qualitative methods. The quantitative sub-studies include:

(1) A 12-month longitudinal sub-study. Twenty to fourty randomly selected third-year university students, whose major was English, were observed for 12 months. In the first and twelfth months, a composition of about 200 words was collected; meanwhile, tests for FAV, PA and CAV were conducted. Then all the scores of the tests were put into SPSS and analysed. The purpose of this part of study was to obtain details on FAV development, and to explore the relationship between L2 learners' FAV knowledge and other vocabulary knowledge.

(2) A sub-study on the cognitive mechanism in FAV development. First, a group of frequently produced words and seldom produced words were selected. The selection process will be introduced in Chapter 5. Then word association tests were conducted to explore the lexical networks of the two kinds of vocabulary in subjects' mental lexicon. Responses to the stimulus words were classified into different categories, and the number of responses

in each category was counted. Then results were put into SPSS and analysed. The purpose of the sub-study was to compare the lexical networks of the two types of vocabulary, which may shed some light on the lexical construction procedure in FAV development.

The qualitative research includes:

(1) Interviews were conducted. The interview aimed to investigate whether students and teachers attached importance to FAV development, and whether effective teaching and learning strategies were adopted to promote FAV growth. Possible reasons for FAV stagnation were investigated as well.

(2) A documentary analysis was conducted. The course structure in the period of the 12-month longitudinal sub-study was examined. The English units taken in the period were analysed. *The Syllabus of English Courses for College English Majors* by the Chinese Ministry of Education (2000) in China was examined as well. The purpose of the documentary analysis was to detect possible factors in course design that may affect FAV development.

1.6   Research Significance

1.6.1   Theoretical Significance

The study further testifies and develops the "Threshold Hypothesis" put forward by Laufer (1991). In addition to testifying the hypothesis, more detailed information on the FAV threshold phenomenon was obtained. The study also helps researchers have a better understanding of FAV stagnation by exploring the different lexical organisation of frequently produced words and seldom produced words. This may shed some light on the cognitive mechanism of FAV development.

1.6.2 Practical Significance

The study helps researchers and ESL teachers to obtain more knowledges on FAV development and a better understanding of the FAV threshold phenomenon. Moreover, effective teaching and learning strategies to tackle FAV stagnation are detected. Teachers and learners can obtain more guidance from this research to tackle the problem.

1.7 Outline of the Book

The book, which is a report of the entire research project, contains ten chapters in total. The ten chapters are: *Introduction*; *Literature Review*; *Methodology*; *The Developmental Process of Free Active Vocabulary*; *Comparison of Lexical Network between Frequently and Seldom Produced Words*; *Interview*; *Documentary Analysis*; *Discussions, Findings, Implications and Recommendations*; *Conclusion*; *Extended Research*. A summary of the content of each chapter is presented below.

Chapter 1: *Introduction*

This chapter serves as an introduction to the entire research project. To justify the necessity to do this research, the chapter first presents research motivation, findings in past research, and limitations of past research. Then it describes the research objectives of this study. The research questions are specified as well, followed by a brief description of participants and research methods. The chapter then presents ethical considerations. The significance of the research, which includes both theoretical and practical significance, is discussed. The chapter ends with the outline of the entire book.

Chapter 2: *Literature Review*

This chapter reviews a range of literature related to the research topic. The aim of the literature review is to provide the project with theoretical foundations. It firstly examines and discusses the classifications of vocabulary knowledge. This step leads to definitions of the key concepts used in this research, including passive vocabulary, controlled active vocabulary, and free active vocabulary. The chapter then examines instruments measuring different types of vocabulary knowledge, which helps to select suitable instruments for this research. Relevant literature on mental lexicon is reviewed as well, which provides theoretical background for the lexical network sub-study in this research. Moreover, the chapter has an in-depth review of past studies on L2 FAV threshold phenomenon; findings and limitations of those studies are investigated and discussed.

Chapter 3: *Methodology*

This chapter is an overview of the methodology adopted in the research. It first introduces the research aim and objectives, then describes the mixed-method approach adopted in the study. The research instruments used in the data collection, together with participants and sampling process, are described as well. The pilot studies and the data analysis methods are also generally introduced. To present in a more cohesive way, the details on the pilot study for each sub-study and data analysis methods used in each sub-study are provided in the following chapters with the formal sub-study.

Chapter 4: *The Developmental Process of Free Active Vocabulary*

This chapter tracks the developmental process of FAV in a 12-month period of time. It also investigates the relationship between FAV and other types of vocabulary (i. e., the passive vocabulary and controlled active vocabulary). The chapter first poses research questions, then presents research method, including instruments, data collection, data preparation and data analysis. This is followed by a discussion of the results. Conclusions are made at the end of the chapter.

Chapter 5: *Comparison of Lexical Network between Frequently and Seldom Produced Words*

This chapter investigates and compares the lexical networks of frequently produced words and seldom produced words. The differences between the two (if any) may shed some light on the lexical network construction in FAV development. Moreover, detecting the differences may help researchers and ESL teachers find effective ways to tackle the stagnation problem. This chapter first raises research questions, then presents research methods, including research instruments, data collection procedures, and data analysis. At the end of the chapter, results are discussed, and conclusions are made.

Chapter 6: *Interview*

This chapter aims to investigate whether students and teachers attach importance to FAV development, and whether effective teaching and learning strategies are adopted to promote FAV growth. Possible reasons for FAV stagnation will be investigated as well. The chapter first poses research aims, then presents research method, including instruments, data collection, data preparation and data analysis. At the end of the chapter conclusions on the findings of this sub-study are made.

Chapter 7：*Documentary Analysis*

This chapter investigates the course structure students took in the period of the 12-month longitudinal sub-study. *The Syllabus of English Courses for College English Majors* in China by the Chinese Ministry of Education（2000）was examined as well. The aim of the documentary analysis is to examine whether there are factors in course design that may affect students' FAV development. The chapter first poses research questions, then presents research method, including data collection, data preparation and data analysis. At the end of the chapter conclusions on the findings of this sub-study are made.

Chapter 8：*Discussions, Findings, Implications and Recommendations*

In light of the previous chapters, this chapter examines whether the five research objectives have been addressed and achieved through the research. Discussion is also made to examine whether the research questions have been answered satisfactorily. It first has a general discussion on the results, then presents findings pertaining to the research objectives and research questions, then discusses the theoretical and pedagogical implications of the findings. At last, recommendations for FAV development are provided.

Chapter 9：*Conclusion*

This chapter is a conclusion of the research. It first provides an overview of the entire research, which involves a reflection of the research journey and achievements from the journey. It also summarises the major findings and discusses the significances of the research. Then limitations of the research are disclosed, and possible directions for future study are provided.

Chapter 10：*Extended Research*

This chapter introduces two additional sub-studies, which

include a 36-month longitudinal sub-study and a documentary analysis. The 36-month longitudinal sub-study was conducted to obtain a more comprehensive picture of the FAV development process. The documentary analysis was conducted to further investigate the factors that may affect FAV growth. Results of the two longitudinal sub-studies in this research were compared, and so were results of the two documentary analyses in this research. Findings of these two sub-studies supplemented those of the primary study in achieving the objectives of the research.

Chapter 2   Literature Review

2.1   Introduction

It has been widely accepted that vocabulary is important in ESL learning. Therefore, to a great extent, "improving our understanding of L2 acquisition depends on improving our understanding of how learners acquire individual words and word parts" (Barcroft, 2004). Meara and Fitzpatrick (2000) hold that communicative effectiveness could be achieved more successfully by learners with a larger vocabulary than by learners with a smaller one. Since the 1990s, L2 vocabulary acquisition study has drawn increasing attention, and a large number of studies have been conducted. Among those studies, the classification of vocabulary knowledge and its measurement play a critical role. However, until now, there have been no agreed standards on how to classify and measure vocabulary knowledge.

In this chapter, past studies on the classifications and measurements of vocabulary knowledge are reviewed, and the classification and measurements adopted in this research are justified. Studies on the L2 mental lexicon, which is a significant part in this research, is presented and discussed as well. Then past studies on free active vocabulary threshold phenomenon, including their weaknesses are introduced and discussed. At the end of the chapter, the terminology and working definitions used in this study are provided.

2.2 The Classification of Vocabulary Knowledge

With the development of vocabulary acquisition research, more and more researchers have realized that knowing a word is not an all-or-nothing phenomenon. On the contrary, knowing a word is a complicated process, which involves various aspects and degrees. Therefore, researchers have attempted to find appropriate ways to classify vocabulary knowledge, either from degree perspective, or from dimension perspective.

2.2.1 Classifying Vocabulary Knowledge from Degree Perspective

One way of categorising vocabulary knowledge is to categorise it by different degrees or levels at which learners acquire the word. Since passive and active knowledge is the most widely used classification, these two types of knowledge will be introduced first.

The first method is to classify vocabulary into passive vocabulary and active vocabulary. Most researchers distinguish passive and active knowledge of a word (Laufer & Goldstein, 2004; Meara, 1990; P. Nation, 2001). According to Laufer and Goldstein (2004), passive knowledge concerns with listening and reading, and it indicates that people are able to comprehend the input. In other words, they are able to "perceive the form of the word and retrieve its meaning or meanings" (Laufer & Goldstein, 2004). Active knowledge is related to speaking and writing. It means that "we can retrieve the appropriate spoken or written word form of the meaning that we want to express" (Laufer & Goldstein, 2004). Passive vocabulary is also called "receptive vocabulary", and active vocabulary is called "productive vocabulary" as well.

Currently, passive vocabulary and active vocabulary have been widely used in L2 vocabulary acquisition research, and provide ESL researchers and teachers with a basic distinction on students' vocabulary knowledge levels. However, the pro-blem of receptive/productive classification is that the distinction is not clear enough (Yue, 2012). Although researchers have widely used receptive and productive vocabulary (or passive and active vocabulary) to evaluate acquisition results, almost no studies have given the exact definitions of the two types of knowledge (Yue, 2012). As pointed out by Read (2004), it is too vague to divide vocabulary knowledge into receptive and productive, and the employment of them has shown great arbitrariness. The vagueness of the classification causes it hard to measure different levels of vocabulary knowledge sufficiently (Yue, 2012). For example, in some studies, if testees can make a sentence with a given word, they are considered to have mastered the active or productive knowledge. However, in a strict sense, productive vocabulary are words that can be activated without external stimulus (Meara, 1990). Therefore, productive vocabulary, in its strict sense, cannot be measured by asking students to make sentences with the given words, as the given words serve as external stimuli (Yue, 2012). Yue (2012) pointed out that *The Vocabulary Knowledge Scale* by Wesche and Paribakht (1996) has been widely used to measure vocabulary knowledge (e. g. File & Adams,

2010；Lei，Wei，Ye & Zhang，2007；J. Wu，Lang & Dang，2007），but it has the same problem. In *The Vocabulary Knowledge Scale* test，the highest level of vocabulary knowledge is demonstrated by sentence-making with the given word. Therefore，the "productive vocabulary"，in its strict sense，is in fact a blind point in the test.

The vagueness of the classification makes different researchers adopt different measuring instruments to measure productive vocabulary，and the instruments in fact test different aspects of vocabulary knowledge. For example，in the studies conducted by Fan（2000），Webb（2009），X. Wu and Chen（2000），productive vocabulary was measured by sentence-completion or L1-to-L2 translation. In the research work of Laufer（1998），Laufer and Paribakht（1998），and Tan（2007），productive vocabulary was measured by compositions. The ability to use a word with prompts and the ability to use the word without prompts are evidently two different capabilities：one needs external stimulus to retrieve the word，and the other does not need it at all. The external stimulus means the external hint. For example，in the sentence "She asked for another opp _____ to take the test. "，the external stimulus "opp" is provided for testees to produce the word "opportunity". The vagueness in productive vocabulary classification tends to create misunderstandings and confusions when researchers attempt to compare different results of different studies，and it may lead them to draw misleading conclusions.

Laufer and Goldstein（2004）developed a hierarchy to overcome the confusion caused by the active vocabulary/passive vocabulary distinction. The hierarchy includes four degrees of knowledge，which are active recall（the ability to spell the word with the L1 equivalent translation），passive recall（the ability to

write equivalent L1 word for the given L2 word), active recognition (the ability to recognise the suitable L2 word according
to the given L1 word), and passive recognition (the ability to
choose the correct meaning of the given L2 word). However, it
can be seen that the highest level in the hierarchy, the active recall,
only involves L2 learners' spelling capability when they encounter
the prompt. The higher level of vocabulary knowledge, the capability to use a word without external stimulus, is still a blind
point in this hierarchy.

Laufer and Paribakht (1998) tried to overcome the deficiency
as well. They further divided the active vocabulary into two categories: the controlled active vocabulary and the free active vocabulary.
According to them, the controlled active vocabulary are words that
can be used with external prompts, and free active vocabulary
are words that can be used automatically and voluntarily by
learners without external prompts. For example, in the task of
filling in the blank "I like to eat ap _____ pies. ", the external
stimulus "ap" is provided to elicit testees to produce the word
"apple". If testees can write the word correctly, they are considered
to have grasped the controlled active vocabulary knowledge of
"apple". If testees can use the word "apple" in speaking or writing
without any external prompt, then they are considered to have
grasped the free active vocabulary knowledge of the word.
Laufer (1998) believed that it is necessary to distinguish controlled
active vocabulary and free active vocabulary, as words produced
with prompts may not be produced when there is no prompt.

The categorisation of passive, controlled active and free active
vocabularies can help researchers to solve the problem of classification vagueness efficiently. Based on this system of categorisation,
it can be seen that the studies by Fan (2000), Webb (2008), X.

Wu and Chen (2000) are on controlled active vocabulary, whereas the studies by Laufer (1998), Laufer and Paribakht (1998) and Tan (2007) are on free active vocabulary. Now it is clear that these two groups of studies cannot be compared with each other, as they in fact focus on different degrees of vocabulary knowledge.

In addition to the classification introduced above, there are other approaches to classify vocabulary knowledge from the degree perspective. For example, Wesche and Paribakht (1996) divided vocabulary knowledge into three levels, including the initial recognition (oral or written), the comprehension of common connotations, and the ability to produce the word quickly and correctly in various contexts. This classification, however, still overlooks the difference between the ability to produce words with prompts, and the ability to produce words without prompts. Therefore, comparing all the classifications above, it is believed that the classification by Laufer and Paribakht (1998) is more comprehensive. This research has adopted the classification by Laufer and Paribakht (1998), which divides vocabulary knowledge into three categories: passive knowledge (i. e. , learners know the meaning of the word), controlled active knowledge (i. e. , learners know the meaning and spelling of the word when given stimulus), and free active knowledge (i. e. , learners can use the word without any prompts).

2. 2. 2　Classifying Vocabulary Knowledge from Dimension Perspective

In addition to the degree perspective, vocabulary knowledge can be categorised from the dimensional perspective as well. It is believed that acquiring a word involves acquiring different aspects of the word (Qian, 1999). As early as in 1976, Richards proposed a "Vocabulary Knowledge Framework", which involves seven dimensions of vocabulary knowledge. The dimensions and their definitions are presented in Table 2.1.

Table 2. 1   Dimensions in the Vocabulary Knowledge
Framework by Richards (1976)

Frequency	the knowledge on the degree of probability of encountering a word in speech or print
Register	the knowledge on limitations of using a word based on its function and situation
Position	the knowledge on syntactic behaviour associated with a word
Form	the knowledge on underlying form and derivatives
Association	the knowledge on the network of associations connecting a word with other words in a language
Meaning-concept	the knowledge on the semantic value of a word
Meaning-association	the knowledge on the different meanings associated with a word

Qian (1999) suggested that vocabulary knowledge should involve pronunciation, meaning, register, spelling, frequency, morphological, syntactic, and collocational properties.

2.2.3 Classifying Vocabulary Knowledge from both Degree and Dimension Perspective

Although most studies categorise vocabulary knowledge from either the degree perspective or the dimension perspective, some researchers attempted to include both perspectives in the categorisation. Nation (1990) classified vocabulary knowledge into two levels: receptive level and productive level. In each of the two levels, he proposed four dimensions: form (spoken/written), position (grammatical patterns/collocation), function (frequency/appropriateness), and meaning (concept/associations). Therefore, Nation's categorisation involves both levels and dimensions of vocabulary knowledge. Nation (1990) framework can be considered as a comparatively comprehensive classification of vocabulary knowledge, as it includes both levels and dimensions of vocabulary knowledge. However, due to the vagueness of productive vocabulary/receptive vocabulary distinction, this classification needs further improvement.

The list of Webb (2005, 2007, 2009) is relatively comprehensive as well. He proposed that vocabulary knowledge includes five dimensions at two levels, which is demonstrated in Table 2.2.

Table 2.2　The Vocabulary Knowledge Classification by Webb (2005,2007,2009)

Level	Dimensions
Receptive Level	Knowledge of orthographic form
	Knowledge of meaning and form
	Knowledge of grammatical functions
	Knowledge of syntax
	Knowledge of association
Productive Level	Knowledge of orthographic form
	Knowledge of grammatical functions
	Knowledge of syntax
	Knowledge of association
	Knowledge of meaning and form

Although the classification by Webb (2005,2007,2009) is comprehensive, the weakness of it is evident. The classification seems to be idealized, and it may be difficult to measure all the aspects in one research.

In summary, there are various classifications of vocabulary knowledge, either from the dimension point of view, or from the degree point of view, or from both. In this research, the vocabulary knowledge was studied from the degree point of view, as it aimed to investigate the development of free active vocabulary, and to check its correlation with other levels of vocabulary knowledge.

2. 3　The Measurement of Vocabulary Knowledge

2.3.1　Breadth and Depth of Vocabulary Knowledge

In order to understand different measuring methods for vocabulary knowledge, it is necessary to review the breadth and depth of vocabulary knowledge first. The breadth of vocabulary knowledge indicates the number of words someone knows. This is also understood as the "size" of one's vocabulary. In other words, the breadth of vocabulary knowledge means how many words a learner knows (Wesche & Paribakht, 1996). The focus of the breadth is on learners' vocabulary as a whole, rather than on a specific word. By contrast, the depth of vocabulary knowledge focuses more on individual words, as it means how well a learner knows about a word (Wesche & Paribakht, 1996). The depth of vocabulary knowledge indicates "the quality of the learner's vocabulary knowledge" (Read, 1993), or the "degrees" of lexical acquisition.

2.3.2 Measuring Vocabulary Knowledge of Individual Words

2.3.2.1 Measuring the Dimensional Knowledge of Individual Words

Qwing to the fact that vocabulary knowledge is multifaceted, measuring vocabulary knowledge is not a simple task. It is usually complicated to measure the multi-dimensional vocabulary knowledge, and various sub-tests are needed. As pointed out by Zareva, Schwanenflugel Nikolova (2005), "although it is theoretically possible to describe what it means to know a word, it is hardly possible in practice to design a test that would measure all of the traits". Webb (2007) is one of the few scholars who attempted to design a package of instruments to measure different dimensions of vocabulary knowledge. His instruments include the measurement of written form, meaning, grammatical function, syntax, and association of the target words. Webb's tests not only assess the different dimensions of vocabulary knowledge, but also take the depth of knowledge into consideration. His tests include aspects of meaning, form, and position in receptive level and productive level respectively. At the productive level, written from, meaning, and grammatical function are assessed by dictation, translation, and sentence construction respectively, while syntax and association are measured by asking testees to produce the syntagmatic or semantic association with the prompt words. At the receptive level, the meaning, form and position are assessed by multiple-choice tests. The description of the measurement is presented in Table 2.3.

Table 2.3   The Vocabulary Knowledge Measurement
Instruments by Webb (2007)

Test type	Knowledge measured
Spelling	Productive knowledge of orthographic form
Multiole-choice	Receptive knowledge of orthographic form
Translation	Receptive recall of meaning and form
Sentence construction	Productive knowledge of grammatical functions
Write a syntagmatic associate	Productive knowledge of syntax
Write a paradigmatic associate	Productive knowledge of association
Multiple-choice	Receptive knowledge of grammatical functions
Multiple-choice	Receptive knowledge of syntax
Multiple-choice	Receptive knowledge of association
Multiple-choice	Receptive knowledge of meaning and form

The strengths of Webb's tests are evident: various dimensions of vocabulary knowledge on different levels are tested, which can offer researchers a comprehensive understanding of the testees' level of knowledge. However, the test has weaknesses as well. First, the productive knowledge in Webb (2007) is only assessed by giving testees prompt words and asking them to make syntagmatic or semantic associations. This means the highest knowledge level the assessment can measure is the controlled active level, and the free active level of knowledge remains a blind point in this assessment. Second, it needs a large amount of time to finish all the sub-tests, as there are ten sub-tests of different formats for each target word, which is time-consuming. Third, it is time-consuming to researchers as well, as researchers need to design a large quantity of test items.

Another instrument measuring different dimensions of vocabulary knowledge is designed by Gina, Jennifer, Jill, Marco and Guy

(2011). Six vocabulary knowledge dimensions are included in the instrument, including recognition, definition, classification/ example, context, application and interrelatedness. An example was provided on how to measure the multiple dimensions of vocabulary knowledge by the instrument, which is presented in Table 2.4.

Table 2.4 An Example of Vocabulary Knowledge Measurement by Gina et al. (2011)

Word-knowledge Dimension	Item
Recognition	How well do you know the word <u>evaporation</u>? ○I have not seen or heard this word before. ○I have seen or heard this word, but I am not sure what it means. ○I have seen or heard this word, and I think I know what it means. ○I have seen or heard this word many times; I know what it means.
Definition	What is <u>evaporation</u>? ○The process by which a substance cools off ○The process by which a liquid changes to a gas ○The process by which a gas changes to a liquid ○The process of mixing together liquids of different temperatures
Example	Which of these is an example of <u>evaporation</u>? ○Rain collecting in puddles ○Wet clothes drying in a dryer ○Water cooling in a refrigerator ○Water dripping from an icicle
Context	Which of these sentences uses the word <u>evaporation</u> correctly? ○Heat slows down evaporation. ○When water evaporates, it remains a liquid. ○Evaporation may cause a river or lake to flood. ○Evaporation may cause a puddle to get smaller.

Continued

Word-knowledge Dimension	Item		
Application	Can a table go through the process of <u>evaporation</u>?	○Yes	○No
	Does temperature affect <u>evaporation</u>?	○Yes	○No
	Is <u>evaporation</u> part of the water cycle?	○Yes	○No
	Is <u>evaporation</u> the opposite of condensation?	○Yes	○No
Relatedness	Which two words are most closely related to <u>evaporation</u>? (Choose two.) ○Air ○Solid ○Runoff ○Water vapor ○Measurement		

Gina et al. (2011) thinks that this instrument needs further development to make it more comprehensive. More dimensions should be included in the instrument, including the ability to recall different meanings of polysemous words and the understanding of the morphological make-up of words. It is noticed that this instrument, just like the instrument designed by Webb (2007), does not measure the free active knowledge of the target words as well.

2.3.2.2　Measuring the Depth of Knowledge for Individual Words

As discussed in previous sections, measurement of the depth of vocabulary knowledge does not only examine whether a learner knows a specific word, but also assess how well he/she knows about the word. The depth of vocabulary knowledge is usually expressed by scales. The four basic stages by Dale (1965) can be considered as the earliest instrument to test the depth of vocabulary knowledge. The four stages are:

Stage 1: I never saw it before.

Stage 2: I've heard of it, but I don't know what it means.

Stage 3: I recognise it in context: it has something to do with _____.

Stage 4: I know it.

The four-stage scale is the earliest effort to measure the depth of vocabulary knowledge. However, upon a closer look, it can be found that this test has a low level of reliability. If the testee chooses the fourth stage, "I know it", then it is assumed that he/she has grasped the word's highest level of knowledge. However, from stage 4, it cannot be judged whether the testee's knowledge on the word is correct or not, or to what extent he/she knows about the word. Therefore, it is evident that this instrument needs further improvement.

The instrument designed by Wesche and Paribakht (1996) can be considered as a development on the four-stage measurement by Dale (1965). This instrument is called the Vocabulary Knowledge Scale (VKS), which is a self-report instrument consisting of five scales. The five scales are five statements describing different levels of the testees' knowledge (or familiarity) with the target word:

Ⅰ. I don't remember having seen this word before.

Ⅱ. I have seen this word before but I don't know what it means.

Ⅲ. I have seen this word before and I think it means _____. (synonym or translation)

Ⅳ. I know this word. It means _____. (synonym or translation)

Ⅴ. I can use this word in a sentence, e. g.: _____. (write a sentence)

Wesche and Paribakht (1996) believed that the VKS can help measure learners' knowledge of the target word effectively, ranging from complete unfamiliarity, to the recognition of the word and partial meaning, then to the use of the word in sentences with grammatical and semantic accuracy. Since the VKS was designed, it has been widely used as an instrument in vocabulary acquisition research. To a great extent, the VKS has overcome the weakness of Dale's (1965) instrument. It does not stop at asking testees whether they know or do not know the word, but further checks how well they know about that word, including its meaning and grammatical use. For example, if the student chooses Ⅳ, "I know this word. It means _____. ", but the meaning he gives is incorrect, the score he gets will be the same as Ⅱ, "I have seen this word before but I don't know what it means. "; also, if he chooses Ⅴ, "I can use this word in a sentence, e. g. : _____. ", but the sentence he writes is incorrect, then his score will be equal to Ⅱ, Ⅲ, or Ⅳ, depending on the knowledge level he demonstrated in that sentence. Therefore, compared with Dale's (1965) assessment, the VKS can provide a more accurate and objective judgment on the subject's depth of knowledge. In the word association sub-study of this research, VKS was adopted to measure testees' depth of knowledge, which was called as the "familiarity level" with the stimulus words used in the word association tests.

2.3.3   Measuring Vocabulary Knowledge of the Entire Vocabulary

2.3.3.1   Measuring the Breadth of Passive Vocabulary

As discussed in previous paragraphs, the breadth of vocabulary refers to the number of words that someone knows. The breadth of vocabulary is also known as the "size" of vocabulary. Different instruments are adopted to measure vocabulary size at different knowledge levels. One of the tests that have been widely accepted to assess the passive vocabulary size is Nation's (1990) Vocabulary Levels Test (VLT). VLT is considered to be the most widely known instrument to measure the size of receptive words (Meara & Alcoy, 2010; Read, 2004). The test provides a rough estimate of a learner's receptive vocabulary size in the form of a vocabulary profile (Meara & Alcoy, 2010). It covers the 10,000 most frequent English words, and consists of five levels according to word frequencies: the first 2,000 word frequency band, the 2,001 to 3,000 word frequency band, the 4,001 to 5,000 word frequency band, the University Word List, and the 9,001 to 10,000 word frequency band. In the test, each frequency level has 10 sections, and each section comprises six words and three definitions. Words in each level of the test are representative of all the words at that level (Laufer & Paribhkt, 1998). Testees are asked to match the target words with the corresponding definitions. An example by Nation (1990) is given below.

1 dozen

2 empire ＿＿＿＿＿＿＿ chance

3 gift ＿＿＿＿＿＿＿ twelve

4 opportunity ＿＿＿＿＿＿＿ money paid to the government

5 relief

6 tax

The strength of the VLT is that it is simple to be conducted and easy to be understood. In the past 30 years, the test has been widely adopted for language teaching and research (e. g. Laufer & Nation, 1995; Laufer & Paribakht, 1998; Meara & Alcoy, 2010; Schmitt & Meara, 1997; Schmitt & Clapham, 2001).

Another test measuring receptive vocabulary size is the Yes/No Test (Meara & Buxton, 1987). Similar to VLT, the test aims to estimate testees' receptive vocabulary size by using a group of sample words that cover multiple word frequency levels. The test requires testees to tick the words that they know in a word list.

The advantage of the test is that it is easy to be conducted. Its simplicity makes it able to cover a large number of words but only need a small amount of time, which increases the reliability of the test (Read, 2000). However, the weakness of the test is evident as well. By simply asking testees whether they know a word or not, researchers cannot judge from the answer whether testees truly know the word or not. It is possible that some testees think that they know a word, but in fact they do not know it, or their knowledge on the word is not correct. Therefore, in this research, the Vocabulary Levels Test (VLT) by Nation (1990) was chosen to be the instrument measuring testees' receptive vocabulary.

2.3.3.2   Measuring the Breadth of Controlled Active Vocabulary

Currently, there is only one test designed to measure the size of controlled active vocabulary. It is possibly due to the fact that controlled active vocabulary has not drawn as much attention as receptive vocabulary and free active vocabulary have. The test was designed by Laufer and Nation (1999). In the test, sentences are provided as contexts, and the first two to three letters of the target words are provided as prompts. Testees are then required to complete the missing words. For example, in the test a sentence is given as: I'm glad we had this opp _____ to talk. Then students are asked to fill in the blank. In this case, the right answer should be "ortunity".

Similar to the VLT, the test of controlled active knowledge includes five sections to represent five frequency levels. Each section has 18 test items, and therefore there are 90 items in total. According to Laufer and Paribahkt's (1998) scoring standard, testees' answers are to be marked as correct if they are semantically correct. Target words will still be marked as correct when they are wrong in grammatical form (e. g. wrong tense), or when there is a spelling error that does not distort the word (e. g. "recieve" instead of "receive").

The controlled active vocabulary test has weakness as well. In the test, the first several letters of the target word are given in a context, and students are required to write the complete word according to the context. In this way, the test's validity can also be questionable. For example, a test item which tests the word "treasure" could be: The pirates buried the trea＿＿＿＿＿ on a desert island. If the testee does not understand the given sentence, or if the designed sentence is semantically not clear enough, testees may not be able to produce the target word, even if they know the word well. In this case, the test would fail to examine what it intends to examine. In order to ensure that the understanding of the sentence is not a barrier for the word production, it is suggested that the L1 translation of the target word or the translation of the sentence is added to the original test. For example, in a test for Chinese testees, the original test sentence "Pup＿＿＿＿＿ must hand in their papers by the end of the week." is suggested to be changed into "Pup＿＿＿＿＿ must hand in their papers by the end of the week. (小学生们必须在本周末之前上交他们的作文)". In this way, the production of the target word will solely depend on the subject's controlled active knowledge, rather than other factors.

2.3.3.3　Measuring the Breadth of Free Active Vocabulary

Free active vocabulary is more difficult to be assessed than receptive and controlled active vocabulary. The reason is that the vocabulary produced by learners are context-specific, and it is almost impossible to calculate the true size or range of someone's entire vocabulary pool from a small sample of produced words (Meara & Fitzpatrick, 2000). Usually there are two test styles to assess the size of free active vocabulary: by discourse or by word associations. These two test styles will be analysed and compared in this section.

Laufer and Nation (1995) designed a discourse-based test to measure free active vocabulary size. It is a profile called Lexical Frequency Profile (LFP). In LFP, the frequency has three levels: Level 1 contains the first 1,000 most frequently used words in English (the frequent words); Level 2 contains the second most frequently used words (the less frequent words); Level 3 is composed of Xue and Nation's (1984) University Word List, which has 836 word families (the infrequent words). The rest of the words are considered to be "not-in-the-lists" words. The LFP's computer version is called VocabProfile (VP). Teachers can analyse students' written essays by inputting the essays into Vocab-Profile, and the program will classify the words in the essays into Level 1, Level 2, Level 3, and "not in the lists". The higher the percentage of infrequent words, the larger the subject's free active vocabulary is estimated to be. According Laufer and Nation (1995), LFP has a high reliability. VocabProfile was later developed into another version which is called RANGE (Heatley, Nation & Coxhead, 2002; Nation & Heatley, 1994).

The discourse-based tests offer researchers a way to assess the elusive free active vocabulary size. The computer-adaptive program of VP and RANGE makes the assessment convenient and efficient. However, it should be noted that the discourse-based tests can only provide researchers with a relative value of testees' free active vocabulary size; it cannot provide them with an absolute number of how many free active words a testee has. Moreover, this test style has drawbacks as well. It is believed that no less than 200 words are needed, to ensure the reliability of the test (Laufer & Nation, 1995). The test therefore is time-consuming, and is especially challenging to low-level learners, who may feel reluctant to produce a long written text for evaluation (Meara & Alcoy, 2010).

An alternative test that attempts to avoid the efficiency problem of discourse-based measurement is the spew test. Instead of asking testees to produce essays, spew tests require subjects to produce words with a specific feature, for example, words that start with a specific letter (Meara & Fitzpatrick, 2000). Compared with discourse-based tests, spew tests overcome the drawback of inefficiency. However, the reliability of spew tests needs more improvement (Meara & Fitzpatrick, 2000). Currently this assessing approach is still in its preliminary stage, and there is no reliable scoring standard yet. Therefore, the spew test is not ready to be used yet.

Another free active vocabulary test based on association mode is the Lex30 test. In the Lex30 test, testees are presented with 30 stimulus words, and they are required to produce four responses to each of the stimulus words. There is no limit for testees' production from the stimuli. The 30 stimulus words are selected according to the following criteria (Meara & Fitzpatrick, 2000). First, the words are highly frequent words from the first 1,000 wordlist in Nation (1984), so that even a low-proficiency learner can recognise them. This makes the test suitable for learners across a wide range of proficiency levels. Second, all the stimulus words can typically elicit various responses. Additionally, all the stimulus words elicit responses in which at least half of them are beyond the first 1,000 wordlist. The reason for this criterion is that infrequent words are believed to be the true indicators of a large productive vocabulary.

Compared with discourse-based test model, the advantages of Lex30 test are evident. It does not require testees to write a long composition, and it does not need to be re-written into computer for analysis. Lex30 can be done on the computer and then scored automatically by the computer program. Therefore, Lex30 is more efficient, less time-consuming (usually 15 minutes), and easier to be conducted. Furthermore, compared with discourse-based tests, Lex30 test surpasses the limit of context, therefore elicits vocabulary in a more varied way (Meara & Fitzpatrick, 2000).

It should be noted that similar to discourse-based tests and the spew test discussed above, the result obtained from Lex30 test cannot inform researchers on the number of free active words a testee has. As pointed out by Meara and Alcoy (2010), "it was not obvious how the profiles provided by the Lex30 test could be converted into proper estimates of productive vocabulary size". The difficulty of measuring the exact size of free active words is understandable. Words produced by learners represent only a portion of their lexicon storage, and it is impossible for researchers to collect all the free active words in their mental lexicon. Therefore, almost all the test approaches for free active vocabulary size can only offer a relative value. It seems that finding an instrument to measure the exact free active vocabulary size is a "mission impossible".

However, Meara and Alcoy (2010) made a brave step for-ward. They were inspired by the way ecologists measure animal populations in the natural environment. In ecology, researchers capture a species of animal, for example, fish, at regular intervals, during a fixed period of time, and then try to estimate the whole size of the species in that area. The capturing and recapturing of fish can help ecologists obtain three numbers: the number of fish captured at the first time, the number of fish captured on the second time, and the number of fish captured on both occasions. Ecologists then designed a formula to calculate the whole population of the fish. Inspired by this approach, Meara and Alcoy (2010) attempted to find out whether the same formula could be used in free active vocabulary size assessment. They claimed that there might be some similarities between assessing free active vocabulary and counting animals in the natural environment. Just like counting wild animals, researchers can only capture part of the learner's free active vocabulary, and it is impossible to "catch" all the words that a learner can produce. The result indicated that the method was partially successful. It indicated that the subjects' free active vocabulary is much higher than that in the raw data, and it is believed that this method can detect the size of free active vocabulary more sensitively than the raw data. However, the method is still not accurate enough. In Meara and Alcoy's (2010) study, the result indicates that the intermediate group and advanced group have a free active vocabulary of 90 and 163 respectively, which is too small to be their real vocabulary size.

Meara and Alcoy's (2010) research is the first effort to measure exactly how many free active words someone knows. They attempted to think outside the traditional thinking style, and to find an innovative solution to this difficult issue. Unfortunately, this method cannot be put into use yet, since it fails to produce reliable and realistic figures for free active vocabulary size, and it is still not sure whether this ecological approach would be a good analogy for what happens with words. Therefore, further studies are needed to justify and improve this methodology.

After reviewing and comparing the measuring instruments for free active vocabulary, it is proposed that essay writing and Lex30 be adopted in this research. As it was discussed, the drawback of essay writing is that it is time-consuming, and it may be too difficult to low-proficiency L2 learners to complete. However, as participants in this research were upper-intermediate to advanced ESL learners, to them an essay of no less than 200 words would not be a task that was too long or too difficult to complete. Lex30 test was also adopted, so that the free active vocabulary could be measured out of context as well. It is believed that adopting both the two instruments can help researchers understand L2 learners' free active vocabulary more comprehensively. The spew approach and the capturing-recapturing approach were not adopted, as both of them need further development.

2. 4   Mental Lexicon

2.4.1   Definition of Mental Lexicon

In recent years, the notion of mental lexicon has drawn increasing attention from researchers in linguistics (especially psycholinguistics), psychology, and anthropology. The study of mental lexicon started from the 1960s (e. g. Treisman, 1960). Various definitions have been given since then. For example, Treisman (1960), the first scholar to propose the notion of mental lexicon, defined it as a repository that a person has on all the information of words in a language. According to Bock and Levelt (1994), mental lexicon is "our mental store of words and basic information about them". The definition of mental lexicon by Aitchison (1994) is the representation of words and their meaning that are stored in permanent memory. Richards (2001) defines mental lexicon as "a mental system that contains all the information a person knows about words". Carroll (1986) holds that mental lexicon is an organisation of vocabulary knowledge that is stored in permanent memory.

Among the definitions, only Aitchison's (1994) definition focuses more on words' semantic aspect. Almost all of others share the same idea that mental lexicon stores all sorts of information on words in people's mind. The information includes words' form (morphological/orthographic knowledge), pronunciation (phonological knowledge), meaning (semantic knowledge), and grammar (syntactic knowledge). Since the knowledge of a word involves not only the semantic aspect but also many other aspects, the idea that mental lexicon is the storage of words in all aspects, including the aspects of form, pronunciation, part of speech, world knowledge of the word, and so on, seems to be more reasonable.

2.4.2　Nature of L2 Mental Lexicon

It is widely believed that the storage of L1 mental lexicon in people's mind is semantically driven (A. Hu & Liu, 2013; Laufer, 1989; Meara, 1984). As for the nature of L2 mental lexicon, researchers have conducted a large number of studies since the 1980s. However, until now there are controversies among researchers.

Some scholars (e. g. Maréchal, 1995; O'gorman, 1996; Singleton, 1999; Söderman, 1993; Wolter, 2001; Zareva, 2007) hold that L1 and L2 mental lexicon are stored in the same way, whereas others (e. g. Channell, 1990; Meara, 1984; Wolter, 2001; S. Zhang, 2003) believe that L1 and L2 mental lexicon cannot be stored in the same style, due to the fact that L1 and L2 are usually acquired at different ages, in different environment, and with learners' different cognitive capability. Generally there are three views on L2 mental lexicon storage.

The first view is phonological view. Representatives supporting this view include Meara (1983, 1984) and Laufer (1989). In the 1980s, Meara hosted the Birkbeck Vocabulary Project, from which he concludes that: (1) the connections of words in L2 learners' mental lexicon are not as stable as those in L1 speakers; (2) phonology plays a more prominent role in L2 mental lexicon than in L1 mental lexicon; and (3) the semantic links of L1 speakers are different from L2 learners (Meara, 1983). Laufer (1989) also supports the idea that L1 mental lexicon is basically semantically organised, while L2 mental lexicon is phonologically organised. S. Zhang (2003) conducted a word association test with some advanced L2 learners. The result reveals that phonological reactions are the main reactions even for these advanced learners. S. Zhang (2003) concluded that semantic connections are not well established even in advanced L2 learners. She therefore supported the phonological view that L2 mental lexicon is mainly phonological rather than semantic.

The second view on the nature of L2 mental lexicon is semantic view. Scholars who support this view believed that just like native speakers, L2 mental lexicon is semantically-driven (Maréchal, 1995; O'gorman, 1996; Singleton, 1999; Söderman,

1993；Zareva，2007）. For example，in O'gorman's（1996）study，word association tests were conducted among 22 teacher trainees who had intermediate English proficiency. They were asked to listen to some prompt words in both English and Chinese，and then write down the first word that they could think of as soon as they heard each prompt word. Results showed that although the responses in L1（Chinese）and L2（English）were different，both languages primarily inspired semantic responses. These results indicate that L2 mental lexicon is also semantically driven. In the research by Maréchal（1995），testees were asked to respond to 50 English（L1）words and 50 French（L2）words. The result is that both the L1 and L2 elicited a large number of semantic responses，including paradigmatic and syntagmatic responses，and very few phonological responses. Singleton's（1999）study also drew similar conclusions. His word association test indicates that for advanced L2 learners the lexical structures are semantic-pragmatic. Zareva（2007）compared three groups of subjects，including native English speakers，advanced L2 learners，and intermediate L2 learners. His study reveals that these three groups' mental lexicons had no significant difference，and all of them had predominantly paradigmatic connections and fewer syntag-matic connections. Therefore，Zavera agrees with the opinion of Söderman（1993）that "adult L2 learners pattern their responses very much like adult native speakers do，even at the lower levels" of proficiency（Zareva，2007）.

Taken a closer look，it can be found that there seems to be inconsistencies in studies of the two views above. First，different researchers chose participants with different L2 proficiencies. For example，in the research by O'gorman（1996），learners with intermediate-proficiency level were chosen to be participants；in

Zareva's (2007) study, two groups of L2 learners (advanced and intermediate learners) were observed. The subjects in Maréchal (1995) were high-proficiency students. Singleton's (1999) subjects were advanced L2 learners. Söderman (1993) selected advanced ESL learners to study L2 lexical connections. There are also researchers who did not take language proficiency into account. For example, although Wolter (2001) required his subjects to have a score of at least 500 in the TOEFL test (or a mock TOEFL test), he holds that the language proficiency variable in his study was not controlled, due to the fact that some of the participants took TOEFL tests several years ago, whereas some had just taken the test at the time of the study. Therefore, it is difficult to compare the results of these studies. Since different studies involved participants with different L2 proficiencies, it would be too hasty to conclude from any single study how L2 mental lexicon is stored in memory. Additionally, there is no consistent standard to judge what proficiencies should be considered as low, intermediate, and advanced proficiencies, and this makes the issue of L2 lexical representation even more complicated and ambiguous.

Second, there is no consistent standard to judge whether a response is "semantic" or "syntactic". This inconsistency makes it difficult to compare the findings of different studies. Some researchers (e. g. McNeill, 1966; Zareva, 2007) distinguished paradigmatic response and syntagmatic (also called "syntactic") response as two different responses, and they considered paradigmatic response as semantic, whereas syntagmatic response as syntactic. Some other researchers (e. g. Henriksen, 2008; Maréchal, 1995; Singleton, 1999; Wolter, 2001; P. Zhang, 2010b) suggested that both paradigmatic and syntactic responses are semantic. A few researchers (O'gorman,1996) opposed to dividing sematic response into paradigmatic and syntagmatic. This inconsistency in the classification causes problems when different conclusions are compared with each other. It also causes misunderstandings and confusions. For example,a large number of research studies, such as those conducted by Cui (2006),S. Zhang (2005),and P. Zhao (2013),summarised relevant theories into three views:the semantic view,the phonological view,and the syntactic view. These studies all took Wolter (2001) as the only representative of the syntactic view. However,Wolter (2001) held that syntactic relation belongs to semantic relation in word connections. Therefore,Wolter's syntactic view,in fact,is still semantic view.

The third problem is that most studies neglect word familiarity (or the depth of word knowledge) as a variable. A large number of theoretical and empirical studies have proved that word familiarity has a significant effect on words' representations in mental lexicon (Caramazza,Laudanna & Romani,1988;S. Chen,2006; S. Chen, Peng, Yang, Hou & Fang, 2011; Wolter, 2001; S. Zhang,2003). However,in studies exploring the nature of L2 mental lexicon,most scholars overlooked this variable. Only a few researchers (e. g. Wolter, 2001; Zavera, 2007) took word familiarity into consideration when they analysed their test results. Therefore,the neglect of word familiarity may affect the reliability of some tests.

Due to the second problem stated above, it may not be appropriate to take Wolter's (2001) syntactic view as the third view on the nature of L2 mental lexicon. It is proposed in this study that the third view is the developmental view. The developmental view considers L2 mental lexicon's construction as a dynamic process,during which its storage nature keeps changing.

Scholars who hold this view include Wolter (2001), Wilks and Meara (2002), S. Zhang (2005), O'gorman (1996), Zavera (2007), R. Li (2003), Cui (2006), and Söderman (1993). For example, Wolter (2001) conducted a research in which 13 Japanese non-native speakers of English and nine native speakers of English were asked to take word association tests. After comparing the native speakers and non-native speakers' responses, Wolter concluded that both L1 and L2 mental lexicon experienced a developmental process from phonological and other non-semantic connections to paradigmatic or syntactic connections. The difference between L1 and L2 mental lexicon is that in terms of words with high familiarity, L1 mental lexicon is primarily paradigmatic, whereas L2 mental lexicon is primarily syntactic. According to Wolter (2001), this is just a difference between L1 and L2; and it does not mean that syntactic connections are inferior to paradigmatic connections. Another example is the research by Söderman (1993), in which four groups of Finnish and Swedish ESL learners with different L2 proficiencies were tested. Söderman (1993) found that the number of paradigmatic responses had a positive relation with the subjects' proficiency levels.

All of the research holding developmental view (Cui, 2006; R. Li, 2003; O'gorman, 1996; Söderman, 1993; Wilks & Meara, 2002; Wolter, 2001; Zareva, 2007; S. Zhang, 2005) share similar opinions that at early stages the links between words are mainly phonological; semantic connections (paradigmatic, syntagmatic, or both, depending on different researchers) would develop with the growth of L2 proficiency. In other words, learners with low L2 proficiency tend to access words by phonological properties, whereas learners with advanced L2 proficiency tend to access words by semantic properties.

Looking back on previous empirical studies, it can be found that most studies with low-proficiency subjects or with words of low familiarities drew phonological conclusions, such as those conducted by Wolter (2001), Meara (1984), and O'gorman (1996). Studies with high-proficiency subjects or with words of high familiarities, such as those by Wolter (2001), Singleton (1999), and Maréchal (1995), tended to draw semantic conclusions. Therefore, most research leading to phonological and semantic views is, in fact, not contradictory to each other. For this reason, this research tends to support the developmental view that the nature of L2 mental lexicon keeps changing with the development of L2 proficiency and word familiarity.

2.4.3　The Organisational Structure of Mental Lexicon

It is believed that rather than being stored randomly and disorderedly, words are stored systematically in humans' memory (Aitchison, 1994; Bock & Levelt, 1994). Both Bock and Levelt (1994) and Aitchison (1994) think this could be evidenced by the fact that humans have a large storage of words in mind, and most of these words can be accessed accurately and quickly when people need to use them. Another evidence is that words can always make people think of their related words. For example, the word "food" may elicit the association of relevant words, such as "milk" "rice" "tea", etc. Therefore, there might be a highly organised and accessible system, or word web, in mental lexicon. There are quite a number of studies probing mental lexicon's organisation, but no consensus has been reached yet. In this section the organisation models are introduced and discussed.

2.4.3.1 The Hierarchy Model

The earliest model on mental lexicon's organisation is the Hierarchy Model, which was proposed by Collins and Quillian in 1969 (Figure 2.1). According to the Hierarchy Model, each concept is a node in a network, and concepts are organised according to their category (or hyponymy) and property relations with other concepts. Therefore, the network has a hierarchical and clustered look, and there are superordinates, subordinates, and coordinates in the web of mental lexicon. A node in the web always locates above some nodes and below some other nodes, as illustrated in Figure 2.1.

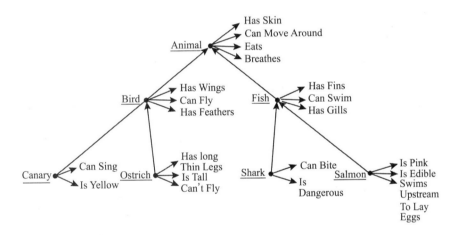

Figure 2.1   The Hierarchy Model by Collins and Quillian (1969)

The Hierarchy Model is a forerunner which describes mental lexicon's organisation on the basis of network representations (Collins & Loftus, 1975). Its idea of network representation in mental lexicon has a significant influence on later studies. However, the model has some limitations.

The first limitation results from the purpose to construct this model. This model was constructed to explore information's retrieval process in humans' semantic memory, so that computers can be programmed to simulate humans' memory search and comprehension. Therefore, only semantic properties or concepts of words are considered in the model; other properties of words, such as phonology, orthography, and grammar (syntax), are all neglected. The model fails to display a complete picture of how words are organised in humans' mind.

The second limitation is that the description of semantic organisation in the model is incomplete. The model overlooks the fact that different nodes may have different strengths of connections with others. For example, in Chinese ESL learners' mental lexicon, the word "apple" may have a closer or stronger subordinate connection with the word "food" than "sushi" does, because "apple" is a more common food in their world knowledge. Therefore, when "food" is discussed, the word "apple" may be accessed more easily and quickly than the word "sushi" in Chinese ESL learners' mental lexicon. The neglect of this factor may cause misunderstandings that all nodes on a specific level in the hierarchy are equally connected with their superordinate node.

The third limitation originates from the model's tree—like structure. As pointed out by Steyvers and Tenenbaum (2005), the tree-structured semantic organisation may only be suitable for concepts that are taxonomically organised. For example, "food" and its subordinate "fruit" and "vegetable" can be presented by the tree—like structure. However, not all concepts are taxonomically organised. For example, the concept of "abstract" may not have subordinates or superordinates. Additionally, even in ideal conditions, "a strict inheritance structure seems not to apply except for the most typical members of the hierarchy"

(Steyvers & Tenenbaum, 2005). Therefore, the hierarchy model fails to offer a complete description of the organisational structure of mental lexicon.

2.4.3.2   The Spreading-activation Model

Based on Collins and Quillian's (1969) spreading-activation idea and network concept in the Hierarchy Model, Collins and Loftus (1975) proposed another model, which is usually called as Spreading-activation Model. The model is presented in Figure 2.2.

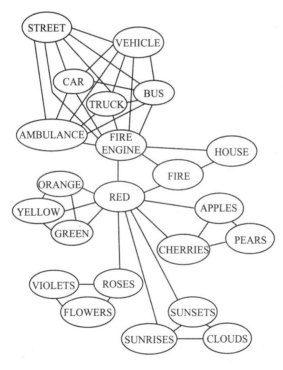

Figure 2.2   The Spreading-activation Model by Collins and Loftus (1975)

The model is a further development of the Hierarchy Model, and it includes the following extensions. First, "When a concept is processed (or stimulated), activation spreads out along the paths of the network in a decreasing gradient" (Collins & Loftus, 1975). This means when a concept (i. e., the semantic property of words) is primed, it activates other related concepts (nodes) in the network, and the activated concepts will continue to activate other concepts that are related to them. This activation expands continuously, but the strength of activation weakens over time, until it disappears completely.

Second, concepts are organised according to their conceptual (semantic) similarities. This indicates that the more properties two concepts share, the more connections they have, and the more related they are to each other (Collins & Loftus, 1975). In Figure 2. 2, the degrees of connectedness between two concepts are described by the lengths of lines between the two nodes. The shorter the line, the stronger the connection is between two concepts (Collins & Loftus, 1975).

Third, concepts are connected with other concepts in semantic network; with regard to the names of concepts, they are stored in the lexical network, which is organised according to their phonemic and orthographic similarity (Collins & Loftus, 1975). This assumption shows that different from the hierarchy model, Collins and Loftus (1975) noticed the existence of phonemic/orthographic connections between words. They called the phonemic/orthographic connections as "names of concepts" (Collins & Loftus, 1975). However, because Collins and Loftus's (1975) Spreading-activation Model aimed to describe semantic processing, they did not further explore this issue. The model also holds that people can decide whether to activate the lexical network (i. e., phonemic/orthographic network), the semantic network, or both of them.

As it is stated in Section 3. 1, the Hierarchy Model was designed to assist computers to simulate humans' semantic storage and processing. The Spreading-activation Model makes a step forward in that it adds more structural and processing assumptions to the former model. Compared with the Hierarchy Model, which mainly concerns with computational linguistics, the Spreading-activation Model is more psychologically and neurologically realistic. Therefore, it is believed in this study that the Spreading-activation Model surpasses the constraint of Hierarchy Model in that it is not limited to computer use, and it can be applied to deal with experiment results in humans' semantic memory and processing.

Another weakness of the Hierarchy Model is the tree—like structure. Unlike the Hierarchy Model, the Spreading-activation Model is not constructed as a tree—like hierarchy; on the contrary, it is "essentially unstructured … with each word or concept corresponding to a node and links between any two nodes that are directly associated in some way" (Steyvers & Tenenbaum, 2005). Therefore, the Spreading-activation Model is not constrained to categorical concepts. It applies to the organisation of all types of concepts in the mental lexicon.

Although the Spreading-activation Model conquers many weaknesses of the Hierarchy Model, it still inherits a limitation of the Hierarchy Model. That is, both of them focus on the structure and processing of humans' semantic memory, and therefore, both of them are a "model of concepts rather than words" (Cui, 2006). As a result, the model is also not complete in describing the organisation or structure of humans' mental lexicon.

To deal with the limitations of the two models, Bock and Levelt (1994) proposed a modified Spreading-activation Model, which is illustrated in Figure 2.3. The modified model has three stratums: the first stratum is the conceptual level, which contains words' semantic properties; the second stratum is the lemma level, which contains words' syntactic properties; and the third stratum is the lexeme or sound level, which contains words' phonological and orthographic properties. This model illustrates a more comprehensive picture of words' storage in people's mental lexicon. As this model notices the existence of syntactic, phonological and orthographic components of words in mental lexicon, many phenomena that cannot be explained by the other two models can find explanations from this model. For example, the Modified Spreading-activation Model may shed some light on the "slip-of-tongue" phenomenon, which is explained below. According to the model, relevant nodes are interconnected with each other, and when a node is activated, its relevant nodes will be activated as well. Then those activated nodes will compete for retrieval. For instance, when someone needs to pronounce a word, all the words' relevant phonological properties, including those similar pronunciations, may be activated. Then these pronunciations are in competition for retrieval, and the person needs to access and pick up the correct one in a short period of time. Due to the limited time or his unfamiliarity with the word, a similar but wrong phonological entry may be retrieved, which would result in the "slip-of-tongue" phenomenon (Cui, 2006).

This section introduces different models on mental lexicon organisation. From the Hierarchy Model, to Spreading-activation Model, then to Modified Spreading-activation Model, each model overcomes some weaknesses of the former one and makes some progress forward. The third model, the Modified Spreading-activation Model, provides researchers with a more comprehensive picture on mental lexicon organisation. This model is also theoretically significant, due to the fact that many linguistic phenomena in experiments and reality can find reasonable explanations from this model. However, it needs to be pointed out that the three models are still hypothetical, and they need to be testified by further studies.

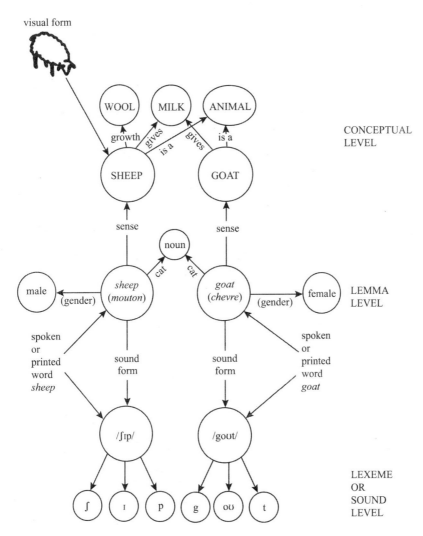

visual form

WOOL   MILK   ANIMAL

growth gives is a gives is a

CONCEPTUAL
LEVEL

SHEEP   GOAT

sense   sense

noun

cat   cat

male   *sheep (mouton)*   *goat (chevre)*   female

(gender)   (gender)

LEMMA
LEVEL

spoken
or
printed
word
sheep

sound
form

sound
form

spoken
or
printed
word
goat

/ʃɪp/   /goʊt/

LEXEME
OR
SOUND
LEVEL

ʃ   ɪ   p   g   oʊ   t

Figure 2. 3   The Modified Spreading-activation Model by
Bock and Levelt (1994)

2.4.4 Bilinguals' Lexical Retrieval

Lexical retrieval, which means "finding the right word in the right context", sometimes is also called as "lexical access" (French & Jacquet, 2004). Forster (1976) likened mental lexicon to a library: words can be retrieved from mental lexicon through various accesses. Forster (1976) thinks that there are three accesses in mental lexicon: orthographic access, phonological access, and semantic/syntactic access. Words can be drawn out from these accesses when they are needed in the processes of reading, listening, and speaking.

Compared with monolinguals, bilinguals' retrieval process seems to be a little intriguing. According to the Spreading-activation Model, a concept may activate several nodes simultaneously, which causes competitions among those nodes for retrieval (Collins & Loftus, 1975). Then a question emerges: how can the target entry be accessed when there are two languages in mental lexicon? Until now this is a controversial issue, and two different views exist. They are the language selective (also called as language-specific selection) view and the language nonselective (also called as language-unspecific selection) view.

From the language selective view, words are retrieved from the specific language in bilinguals' word searching process, or in other words, only word candidates from the target language will be activated by bilinguals (van Hell & Tanner, 2012). Words from the other language will not take part in the competition, since they are not selected to be candidates at all (W. Zhang & Zhang, 2007). There are a large number of studies supporting the language selective view (e. g. Costa, 2005; Costa, Miozzo & Caramazza, 1999; La, 2005; Roelofs, 1998; van Hell & Tanner,

2012; W. Zhang & Zhang, 2007).

The language nonselective view holds a different opinion. It holds that words from both of the two languages will be activated, and all of them will join the competition for retrieval (French & Jacquet, 2004; Green, 1998; van Hell & Tanner, 2012; Von & Mani, 2012). However, in the competition, there is an inhibitory mechanism which ensures that only words in the target language will be accessed and picked up. This mechanism is called the "inhibitory control", or briefly "IC" (Costa & Santesteban, 2004; Green, 1998; Meuter & Allport, 1999). According to Costa and Santesteban (2004), the IC mechanism ensures the access of words in the target language by intentionally inhibiting the retrieval of candidate words in the non-target language(s).

It can be noticed that Costa supports both selective and nonselective views (Costa, 2005; Costa et al. , 1999; Costa & Santesteban, 2004). In fact, Costa holds a developmental opinion, and he believes that bilinguals' retrieval mechanism changes with the growth of their L2 proficiency. After investigating the retrieval process of both fluent and influent bilinguals, Costa (2005) concluded that influent bilinguals' retrieval system is nonselective; and with the development of L2 proficiency, the selective retrieval system replaces the nonselective retrieval system gradually.

2.4.5   Significance of Mental Lexicon Study to This Research

The study of mental lexicon is of great significance to this research. Humans' memory system is like a "dark box", which cannot be observed directly. Since the 1980s, increasing attention has been paid to L2 learners' mental lexicon. It is believed that the transition from solely focusing on vocabulary size to also paying attention to mental lexicon is a great leap forward in L2 vocabulary acquisition research (P. Zhang, 2009). Exploring the inner structure of mental lexicon may offer researchers an effective channel to know how words are stored and retrieved in memory. In this way, researchers may find more effective methods to assist vocabulary learning.

As for the threshold phenomenon in L2 FAV acquisition, previous studies have tried to seek reasons for the emergence of threshold, but conclusions are usually superficial. Ineffective teaching methods or learning strategies have always been blamed for the failure of FAV's constant growth (Cui & Wang, 2006; Gu & Li, 2013; Laufer, 1998; Lu, 2008; Tan, 2006; G. Zhang et al., 2005). For example, Laufer (1998) attributed the stagnation of FAV to students' lack of incentive to use more advanced words, and to the lack of teachers' reward for lexical richness. Moreover, Laufer (1998), Cui and Wang (2006), and Lu (2008) believed that the overlook of output practice, such as speaking and writing, is another cause. Students' tendency to avoid mistakes is also blamed for the stagnation (Gu & Li, 2013; G. Zhang et al., 2005). It is admitted that these factors may be reasons for FAV stagnation, but they may not be the whole truth. This research assumes that more reasons for the FAV stagnation may lie in learners' cognitive mechanism. Therefore, attention should be paid to learners' cognitive mechanism as well. Investigating the storage characteristics of FAV in mental lexicon may help researchers detect the root causes for the occurrence of FAV threshold, and thereby more effective teaching and learning methods can be identified to help students overcome the plateau in L2 FAV vocabulary acquisition.

2.4.6　Word Association Tests in Mental Lexicon Study

Since people's mental lexicon is like a "dark box" and cannot be observed directly, various investigative instruments have been adopted to explore its nature. These instruments include word association test, reaction time test, event-related potentials test, lexical naming test, error analysis, and stroop test. Among them, word association (WA) test may be the most simple, quick, and direct way to collect data for mental lexicon study (Schmitt, 1998; P. Zhang, 2009). WA test is widely used in mental lexicon research, and is used in this research as well.

2.4.6.1　The Fundamental Assumption behind WA Tests

The fundamental assumption behind the use of WA tests in mental lexicon research is that the automatically responded words in WA are strongly connected with the stimulus words in mental lexicon (Nissen & Henriksen, 2006; Schmitt, 1998). This assumption is consistent with the widely accepted metaphor that words are stored in a "network" where lexical nodes are linked with each other in particular ways (Fitzpatrick & Izura, 2011). Based on this assumption, it is believed by many psychologists and linguists that the associated behaviour activated by WA tests reveals people's cognitive processes, their concept building in thoughts, the connection features between words in mental lexicon, and the structure of word web in mental lexicon (Albrechtsen, Haastrup & Henriksen, 2008; Cramer, 1968; Fitzpatrick, 2007; Riegel & Zivian, 1972; van Hell & de Groot, 1998; Wolter, 2002; Zareva & Brent, 2012).

2.4.6.2 Selection of Stimulus Words in WA Tests

WA test has been widely used in mental lexicon research. However, there are numerous factors that need to be treated carefully, owing to the fact that they may affect the reliability, re-testability, and comparability of the results. Numerous researchers (Cui, 2010; Fitzpatrick, 2006; Wolter, 2002; P. Zhang, 2010a) have expressed concerns that WA stimuli may not have been chosen in a standard, consistent, and principled way. There are seven variables of cue words which may affect the WA result, and they need to be treated carefully. These variables include word class, frequency, familiarity, concreteness, cognate/noncognate, word length, cultural connotation, and routine-elicitation tendency. Adequate attention should be paid to these factors to ensure the reliability of WA tests.

The first variable that needs to be controlled is the word class of cue words. Numerous researchers (e. g. Clark, 1995; Cramer, 1968; Deese, 1962, 1966; Fitzpatrick, Wray, Playfoot & Wright, 2015; Källkvist, 1999; Lotto & de Groot, 1998; Navracsics, 2007; K. Nelson, 1977; Nissen & Henriksen, 2006; Palermo, 1971; Sökmen, 1993; Zareva & Brent, 2012) believe that the word class of cues may significantly affect response behaviours. For example, Cramer (1968), who is a psychologist, concluded from his study that nouns elicit the most paradigmatic responses, verbs and adjectives elicit less, and adverbials elicit the least; on the other hand, adverbials produce the most syntagmatic responses, verbs and adjectives produce less, and nouns produce the least. Similarly, study by Zhang (2006) indicates that L2 nouns produce more paradigmatic responses, whereas verbs produce more syntagmatic responses. The WA study by Nissen and Henriksen

(2006) indicates that in terms of both L1 and L2 prompt words with high familiarity and high frequency, nouns seem to be predominantly organised paradigmatically, while verbs and adjectives are predominantly organised syntagmatically. P. Zhang (2009) thinks that the reason why verbs elicit more syntagmatic responses than other word classes is verbs carry more syntactic functions in sentences. Therefore, in WA tests, the word class should be taken into account when researchers choose words as cues.

Another factor that influences the robustness of WA study is the frequency of cue words. A number of researchers (Postman & Keppel, 1970; Söderman, 1993; Wolter, 2001; Zareva & Brent, 2012) point out that stimulus words' frequency of occurrence may affect testees' association behaviours. P. Zhang and Wang (2012) conducted WA tests to check the effect of word frequency on word association behaviours. The results show that high frequency words tend to produce semantic reactions, whereas low frequency words tend to produce non-semantic reactions. The tests in Postman and Keppel (1970) and Wolter (2001) had similar findings that low frequency words tend to produce more non-semantic responses than high frequency words.

Although there are not as many empirical studies on word frequency effect as on other variables, such as on word class, it seems to be reasonable to postulate that word frequency would affect association behaviours. High-frequency words are encountered by individuals more frequently than low-frequency words in reading, writing, listening and speaking. Therefore, high-frequency words may set up semantic connections more easily than low-frequency words do. Therefore, word frequency should be taken into account, and word frequency lists should be referred to when researchers choose words as cues.

The third variable that was found to influence language users' associative behaviour is the degree of familiarity (Zareva & Brent, 2012), or the depth of individual vocabulary knowledge, as Wolter (2001) calls it. According to Namei (2004), barely familiar words tend to be form-based, moderately known words tend to be syntagmatic, fairly well-known words tend to be paradigmatic, and well-known words tend to be paradigmatic or late syntagmatic. Entwisle (1966) holds that knowledge of an individual word develops with the change of association patterns in mental lexicon, from clang response to syntagmatic response, to paradigmatic response, and then to late syntagmatic response. P. Zhang and Wang (2012) conducted WA tests to investigate the effect of stimulus words' familiarity on associative behaviours and found that words with high familiarity primarily elicit semantic responses, and words with low familiarity mainly elicit non-semantic responses. The widely used instrument to measure words' degree of familiarity is the Vocabulary Knowledge Scale (VKS) test by Wesche and Paribakht (1996). For example, Wolter (2001) thinks that the depth of individual vocabulary knowledge determines the word's degree of integration into mental lexicon. Therefore, he tried to control this variable by using VKS test to measure stimulus words' depth of knowledge before selecting cue words and analysing WA data. It is proposed in this research that VKS test be conducted before the WA test, so that the familiarity effect can be controlled in WA analysis.

The fourth variable that needs to be controlled in stimulus word selection is the length of word. It seems that currently there is little research into the effect of word length on word association behaviours. However, indirect evidence can be found from studies that investigate the word length effect on lexical storage and retrieval. The length of word can be measured by the number of letters, syllables, and morphemes in the word. Zhuang and Zhou (2001) used picture naming experiment to examine the effect of word length (the number of syllables in this case) and found that the number of syllables significantly affect the retrieval speed of words. Disyllabic words are retrieved from memory more slowly than monosyllabic words. New, Ludovic, Christophe, and Marc (2006) conducted word decision tests and found that there was a word-length effect on lexical decisions when the word was three to five letters long or eight to thirteen letters long. Y. Zhang and Zhang (2014) conducted lexical naming and picture naming tasks and found that the time needed to retrieve long words is significantly longer than the time needed to retrieve short words. This finding is similar to the picture naming test by Zhuang and Zhou (2001), which indicates that disyllabic words' retrieval speed is significantly slower than monosyllabic words. S. Chen et al. (2011) examined word length effect by lexical naming tasks and also discovered that word length affects lexical retrieval speed. These studies indicate that word length may affect words' storage and retrieval in mental lexicon. Therefore, it may also affect WA behaviours. Although there are some studies that drew different conclusions in that no robust connections between word length and word retrieval were found (Bachoud-Lévi, Dupoux, Cohen & Mehler, 1998; Lovatt, Avons & Masterson, 2000; Neath, Bireta & Surprenant, 2003), it is proposed in this research that a cautious attitude be adopted and word length be treated as a variable to be controlled. Some researchers (Fitzpatrick & Izura, 2011; P. Zhang, 2011) who hold the same opinion suggest that words that are too short (e. g. less than three letters) and too long

(e. g. more than ten letters) should be avoided when researchers select cue words.

The next variable that needs to be treated carefully when researchers select stimulus words is the words' social and cultural connotation. According to the semantic classification by Leech (1974,1983),words not only have conceptual meaning,but also have associative meaning. The associative meaning includes the words' social, cultural, affective, and connotative meanings. Therefore,words that share the same conceptual meaning may differ in associative meaning. It is believed that words' associative meaning is affected by culture (Y. Hu,2013;Q. Li,2008;R. Li, 2003;S. Li,2004). The effect of culture can be evidenced in WA research. Carolyn et al. (2004) conducted WA tests on a group of Chinese and Americans and found that testees from similar cultural background tend to yield similar reactions to cue words, whereas testees from different cultural background tend to yield different responses. Son et al. (2014) explored consumers' per-ception toward rice by using a word association task among people from four countries:Korea,Japan,Thailand,and France. The prompt words were "rice" and "good rice". Their results showed that there were significant associative differences among people from different regions:French respondents produced more words related to symbolic motivations,such as "travel""culture" and "exoticism";Asian respondents produced more associations related to utilitarian motivations,such as "agricultural products" and "necessary goods". Chow,Inn,and Szalay (1987) compared word associations between American and Chinese respondents. A list of more than 100 words which were believed to contain culturally relevant themes for participants was selected to be cues. The study by Chow,Inn and Szalay (1987) shows that words with culture-specific meanings tend to elicit unique associations.

There is also research that used words without obvious culture-specific meanings as cue words. For instance, B. Zhang (2008) chose 50 nouns which did not have obvious cultural features, such as car, hungry, table, quickly, word, etc., as cues. The results indicate no significant culture effect on associative pattern. Therefore, unless there is special research needs, words with rich cultural connotations should not be used as stimulus words.

The degree of concreteness also affects WA results (de Groot, 1989, 1993; Fitzpatrick et al., 2015; Kolers, 1963; D. L. Nelson & Schreiber, 1992; van Hell & de Groot, 1998; P. Zhang, 2010a, 2011). Concreteness is sometimes called as imageability, which means the degree to which a word can evoke a mental image (Fitzpatrick & Izura, 2011). It has been demonstrated repeatedly that compared with abstract words, concrete words tend to have cognitive advantages (Binder, Westbury, McKiernan, Possing & Medler, 2005; X. Chen & Zhang, 2008; Romani, McAlpine & Martin, 2008). X. Chen and Zhang (2008) pointed out that this is because concrete words contain more image information than abstract words do. Schwanenflugel (1991) and Crutch and Warrington (2005) hold that concrete words are organised differently from abstract words. According to Schwanenflugel (1991), concrete words may represent more diversely than abstract words in mental lexicon. Ferré and Sánchez-Casas (2014) further pointed out that concrete and abstract words may contain different quantity of sensory, motor, affective and linguistic information.

Although numerous studies have been conducted on the concreteness issue, almost all of these studies focused on the concreteness of nouns only. P. Zhang (2010a) made a step forward in that she extended this issue to adjectives and verbs, and she devised a concreteness scale. The scale helps researchers to determine whether a word is a concrete word or an abstract one based on consistent and standard criteria. The scale is demonstrated in Table 2.5.

Table 2.5 The Concreteness Scale for Words of Different Lexical Classes (P. Zhang, 2010a)

Concrete nouns	Anything that exists in real world and can be felt by the five senses of seeing, smelling, tasting, touching, and hearing. Examples: cat, pencil
abstract nouns	Concepts, properties, or conditions that do not have corresponding objects in real world. Examples: bravery, convenience
Concrete verbs	Observable behaviours or movements that can be conducted or practiced by living beings. Examples: jump, write
Abstract verbs	• Invisible states of mind or psychological activities. Examples: guess, presume • Copulas and modal verbs. Examples: seem, should
Concrete adjectives	Adjectives describing features that can be felt by the five senses of seeing, smelling, tasting, touching, and hearing. Examples: smooth, velvety
Abstract adjectives	Adjectives describing features that cannot be felt directly by the five senses of seeing, smelling, tasting, touching, and hearing. Examples: ambiguous, discriminatory

The next factor that should be paid attention to in L2 WA test is whether the cue words are cognates of L1 or not. Cognates are words that are similar in meaning and form across languages (Fitzpatrick & Izura, 2011; Wolter, 2001). For example, the German word "ael" and the English word "eel" are cognates. It is believed that whether the words are cognates or not would affect their integration in mental lexicon, and hence it would influence the response patterns in WA tests (de Groot, 1993). Cognates are also believed to be processed more efficiently by bilinguals (Jared & Kroll, 2001). Therefore, cognates may elicit responses different from non-cognates may when they are used as stimulus words in WA tests.

Words that tend to yield a particular response should be avoided, too, unless there are specific research goals that need to use these words as cues. For example, words in highly probable collocates, such as "bread butter", should be considered carefully when researchers select cue words (Fitzpatrick et al., 2015). This is because when cue words have a high possibility to elicit a routine reaction, the validity of the WA test may be affected and some association features may be concealed by the cue words.

2.4.6.3   The Response Categorisation in This Research

The categorisation adopted in this research is demonstrated in Figure 2.4.

The categorisation is based on that of P. Zhang (2010a), but minor changes were made. First, the syntagmatic response was classified into two subcategories: the compound/chunk response (e. g. heart→heart attack, give→give up) and the syntactic response (e. g. apple→an apple, drink→drink water). By contrast, the subcategories of syntagmatic response in P. Zhang's (2010a) framework include "position" "modifier" "tool" "supplement" "consistency""feature" and "containing". The change was made to ensure that the new categorisation is easier for operation while reflecting the essential characteristics of the lexical network in mental lexicon. Second, the response subcategory of "translation" was added to the non-semantic category. The "translation" involves responses that translate the cue word into its L1 equivalent. It should be noted that although translations contain equivalent meanings of the stimulus words, the translation of a target word does not embody any semantic relation with the cue like paradigmatic, systematic, or encyclopaedia does. It is because a L2 word and its translated L1 word are equal in meaning, and they don't form semantic relations. Therefore, in this research "translation" was categorised as non-semantic nodes. Of course, categorisation may change according to different research purposes. The "translation" may need to be categorised as semantic response in some circumstances.

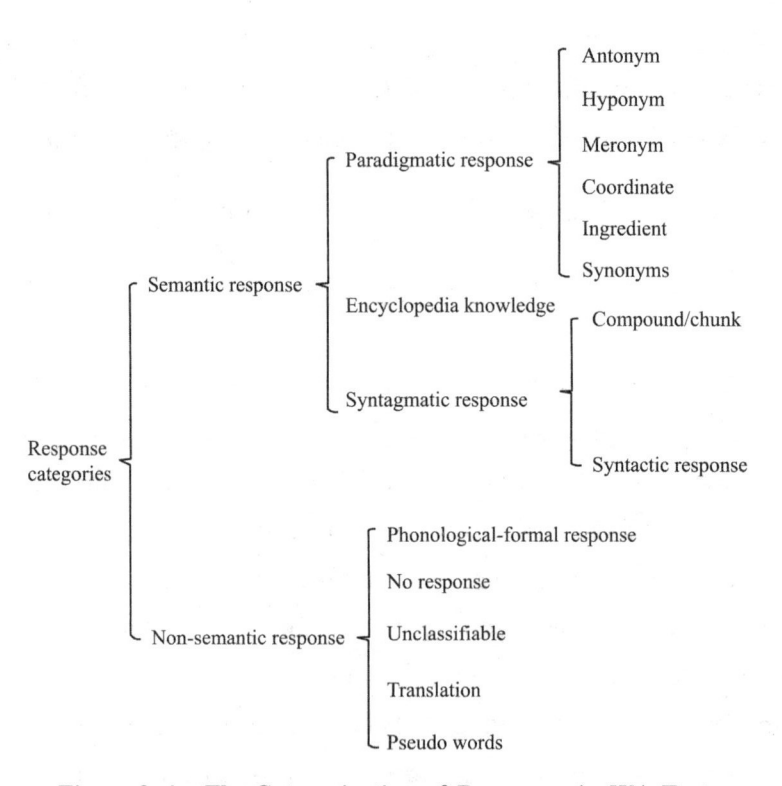

Figure 2.4　The Categorisation of Responses in WA Tests

It is admitted that the new categorisation still has some weaknesses that former categorisations have. First, although most categories are clear cut, there are responses that inevitably and reasonably belong to more than one category. This problem may be due to the fact that in WA tests only elicited words can be collected, and no context information of the elicited words can be obtained. For example, the cue word "black" may elicit the response "white", and this response can either be classified as syntagmatic, as in "black and white television", or be classified as paradigmatic, as both of them are colours (Fitzpatrick & Izura, 2011). To deal with this problem, different measures are adopted. Some researchers, such as Fitzpatrick (2006), conducted post-test interviews to decide which exact category the response in question should be assigned to; some other researchers, such as Fitzpatrick and Izura (2011) and Wolter (2001), had the response evaluated by two judges separately. If there was disagreement, discussions would be conducted until a consistent conclusion was drawn; or a final decision would be made by the third party.

These two measures offer some ways to solve the problem. However, both of them have deficiencies. The first measure is time-consuming. When there is a big sample size, interviews may not be feasible to be conducted. In addition, if the samples are anonymous and unidentifiable, it will not be possible to be conducted. The second measure in fact does not overcome the deficiencies brought about by the lack of context information. Even if there are two judges or the third party to make decisions, without referring to the testees, the conclusion is inevitably subjective and speculative.

There are other researchers, such as Maréchal (1995), who used "paradigmatic-syntagmatic" category to include those responses that could either be paradigmatic or syntagmatic. Zareva (2007), and Zareva and Brent (2012) treated this issue in a different way. They assigned these responses to paradigmatic group instead of syntagmatic group. These two methods are not perfect, either.

They may affect accuracy, and conceal some essential characteristics of the lexical network. Due to the fact that all these measures have weaknesses, further studies are needed to identify more efficient ways to solve this problem. Maybe the key solution, as pointed out by Zareva and Brent (2012), is consistency and transparency, so that the whole research procedure is clear enough for future empirical interrogations.

2.5 The Threshold Phenomenon in Free Active Vocabulary Acquisition

The threshold phenomenon in L2 FAV acquisition was discovered by Laufer in 1991. Laufer (1991) observed 47 first-year university students, whose major was English, for 28 weeks. During this period, students' compositions on the same topic were collected for three times (i. e. , the first week, the fourteenth week, and the twenty-eighth week). Then four variables representing lexical richness were calculated. These variables include lexical variation, lexical density, lexical originality, and lexical sophistication. The result showed that there was no significant progress in testees' lexical richness, especially in lexical variation, lexical density, and lexical originality. It indicates that there is no FAV progress after students reach the average level of L2 proficiency. Laufer (1991) therefore postulated the "active vocabulary threshold hypothesis", which assumes that even though L2 learners' passive vocabulary develops throughout their lifetime, their FAV would grow "only until it reaches the average level of the group in which they are required to function" (Laufer, 1991). In other words, FAV will stop progressing after reaching a certain degree, no matter how much input is given to the learners. After Laufer's (1991) research, numerous studies have been conducted and the FAV threshold phenomenon was detected in most of them (Gu & Li, 2013; Huang, 2012; Lu, 2008; Tan, 2006; X. Wu & Chen, 2000; Y. Zhao, 2011).

In 1998, Laufer conducted another research exploring the development of passive vocabulary, controlled active vocabulary, and free active vocabulary. Two groups of Israeli students, whose second language was English, participated in the study. The first group consisted of 26 16-year-old students who had studied English for six years, and the second group consisted of 22 17-year-old students who had studied English for seven years. The two groups were given the same tests (passive vocabulary test, controlled active vocabulary test, and free active vocabulary test), and results between the two groups were compared. The test for FAV was a composition of 300 – 400 words, and it was analysed using Lexical Frequency Profile (Laufer & Nation, 1995). The Lexical Frequency Profile was a computer software that analyses word frequencies in writings. Results of the tests showed that learners' passive vocabulary size correlated with their controlled active vocabulary size. However, as for FAV, no significant difference was found between the two groups. Laufer (1998) therefore concluded again that "the free active vocabulary reached a plateau and might therefore defy further development".

In recent years, the development of L2 FAV obtained increasing attention from researchers, and more quantitative studies have been conducted to explore this issue (Gu & Li, 2013; Huang, 2012; Lu, 2008; Tan, 2006; Tong, 2009; X. Wu & Chen, 2000; G. Zhang et al., 2005; Y. Zhao, 2011). Most of these studies proved the existence of threshold, except for two studies by Tong

(2009) and G. Zhang et al. (2005). In Tong's (2009) research, 11 year-one university students of English major were observed for 3 semesters. In each semester, their spoken English was collected and scored. Then the breadth and depth of students' FAV was analysed. The results showed that both the breadth (in this study measured by lexical frequency, lexical variation, and lexical density) and depth (measured by error analysis) of FAV kept growing, and there was no "plateau" in the whole process. In G. Zhang et al.'s (2005) study, students from both English major and other majors took part in the tests. The researchers found that there was a continuous FAV growth in non-English-major students, whereas there was a threshold in English-major students.

However, the non-existence of the FAV threshold pheno-menon in the two studies seems to be rational. In Tong's (2009) research, the subjects were year-one university students, who may still be at a progressing stage in their language study and may not have reached the stagnation stage yet. G. Zhang et al.'s (2005) study was a similar case. Only year-one and year-two university students were tested, and the participants may not have reached the stagnation stage yet. In addition, the language samples collected in Tong's (2009) research were students' oral presentations with the topic of campus life. Both the topic and the style (spoken language) of the data may not be challenging enough to elicit the participants to produce enough low-frequency words.

2.6 The Working Definitions and Terminology in the Research

In this section the working definitions for the key terms used in this research are clarified. Based on Laufer (1998) and

Laufer and Paribakht (1998), the receptive vocabulary is defined as words whose meanings can be retrieved when being seen or heard; the controlled active vocabulary is defined as words that can be produced in writing or speaking with external stimulus; the free active vocabulary is defined as words that can be produced in writing or speaking without external stimulus.

In this research "receptive vocabulary" and "passive vocabulary" are used interchangeably; "productive vocabulary" and "active vocabulary" are used interchangeably as well. Additionally, unless otherwise noted, "productive vocabulary" and "active vocabulary" refer to free active vocabulary in this research. "Controlled active vocabulary" is used to specifically refer to words that can be produced in writing or speaking with external stimulus.

The terms of "learning" and "acquisition" are distinguished sometimes (Yue, 2006). Krashen (1981) may be the first scholar who pointed out that "acquiring" and "learning" are different. He pointed out that "learning" is the conscious study of the explicit knowledge, whereas "acquiring" is the unconscious internalizing of the implicit knowledge. As in this study participants' English study involves both conscious study of the explicit knowledge and unconscious study of the implicit knowledge, the terms of "acquiring" and "learning" are not distinguished. They are used interchangeably to refer to both conscious learning and unconscious learning, unless otherwise specified.

2.7　Conclusion

This chapter reviewed the literature on vocabulary knowledge classification and measurement, L2 mental lexicon, and the threshold phenomenon in L2 free active vocabulary acquisition. The working definitions and terminology used in this research is clarified as well. In the next chapter, the research methods and instruments adopted in the study will be introduced and justified.

Chapter 3   Methodology

3.1   Introduction

This chapter is an overview of the methodology adopted in the research. It first introduces the research aim and objectives, and then describes the mixed-method approach adopted in the study. The research instruments used in the data collection, together with the participants and sampling process, are described as well. The pilot study and the data analysis methods are also introduced.

3.2   Research Aim and Objectives

The aim of the research was twofold: first, to have a deeper understanding of the free active vocabulary (FAV) developmental process; second, if FAV experiences stagnation, to find possible reasons for the stagnation and possible ways to tackle the problem. The research aim served as an axis around which the entire research project was designed and carried out. Following the method by Leedy and Ormrod (2005), the research aim was broken into sub-problems to make it more manageable. The sub-problems are stated as research objectives in this study, which are explained below.

Research Objective 1: To investigate the developmental process of FAV in upper-intermediate to advanced L2 learners. This objective was to track the development of FAV in L2 learning, to testify the FAV threshold hypothesis proposed by Laufer (1998), and to explore the features of the threshold phenomenon if it exists.

Research Objective 2: To investigate the relationship between FAV and passive vocabulary (PV), and the relationship between FAV and controlled active vocabulary (CAV). This research objective was to compare the development pattern of FAV with that of PV and CAV, and to investigate the correlation between FAV and the other two types of vocabulary knowledge.

Research Objective 3: To explore how lexical network in mental lexicon is constructed in the process of FAV development. This research objective was to detect possible factors in mental lexicon construction that help promote FAV development.

Research Objective 4: To identify factors in learning and teaching that may affect FAV development. This research objective was to investigate whether some teaching and learning activities, and factors in course design, may affect FAV acquisition.

Research Objective 5: If the threshold phenomenon is detected in the longitudinal sub-study, a fifth research objective and corresponding research questions will be proposed. The fifth research objective is to find effective ways that may help tackle the FAV threshold phenomenon.

3.3 Research Approach and Methods

This research adopted a mixed-method approach, which involved both quantitative and qualitative methods. Following

Tashakkori and Teddlie (1998), the quantitative and qualitative methods were adopted separately in different research phases. Compared with the approach that only uses either quantitative or qualitative method, the advantage of mixed-method approach is that it has complementary strengths and non-overlapping weaknesses, which helps to improve the research quality (Johnson & Christensen, 2014). In this research, the quantitative sub-studies included a longitudinal sub-study and a word association sub-study. The qualitative sub-studies included interviews and documentary analysis. It was believed that the mix-method approach enabled the researcher to obtain more significant ideas and deeper investigation into the issue. The research approach and methods are demonstrated in Figure 3.1.

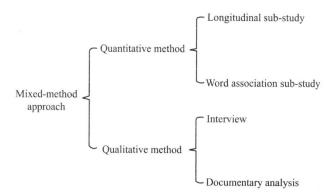

Figure 3. 1   The Research Approach and Methods Adopted in This Study

As demonstrated in Figure 3.1, there were two sub-studies adopting quantitative method, and two sub-studies adopting qualitative method in this research.

3.4 Instruments and Data Collection

3.4.1 Instruments and Data Collection in the Longitudinal Sub-study

As it was introduced in Section 3.3, this research involves four sub-studies. In this section, the instruments used in each sub-study and the data collection procedure are introduced. The first sub-study was the 12-month longitudinal study. In the longitudinal sub-study, the test instruments adopted were: (1) Receptive Vocabulary Levels Test (RVLT); (2) Controlled Active (or Controlled Productive) Vocabulary Levels Test (CAVLT or CPVLT); (3) Lex30 test; and (4) a composition of no less than 200 words. The reliability of PVLT was tested by Read (1988) and Bayazidi and Saeb (2017), and both of them concluded that it was a reliable test. The reliability of CAVLT was tested by Laufer and Nation (1999), and they concluded that it was a reliable test. The reliability of Lex30 was repeatedly tested and confirmed by Walters (2012), Fitzpatrick and Meara (2004), and Fitzpatrick and Clenton (2010). Laufer and Nation (1995) tested the reliability of Lexical Frequency Profile (LFP) for compositions, and they concluded that the reliability was satisfactory.

It should be noted that FAV include words that are used spontaneously in both writing and speaking. In this part of research, however, only writing data was collected and analysed. It was believed that spoken data was not as efficient to measure L2 learners' FAV as written data was. According to Cobb (2003),

" Spoken language, especially conversation, does not require nuanced vocabulary since nuancing of meaning can be provided by shared context, deixis, facial expression, and so on. Most forms of writing, on the other hand, have greater need of nuanced vocabulary since written texts must be able to bridge gaps over space and time between unshared contexts. " Therefore, in this part of research only written data was applied to FAV measurement. Two tests were adopted for the task. One was the Lex30 test, in which the testees were required to instantly write four response words to the given stimulus words. The other was a composition of no less than 200 words. The difference between the two tests is that the Lex30 test measures FAV out of contexts, whereas compositions measure FAV in contexts. Adopting both of the two tests enables the researchers to measure FAV from various perspectives, so that a more comprehensive portrait could be obtained.

The longitudinal study is considered to be a more appropriate choice than the cross-sectional study in this research. Although the cross-sectional study enables researchers to collect data in a relatively short period of time, it can be misleading if used to study developmental trends (Johnson & Christensen, 2014). In other words, if the study is to establish a time-over, the conclusion from cross-sectional studies tends to be weaker than that of longitudinal studies. By contrast, a longitudinal study occurs over time, which provides stronger evidence on developmental trends (Johnson & Christense, 2014). In this sub-study, a battery of vocabulary knowledge tests, including the passive vocabulary test (PVLT), the controlled active vocabulary test (CAVLT), and the free active vocabulary tests (Lex30 and compositions) were conducted both in the first month and in the twelfth month.

The longitudinal sub-study in this research was a panel

study, as the same individuals were studied for a period of time. The goal of a panel study is to understand how and why the panel members change with time passing by (Johnson & Christensen, 2014). By contrast, in a trend study, individuals are taken from a population to be studied over time, but each time the individuals may be different (Johnson & Christensen, 2014). As the sample kept the same over time, the panel study is believed to be stronger than the trend study (Johnson & Christensen, 2014). Meanwhile, this longitudinal sub-study was a prospective study, as it started in a present time and continued forward in time (Johnson & Christensen, 2014).

This section has provided an overview of the instruments and data collection in the longitudinal sub-study. More details on each of the instruments and on the data collection procedure are provided in Chapter 4.

3.4.2 Instruments and Data Collection in the Word Association Sub-study

The second sub-study, which was quantitative as well, was a word association study. In the word association sub-study, two types of instruments were adopted. One was Vocabulary Knowledge Scale (VKS) test, and the other was a word association test. As was discussed in Chapter 2, the word association approach is a well-established approach to investigate testees' lexical organisation in mental lexicon. The strength of word association test is that it is easy to be conducted, and it is time-efficient. However, testees' word associations to the target words tend to be affected by their level of familiarity to the words. Therefore, VKS tests were conducted to control the extraneous variable of familiarity.

In the sub-study, high-frequency words that tended to be frequently produced and that tended to be seldom produced by upper-intermediate to advanced L2 learners were selected. In the first month, the testees were tested with the VKS test and the word association test on words that were frequently produced. In the second month, the testees were tested with the VKS test and the word association test on words that were seldom produced by upper-intermediate to advanced L2 learners. The interval between the two tests was one month, so that reminding effects would be avoided. More details of the sub-study are provided in Chapter 5.

3.4.3   Instruments and Data Collection in the Interview

The third sub-study, which was qualitative, involved interviews. The sub-study was administered to achieve the fourth and fifth research objectives. The fourth research objective was to find possible factors in learning and teaching that may affect FAV development. The fifth research objective was to find effective ways to tackle the FAV threshold phenomenon if the threshold phenomenon is detected in the longitudinal sub-study.

All the questions in the interview were open-ended questions, as to answer the questions, the participants need to provide their own answers (Johnson & Christensen, 2014). By contrast, close-ended questions have predetermined answers, and participants need to select their answer(s). Open-ended questions were used in this sub-study, as the researchers need to know the interviewees' views in details, and the open-ended questions can provide researchers with more detailed information. The advantage of open-ended questions is that they can give researchers rich and in-depth information on the topic (Johnson & Christensen, 2014), and can help avoid misleading information and bias (Seidman, 1998). The interview used in this part of research was a standardized open-ended interview, as the questions had been written out in advance, and they would be read "exactly as written and in the same order to all the interviewees" (Johnson & Christensen, 2014).

The interview was in a face-to-face form. Face-to-face interviews not only give researchers chances to have verbal communications with interviewees, but also provide them chances to observe interviewees. In other words, non-verbal communication and visual support can be provided in face-to-face interviews, which may bring better results (Neuman, 2004a).

This interview was also semi-structured. Different from non-structured interviews, questions in semi-structured interviews are prepared in advance, and all interviewees are treated in a like manner (Fontana & Frey, 2000). Different from structured interview, the semi-structured interview is more flexible, and it allows the researchers to ask questions in addition to prepared ones when necessary (Kvale & Brinkmann, 2015).

Fourteen questions were designed, which was believed to be at a manageable level to interviewees. Follow-up questions may emerge when more details were needed. The questions were designed surrounding four aspects, leading to four sets of questions. To ensure the validity of the interview, content-related evidence needs to be found. Content-related evidence refers to the evidence that can help researchers "judge the degree to which the evidence suggests that the items, tasks, or questions on your test adequately represent the domain of interest" (Johnson & Christensen, 2014). According to Johnson and Christensen (2014), three questions should be asked to examine the content-related evidence. First,

"Do the items appear to represent the thing you are trying to measure?" Second, "Have you excluded any important content areas or topics?" Third, "Have you included any irrelevant items?" Guided by the three questions, discussions were conducted between the researcher and the supervisor. In this way, the interview questions were examined and revised repeatedly. The final version of interview questions was believed to represent the four aspects, and it was believed that no important contents were excluded, and no irrelevant items were included in the interview. The interview questions are provided in Chapter 6.

The interviewees were interviewed by the researcher in a random order. The entire interview procedure was audio recorded with the interviewees' consent. The researcher was awared that the interview settings might affect the interview result. According to Neuman (2004a, 2004b), the interview setting should make interviewees feel safe, relaxed, and confidential. Therefore, in order to get the best from the interviewees, the interview was carried out in a quiet place, and no third-party was present in the entire process. In the interview, adequate time was provided to the interviewees, so that they had enough time to think and express their views without interruption. In addition, the interviewees were all volunteers to participate, as only those who agreed to participate would be interviewed. In other words, they were willing to be interviewed on the issue. Therefore, it was believed that interviewees answered the questions with a serious attitude, which was later evidenced by the interview recordings as well. If the interview was conducted again, most likely these interviewees would provide similar answers. Therefore, the validity of the interview was ensured.

3.4.4 Instruments and Data Collection in the Documentary Analysis

The fourth sub-study, which was qualitative as well, was documentary analysis. In the sub-study, the documents, including the course structure that participants took in the period of the longitudinal sub-study and *The Syllabus of English Courses for College English Majors*, were collected and analysed. The documentary analysis was adopted in this research, as it may be the most achievable way to obtain the unit information needed in this research. Documents are a type of data that are frequently used in qualitative study (Johnson & Christensen, 2014). According to Johnson and Christensen (2014), documentary data usually fall into two categories: personal documents and official documents. The official documents are written, photographed, or recorded documents by some type of public or private organisations (Johnson & Christensen, 2014). As the course structure was made by school, it belonged to the official documents. The data in this sub-study belongs to secondary data. Secondary data is data that has already existed (Johnson & Christensen, 2014). The reliability of the data is high, as the official documents are usually formal and accurate.

The research instruments and data collection in the longitudinal, word association, and interview sub-studies have all been tested in the pilot study. Details of the pilot study will be introduced in Section 3.5 and in the following chapters.

3. 5   Sampling and Participants

3.5. 1   Sampling and Participants in the Longitudinal Sub-study

The participants were sampled from year-three university students, and their major was English. All these students had experienced standard elementary and middle school education in China, indicating that they had already been studying English for at least six years before they entered the university. Therefore, students in the sampling pool had been studying English for approximately 9 years at the beginning of this part of research, and around 10 years at the end of it.

The university that was chosen to conduct the study was a public university in China, thus students studying at this university had passed the competitive nation-wide university entrance examination, in which English was one of the test subjects. At the beginning of this part of research, they were almost at the end of their year-three university study. Having English language as their major, these students had an intensive course in English, which offered English training in various perspectives, such as reading, writing, speaking, Western culture, grammar, etc. The course structure was designed on the basis of *The College English Syllabus for English Majors* by the Chinese Ministry of Education in 2000; thereby students would take ten to fifteen hours' English classes each week. In the four years, the units students took were listed below:

- Intensive Reading.
- Introduction to Linguistics.
- British Literature and Anthology.
- Theory and Practice of Translation.
- Phonemic.
- Selected Reading in English Essays.
- American Literature and Anthology.
- Selected British and American Newspaper Reading.
- English Academic Thesis Writing.
- Research methods in English Teaching.
- Phonetics.
- English Speaking.
- English Listening.
- English Speech.
- Introduction to Western Culture.
- Introduction to English Literature.
- Lexicology.
- Pragmatics.
- Advanced English Writing.
- Audio-visual English.
- English Writing.
- English Pedagogy.
- Overview of English-speaking Countries.
- English Grammar.

All of these units were taught in English, and most teachers who taught the units were Chinese teachers with master's degrees in foreign language study, such as linguistics, applied linguistics, literature and translation. A few teachers teaching in the department had obtained doctor's degree in these areas. English Speaking and sometimes Introduction to Western Culture and Advanced

English Writing as well, were mainly taught by teachers whose native language was English.

There was no unit in the course that was specifically designed to assist word acquisition. Although lexicology was provided in year three, this unit primarily dealt with vocabulary in a linguistic point of view. The content of the unit was primarily on English words' origin, their structure, history, development, and formation. New words were usually learned explicitly in Intensive Reading, or acquired implicitly in other units. In addition to studying the language from formal university instruction, most of the students would try to have more English learning out of class, such as from English TV and radio programs, and from the Internet; they also sought chances to have oral practice with native-speakers, through English Corner, for instance, which was usually a weekend activity for oral English practice with others.

Most of the students would seek discipline-related work after they graduate from the university. For example, they may become English teachers, translators or staff in companies doing international businesses. It thus seemed reasonable to assume that most of them have a relatively high level of motivation to study the language. Taking all the above factors into consideration, it was concluded that the sampling pool represent the upper-intermediate to advanced L2 learners in China.

The sampling method adopted in the longitudinal sub-study was convenience sampling. In convenience sampling, people, who are available, who can be easily accessed, or who are willing to volunteer, are included in the sample (Johnson & Christensen, 2014). Convenience sampling is different from random sampling, as in convenience sampling, not everyone belonging to the population will have equal chances to be included in the sample. Technically speaking, a population cannot be generalized from a convenience sample (Johnson & Christensen, 2014). However, in reality the majority of experimental researchers tend to use convenience samples instead of random samples, due to practical constraints or ethical considerations (Johnson & Christensen, 2014). In this part of research, convenience sampling was adopted, as according to the ethics requirement, only those who agreed to participate in the research could be included in the sub-study.

It should be noted that when convenience sampling is adopted, researchers should describe the characteristics of the participants, and decide whom the participants may represent (Johnson & Christensen, 2014). It was believed that the convenience sampling in this part of research did not undermine the representation of the target population, which was the upper-intermediate to advanced L2 learners in China. There were 27 volunteers who took part in the sub-study, and all the volunteers shared the characteristics with the rest in the sampling pool. The reason why they were willing to participate in this part of research may most likely be because they felt interested in it, or they wanted to test their vocabulary sizes by using this sub-study as an opportunity.

The average age of the participants in the 12-month longitudinal sub-study was approximately 20 years old, and at the end of the longitudinal sub-study, the average age of the participants was around 21. Among the 27 participants, there were 21 (77.8%) females and 6 (22.2%) males. The gender imbalance of the subjects was normal, due to the fact that female students to a great extent outnumbered male students in the department.

3. 5. 2   Sampling and Participants in the Word Association Sub-study

The participants of this sub-study were sampled from the same sampling pool as the participants of the longitudinal sub-study. The word association sub-study adopted convenience sampling as well, in which only students who were willing to do this part of research participated in it. The convenience sampling did not see significant impact on participants' representation of the upper-intermediate to advanced L2 learners, as participants shared the same key features with the target population in education background and motivation to study English.

In total, 30 participants took part in the word association sub-study. The participants were year-three undergraduate students, whose major was English as a foreign language. The average age of the participants was around 20. Among the participants there were 23 females, which accounted for 76.7% in the sample; and 7 males, which accounted for 23.3% in the sample. Again, the gender imbalance of the subjects was normal, owing to the fact that female students to a great extent outnumbered male students in the department.

3.5.3   Sampling and Participants of the Interview

Three participants were involved in the interview, including 1 male and 2 females. The reason why no more interviewees were interviewed is that the interview is considered to be a supplement to the word association sub-study. In the word association sub-study, the cognitive reasons for FAV stagnation were investigated. As is discussed in Chapter 1, this research assumes that underlying the effective teaching and learning methods, it is the cognitive mechanism that works in FAV development. In other words, the cognitive mechanism behind those methods is the root cause for FAV growth. For this reason, it is suggested that more attention should be paid to the mental lexicon construction in FAV development. Guided by the findings of the mental lexicon construction, effective teaching and learning methods may be identified more effectively, and new teaching and learning strategies may be designed. The interview in this research serves as a supplement for the word association sub-study. The effective learning and teaching methods that the interviewees felt effective were cross-compared with the findings from the word association study, and to check whether those strategies can be explained by findings from the word association study. Results of the pilot interview also show that three interviewees were enough, as the strategies interviewees reflected were limited and similar, and their reflection on the attention to FAV teaching and learning was relatively consistent. After three interviewees no new themes came out.

The participants were sampled from the same sampling pool as participants of the longitudinal sub-study and the word association sub-study were. Like the two previous sub-studies, convenience sampling was adopted due to ethical considerations. Before the interview was conducted, the researcher called on students to participate in it. Only those who showed interest and willingness to do the interview would be recruited. The consent form for the participation was signed by participants as well. The time to conduct the interview was in June, 2016. At the time of the interview, the interviewees were around 21 to 22 years old, and they were seniors in the second semester. They had completed all the courses required for the 4-year university study. In addition, they had just completed a thesis writing of about 5,000 words, which was a compulsory requirement for graduation. The topics of the thesis were required to be related to L2 linguistics and applied linguistics, literature, translation, or culture. All the interviewees participated in TEM8 exam in March, 2016. TEM8 is a national test of English as a foreign language in China. The full name of TEM is Test for English Majors. TEM has two levels, TEM4 and TEM8. Certificates of TEM4 and TEM8 are important to English-major students, as they are usually required by recruiters in English related jobs. Meanwhile, TEM tests, especially TEM8, have relatively high ESL requirements to testees, and are relatively difficult to pass. The high level of difficulty can be evidenced by the average national passing rate of TEM4 being 49.92% (Renmin University of China, 2017), and that of TEM8 being 40.60% (Tongji University of China, 2017) in 2016. In order to pass TEM8, students usually spend a great amount of time to prepare for it. In addition, all of the three interviewees participated in the postgraduate entrance examination in January, 2016, in which English was one of the subjects.

3.6   Data Analysis

There were two types of data in this research: numerical data from quantitative sub-studies, and textual data from qualitative sub-studies. The analysis methods for both of the two types of data are introduced in this section.

3.6.1　Quantitative Data Analysis

The Statistical Package for Social Science (SPSS) software was adopted to analyse the data obtained from both the longitudinal sub-study and the word association sub-study. The data that was processed by SPSS included the scores of passive vocabulary test, controlled active vocabulary test, Les30 test, LFP from compositions, and word association tests. The Vocabulary Knowledge Scale (VKS) test, which was a Likert-scale test used to measure testees' familiarity level with the cue words in the word association sub-study, was analysed by SPSS as well. The statistical analysis methods included Descriptive Statistics, Paired-sample T test, and One-way Repeated Measures ANOVA. Details of the statistical analysis for each sub-study are provided in the following chapters. SPSS was considered to be an appropriate tool, as it met all the calculation needs in the two studies. In the word association sub-study, the software AntConc 3.5 was adopted as well. AntConc 3.5 was used to count the frequencies of candidate cue words in the word association tests. Details of the quantitative data analysis are provided in Chapter 4 and Chapter 5.

3.6.2　Qualitative Data Analysis

The first qualitative sub-study in this research was the interview. The analysis of the interview was guided by the constructive grounded theory. According to Charmaz (2006), the constructivist grounded theory "consists of systematic, yet flexible guidelines for collecting and analysing qualitative data to construct theories 'grounded' in the data themselves". Based on the constructivist grounded theory, the data analysis in this sub-study took a series of steps. First, the entire process of the interview was recorded. Then the interview was listened to by the researcher, and was transcribed by the researcher. Second, the transcripts were rechecked by the researcher to ensure that every word had been transcribed correctly. In the next step, the transcript was segmented. Units in the transcript that contained valuable information were found and marked. Then coding was conducted. The researcher read the transcript line by line, and put descriptive phrases as codes beside each segment. In the sub-study, both pre-existing and inductive codes were used. The pre-existing codes were designed in advance based on the research objectives of the interview. For example, the pre-existing code of "effective learning strategies" was made to capture learning activities that may be effective in FAV learning; the pre-existing code of "effective teaching strategies" was made to detect teaching methods that may be helpful to FAV learning. Inductive codes were not prepared in advance, but came into being when the researcher found some unexpected valuable information from the data. For example, one of the inductive codes in this sub-study was "the number of learning strategies used by the interviewee", which was valuable information to judge whether students adopted a variety of activities in FAV learning. After the coding was completed, the codes were re-examined by the researcher and the supervisor. When there was inconsistent coding, discussions were made until agreement was achieved. In this way the intercoder reliability and intracoder reliability was ensured. All the codes were put into a master list. Then the codes were enumerated and categorised. The researcher systematically analysed the categories and codes, and attempted to construct themes and theories that were grounded in them.

3.7　Conclusion

This chapter serves as a methodological foundation for the entire research project. It first introduces the research aim and objectives, then introduces the research method used in this study. Information on the research instruments, participants, sampling process, pilot study, and data analysis methods are provided as well. In the next chapter, the first quantitative sub-study, the 12-month longitudinal sub-study, is presented and discussed.

Chapter 4   The Developmental Process
of Free Active Vocabulary

4.1   Introduction

This chapter explores the developmental process of free active vocabulary (FAV) in a 12-month period of time. Moreover, it investigates the relationship between FAV and other types of vocabulary, $i.e.$, the passive vocabulary (PV) and the controlled active vocabulary (CAV). The chapter first poses research questions, and then presents research method, which includes instruments, data collection, data preparation and data analysis. At the end of the chapter, results are reported, and answers to the research questions are discussed.

4.2   Research Questions

The questions that are explored in this chapter are:
• What is the development pattern of FAV when L2 learners reach upper-intermediate to advanced proficiency level?
• If the threshold phenomenon occurs in the FAV development, what are the features of the threshold phenomenon?
• What is the developmental process of PV when L2 learners reach upper-intermediate to advanced L2 proficiency

level?

- What is the relationship between FAV and PV?
- What is the developmental process of CAV when L2 learners reach upper-intermediate to advanced L2 proficiency level?
- What is the relationship between FAV and CAV?

4.3　Research Method

This section presents the major components of the research method adopted in the sub-study, including instruments, procedure of data collection, data preparation, and data analysis.

4.3.1　Instruments

The participants in this longitudinal sub-study have been introduced in Chapter 3. The instruments adopted in the sub-study included three vocabulary tests and two writing tasks, which are detailed and explained in this section.

4.3.1.1　Test of Receptive Vocabulary

The test of receptive vocabulary adopted in this sub-study was the VLT. It should be noted that the Vocabulary Levels Test (VLT) in fact has two types. The first type is for measuring passive vocabulary, and the second type is for measuring controlled active vocabulary. Therefore, in order to be more accurate, it is proposed in this research that the two types of Vocabulary Levels Test be renamed as Passive Vocabulary Levels Test (PVLT) and Controlled Active Vocabulary Levels Test (CAVLT), according to their different functions. In PVLT, there are five sections: Section A for words from the first 2,000 (i. e. ,1—2,000) word frequency band, Section B for words from the 3,000 (i. e. ,2,001—3,000) word frequency band, Section C for words from the 5,000 (i. e. , 4,001—5,000) word frequency band, Section D for words from the 10,000 (i. e. , 9,001—10,000) word frequency band, and Section E for academic words.

The original Passive Vocabulary Levels Test was designed by Nation (1983,1990), and its reliability was tested and verified by Read (1988). The PVLT adopted in this research was the revised and expanded version designed by Schmitt et al. (2001). In the early version of PVLT by Nation (1983,1990), one-third of the tested words in Section A are sampled from the first 1,000 (i. e. ,1—1,000) word frequency level, and the rest two-thirds of the tested words in Section A are sampled from the second 1,000 (i. e. ,1,001—2,000) word frequency level. In the revised version designed by Schmitt et al. (2001), half of the tested words in Section A are sampled from the first 1,000 word frequency level, and the other half are from the second 1,000 word frequency level. Other sections are similar to those of the original PVLT. The tested words in Section B are from the 3,000 word level, i. e. , they are sampled from the 2,001—3,000 word frequency band. Similarly, in Section C the tested words are from the 5,000 word level, i. e. , the 4,001—5,000 word frequency band, and in Section D the tested words are from the 10,000 word level, i. e. , the 9,001—10,000 word frequency band. The word frequency bands are constructed primarily on the basis of the General Service List (GSL). Schmitt et al. (2001) devised three revised versions of PVLT, and tested their validity. In these revised versions, the tested words in the academic section are from the Academic Word List (AWL). In the original version by Nation (1983, 1990), however, the tested words in this section are from the University Word List (UWL), as there was no AWL yet at the time when it was compiled. All these versions of PVLT are in the form of matching tests. In the revised PVLT, each section has 10 clusters, as compared to 6 clusters in the original version by Nation (1983, 1990). Each cluster is composed of 3 tested words on the right column, and 6 paraphrases on the left column. An example from Schmitt et al. (2001) is shown below:

1 copy

2 event ＿＿＿＿＿ end or highest point

3 motor ＿＿＿＿＿ this moves a car

4 pity ＿＿＿＿＿thing made to be like another

5 profit

6 tip

Since the revised PVLT contains 5 sections, and each section contains 30 test items, the test has 150 test items in total. In each section, the ratio of noun, verb, and adjective is 3 : 2 : 1. According to Schmitt et al. (2001), the average time needed to take the test is 31 minutes.

PVLT has numerous strengths. It is easy and quick to be conducted and scored, and needs no special equipment. It can provide researchers and teachers with a relatively comprehensive picture on test takers' passive vocabulary knowledge, since the test contains various sections to test words from different frequency levels. Compared with the original version of PVLT by Nation (1983, 1990), the revised versions by Schmitt *et al.* (2001) are more updated, as they adopted AWL instead of UWL to sample tested words in the academic word section. The revised versions also sample tested words in a more balanced and rational way. As has been introduced, in the early version of PVLT by Nation (1983,1990), one-third of the tested words in Section A are sampled from the first 1,000 (*i.e.*, 1—1,000) word frequency level, and the rest two-thirds of the tested words in Section A are selected from the second 1,000 (*i.e.*, 1,001—2,000) word frequency level. In the revised version designed by Schmitt *et al*. (2001), half of the tested words in Section A are sampled from the first 1,000 word frequency level, and the other half are from the second 1,000 word frequency level. Moreover, the revised versions cover more tested items than the original version. There are 18 test items in each section in the original version. By contrast, there are 30 test items in each section in the revised version. Bayazidi and Saeb (2017) tested the reliability of two of the three revised versions by Schmitt *et al*. (2001), and they concluded that the two are reliable tests. Due to the strengths of the revised PVLT, one of the revised versions was adopted in this sub-study. The reliability of the adopted version was tested and proved by Bayazidi and Saeb (2017).

It should be noted that only one version of PVLT by Schmitt et al. (2001) was adopted in this longitudinal sub-study. In the first month and the twelfth month, the test was conducted twice, and then the test results were compared. It was due to the consideration that although Schmitt et al. (2001) tested and proved the revised versions' validity, they did not test whether those versions were parallel to each other. In addition, as the interval between the two tests was as long as 12 month, the possibility that the first-month test would have a great reminding effect on the twelfth-month test was low. Therefore, only one version was adopted. In 2017, Bayazidi and Saeb (2017) tested two of the three revised PVLT versions by Schmitt *et al*.(2001), including the one that was applied in this sub-study. He found although both of the two versions were highly reliable tests, they were not equivalent or parallel. Therefore, the two should not be treated as equal forms and used as parallel tests, particularly in longitudinal studies (Bayazidi & Saeb, 2017). Appendix A presents the PVLT version adopted in this sub-study.

4.3.1.2 Test of Controlled Active Vocabulary

The structure of CAVLT is parallel to that of PVLT. The CAVLT contains 5 sections as well, *i.e.*, Section A for the 2,000 word frequency level, Section B for the 3,000 word frequency level, Section C for the 5,000 word frequency level, Section D for the 10,000 word frequency level, and Section E for the university words. In total, CAVLT contains 90 test items, with each section having 18 test items. CAVLT is in the form of cued recall. In the test, full sentences with blanks for the target words are provided. The first two letters of the target words are provided as well.

It is necessary to note that in the revised PVLT by Schmitt *et al*.(2001), which was adopted in this sub-study, the tested items in the academic section (Section E) are sampled from the Academic Word List (AWL). However, in CAVLT tested items in the academic section (Section D) are selected from the University Word List (UWL). Therefore, it is necessary to investigate the similarities and differences between UWL and AWL. The UWL, which was designed by Xue and Nation (1984), is a list of words that are used in academic texts with various subjects. The list contains 836 words. These 836 words are the most frequently used academic words that do not belong to the first 2,000 words in the General Service List (GSL) by West (1953).

The AWL is a new version of UWL, and it was designed by Cox-head (2000). Coxhead (2000) holds that the first 2,000 words in GSL are basic words that any ESL learners need to grasp before studying the academic vocabulary. Therefore, just like UWL, AWL does not contain the first 2,000 words from GSL. AWL contains 3,100 words belonging to 570 words families which originate from the 836 words of UWL. According to Schmitt *et al*. (2001), AWL gives better coverage of academic texts while listing fewer words than UWL, as AWL presents academic words in form of word families. Different from other sections in PVLT and CAVLT, the academic section in PVLT and CAVLT is not primarily frequency driven. In fact, the AWL and UWL contain words of various frequency levels above the 2,000 word frequency level. In other words, the academic section in the original and revised PVLT and CAVLT contains words of frequency levels from 2,000 to 10,000 (i. e., 2,001—10,000). The reason why UWL is adopted in CAVLT but AWL is adopted in the revised PVLT is because AWL was not compiled yet when CAVLT was devised. However, since AWL was devised based on UWL, the two are basically consistent to each other.

Laufer and Nation (1999) tested the validity and reliability of CAVLT. They concluded that it is a reliable and valid test, and just like PVLT, the advantage of CAVLT is that it is easy to conduct and score. The version of CAVLT adopted in this sub-study is presented in Appendix B.

4.3.1.3　Test of Free Active Vocabulary

4.3.1.3.1　Lex30 Test

One of the tests conducted to measure the testees' FAV in

this sub-study is the Lex30 test, which was designed by Meara and Fitzpatrick (2000). Lex30 is in the form of word association tasks. However, by nature it is not a word association test, as its score is based on the frequencies the associations belong to, rather than association types they are of. There are 30 cue words in Lex30, and testees are required to produce four responses to each of the cue words if they can. All the 30 cue words are sampled from the first 1,000 word frequency band. It is believed that words from that frequency level can be recognised by test takers of various language proficiencies, and is therefore suitable to be used as cues for a wide range of testees (Meara & Fitzpatrick, 2000). In addition, the 30 cues are believed to be able to elicit responses that do not fall into the first 1,000 word frequency level, and do not tend to elicit strong primary associations (Fitzpatrick & Clenton, 2010) as well. Lex30 is easy and time-saving to be conducted, as it only takes 15 minutes to complete (Fitzpatrick & Clenton, 2010). Moreover, it gives testees chances to produce responses more freely, without the confine of context (Meara & Fitzpatrick, 2000). The validity and reliability of Lex30 has been repeatedly tested and proven (Fitzpatrick & Clenton, 2010; Fitzpatrick & Meara, 2004; Walters, 2012). The Lex30 test adopted in this sub-study is presented in Appendix C.

4.3.1.3.2　Writing Tasks

Although writing tasks are not as time-saving and convenient to be carried out as Lex30 is, both of them were conducted to measure FAV in this sub-study. The first reason is that although Lex30 possesses many strengths in measuring FAV, it is believed by some scholars that "producing response words to stimuli … is not the same as spontaneously producing words in a composition, of course" (Siok & James, 2006). In other words, measuring FAV in context may offer researchers more accurate information on FAV, although it exerts on testees a limit of context in word production. The second reason is that although Meara and Fitzpatrick's (2000) original Lex30 test can show scores of FAV at various frequency levels by using a software, the software seems not available to other researchers. The Internet version of Lex30 can generate a general score, but cannot generate scores for responses at different word frequency levels. According to the scoring standard of Lex30 (Meara & Fitzpatrick, 2000), the test result of Lex30 can only reflect the number of responses that fall out of proper nouns, numbers, high-frequency function words, and the first 1,000 most frequent words. More detailed information on FAV cannot be obtained from it. The writing tasks, however, may offer researchers more detailed information on FAV. Owing to the consideration that both Lex30 and writing tasks have strengths and weaknesses in evaluating FAV, to get more accurate and comprehensive information on it, both of them were adopted in this research as measuring tools.

As has been pointed out in Chapter 2, there is no instrument that can directly measure the size of FAV. The size of FAV therefore is usually expressed by lexical richness. It is believed that if the lexical richness is high, then the test taker may have more FAV available in his lexical repertoire (Laufer, 1991). There are two ways to measure lexical richness. One is by Lexical Frequency Profile (LFP), and the other is by four indexes including lexical variation (LV), lexical originality (LO), lexical sophistication (LS), and lexical density (LD). The first method, the Lexical Frequency Profile (LFP), measures the richness of a text by calculating how many words in the text belong to different frequency categories. LFP usually includes four categories. The first category, which is called Band 1, contains the first 1,000 frequent words in English; the second category, Band 2, contains the second 1,000 frequent words in English; the third category, Band 3, contains the academic words; and the fourth category, "Not in the lists", are words that do not belong to any of the 3 categories mentioned above. LFP shows the distribution of words (including tokens, types and word families) of a text in the four categories. The computer program that conducts LFP calculation is Vocabprofile, which was later updated to be RANGE. In Vocabprofile, UWL was adopted to be Band 3, the academic words. In RANGE, AWL was adopted to be the academic words.

RANGE was developed by Paul Nation, Alex Heatley, and Averil Coxhead at Victoria University of Willington. It can be downloaded from Nation's website as part of the website of the Victoria University of Willington (Heatley, Nation & Coxhead, 2002). RANGE contains three word lists. The first word list (BASEWRD1) contains the first 1,000 frequent word families of English; the second word list (BASEWRD2) contains the second 1,000 frequent word families; and the third word list (BASEWRD3) is the Academic Word List. Both BASEWRD1 and BASEWRD2 are compiled based on the General Service List. All the three lists contain words' base forms, derived forms, and inflectional forms. Results by RANGE show the numbers and percentages of tokens and types that fall into each of the three word lists, as well as the numbers and percentages of tokens and types that are not in the three lists. The number of word families that belong to the three lists and those that are not in the lists are counted as well.

The second way that is widely used to measure lexical richness is by lexical variation (LV), lexical originality (LO), lexical density (LD), and lexical sophistication (LS). Laufer (1991) may be one of the earliest scholars using these four indexes to measure FAV size. According to Laufer (1991), LV is the type/token ratio, the formula of which is LV = (number of types ÷ number of tokens) × 100%. LV indicates how testees incline to repeat the same words in writing. The higher of the LV, the more varied the words are in writing. According to Laufer (1991), LD refers to the percentage of lexical words in the text. The lexical words are also called content words, which include nouns, verbs, adverbs, numerals, and adjectives. Information is usually conveyed by lexical words. Functional words, however, do not convey as much information, and they are usually used to show relations between words and sentences (Thoughtco, 2017). Functional words include conjunctions, prepositions, articles, and auxiliaries (Thoughtco, 2017). Since a word is either a lexical word or a functional word, the total number of tokens can be calculated by adding the two types of words together. The formula for calculating LD is LD = (number of lexical words ÷ number of tokens) × 100%. The higher of the LD is, the "denser" the text is, since there are more lexical words in the text to convey information. According to Laufer (1991), LO is the percentage of unique words that are used by a writer but not by other writers in the group. The higher of the LO is, the more words there are that can be produced by the testee than by his peers. The formula of LO is LO = (number of lexemes unique to one writer ÷ total number of tokens) × 100%. According to Laufer (1991), LS refers to the percentage of "advanced words" used in writing. There is no set standard to judge which words are "advanced words". Instead, the judgment of "advanced words" is flexible, depending on the testees' profi-

ciency level. For example, in Laufer's (1991) study, the participants were year-one university students in English language
department; therefore, the researcher decided that "advanced
words" were those from UWL. He pointed out that for testees
who were school learners, "advanced words" could be those
taught in upper grades.

All the four indexes of LD, LV, LO, and LS may be appropriate tools to measure the quality of a piece of writing, but they
seem to be problematic as an indicator of FAV size. The problem of
LV and LD is that the two seem to ignore the factor of word
frequency in calculation. According to Schmitt et al. (2001),
words are usually learned in layers. Specifically, "learners acquire
more frequently used words before they acquire less frequently
used ones" (Schmitt et al., 2001). Testees may need to learn
more words in higher frequencies before they can grasp more
words in lower frequencies. Therefore, if more FAV fall into
lower frequencies, it may indicate that the testee has a bigger FAV
repertoire. However, the LV and LD do not consider LFP in
their calculation, which may make the two not sensitive to FAV
size. For example, two testees are asked to write a composition of
200 tokens. The first testee produces 60 different types, and all
the 60 types are from the first 2,000 frequent words; the second
testee produces 60 different types as well, but 40 of them are
from the words beyond the first 2,000 frequent words. According to
the formula LV = (number of types ÷ number of tokens) × 100%,
the two testees have the same LV value. However, it may not be
rational to draw a conclusion from this result that the two testees
have the same FAV size. More likely, they have different FAV
repertoires, since the second testee can produce more lower-
frequency words than the first testee. LD shares the same defi-

ciency. For instance, two testees are asked to write a composition of 200 tokens, and in both of their writings there are 80 lexical words. All the first testee's lexical words are from the first 2,000 frequent words, and 60 of the second testee's lexical words are from the words beyond the first 2,000 frequent words. According to the formula LD=(number of lexical words ÷ number of tokens) × 100%, the two compositions result in the same LD value. But the two testees may have different FAV size, since the majority of their lexical words are from different word frequency bands. Therefore, LV and LD seem to be inappropriate measures of FAV size. LO and LS to some degree share the same idea as LFP in that they all indicate that words at lower frequencies may convey important information on FAV size. In LO, lower-frequency words are represented by "unique words"; in LS, they are expressed by "advanced words". However, both "unique words" and "advanced words" are problematic in that there are no set standards for them. This weakness may make researchers' judgment subjective and arbitrary, and therefore make it hard to have cross-comparisons of research findings. In addition, the list of "unique words" and "advanced words" has to be compiled by researchers themselves, which is not time-efficient.

Due to the weaknesses of LO, LD, LV, and LS in FAV evaluation, it is proposed in this research that LFP be adopted to evaluate FAV size. Laufer and Nation (1995) tested the reliability and validity of LFP, and they concluded that the reliability and validity is satisfactory.

In this sub-study, two topics were selected for students' writing tasks. Both of the two topics were referenced from IELTS, but minor changes were made according to the purpose of the sub-study. The length of writing was changed to be no less than 200 words, so that the work load of testees was rational, meanwhile enough tokens could be obtained for reliable LFP results (Laufer & Nation, 1995). The two topics were at the same difficulty level. Both of them were of a discussion type that could elicit testees to express their own opinions. In this way, primary responses could be avoided. Topics that seemed to be too easy, such as those on food, entertainment, and travelling, were not chosen, owing to the fact that those topics may elicit mostly high-frequency words. The two topics were presented in Chinese, so that testees' FAV production would not be affected by the given information. The topic in the first-month test was on factors that could help people achieve success, and the topic in the twelfth-month test was on factors that could help a country develop. Detailed information on the two writing tasks is presented in Appendix D and E.

4.3.2　Data Collection Procedures

4.3.2.1　Pilot Study

A pilot study was administered before the formal data collection. 11 year-three students who were studying in the same major and from the same university took part in it. They were asked to do the PVLT, CAVLT, Lex30, and a writing task with one of the two topics in the formal tests. The pilot study aimed to ensure that the test instruction and test items were clear enough to test takers, and to find the suitable length of time for testees to complete each test. Based on the results and testees' feedback, test instructions were changed to be in Chinese. The pilot study showed that some participants were able to spell the tested words in CAVLT, but they did not pay adequate attention to grammar. Therefore, in the instruction of CAVLT, a reminder was added. The reminder was: "Please pay attention to grammar such as number, tense, person, and possession. Please write the target words with correct grammatical forms." Moreover, in order to assist test takers to choose the right word to spell in CAVLT, Chinese translation of the target words was added after the blanks. It was found that some participants did not notice that on the other side of the paper there were also test items. Therefore, at the end of each page a short note was provided, saying that there were more test items on the other side of the paper. The length of time for each test was decided as well. There would be 30 minutes for PVLT, 30 minutes for CAVLT, 15 minutes for Lex30 test, and 40 minutes for the writing task. Before the writing task, there would be a 5-minute break. Therefore the formal tests would take 120 minutes in total.

4.3.2.2　Formal Data Collection

Due to the fact that the sub-study is a longitudinal one of 12 months, formal data collection was conducted twice, with the first one being conducted in May, 2015, and the second one being conducted in May, 2016. May was considered to be a suitable time to collect data, since it was in the middle of a semester, and students were in their normal track of study at the time. Before the data was collected, instructions for PVLT, CAVLT, Lex30 and the writing tasks were orally presented to the testees by the student investigator. Extra time was offered to test takers to read the written instructions as well. If they had any doubts on the test formats or requirements, they were encouraged to raise questions. The testees were reminded on the length of time allotted to each test, and they were suggested to manage their time according to it. Then test papers were handed out to the testees. When there were 5 minutes left for each test, the testees were notified on it, and they were suggested again to manage their time. It was noticed that most of them could complete the tests on time. In both the first data collection and the second one, the procedure was the same. After the tests were completed, all the test paper was collected. Since the interval between the first and second data collection was 12 months, it was assumed that the interval time was long enough, therefore the reminding effect was minimal. In addition, no results were released to the participants after the first-month test, so the possible influence of the first-month test on the twelfth-month test was minimal. In the PVLT test, the investigator repeatedly reminded testees that if they did not know which paraphrase a tested word should be matched with, they should not guess and should just leave the blank empty. The purpose was to ensure that results of PVLT were not affected by guessing. The detailed information on the tests is demonstrated in Table 4.1.

Table 4.1   Tests Adopted in the Longitudinal Sub-study

Test type	Activity	Purpose
The Passive Vocabulary Levels Test	Match the tested words with their equivalent paraphrases	To measure testees' passive vocabulary size
The Controlled Active Vocabulary Levels Test	Complete the tested words according to the given context	To measure testees' controlled active vocabulary size
Lex30 Test	Instantly write down four responses that come into the testees' mind when encountering the cue word	To measure testees' free active vocabulary size

Continued

Test type	Activity	Purpose
Writing Task One	Write a composition of no less than 200 words on the given topic	To measure testees' free active vocabulary size
Writing Task Two	Write a composition of no less than 200 words on the given topic	To measure testees' free active vocabulary size

4.3.3　Data Preparation

4.3.3.1　Selection of Valid Data

Test papers were collected after the testees completed the tests. Then valids datas were selected. Since the sub-study was longitudinal, test papers done by the testees who failed to participate twice were removed. Only the data done by subjects who participated in both the first-month and the twelfth-month tests were kept for further selection. Datas with handwritings that were difficult to be recognised, and datas that were suspected to be done carelessly were removed. In total six participants' datas were removed. After the selection, 21 subjects' test papers were determined as valid data for final analysis.

4.3.3.2　Scoring of PVLT

In PVLT test, if a tested word is matched with the right paraphrase, one point will be given. Since there are 30 tested words in each section, and there are 5 sections in the test, the total score of PVLT is 150 points, with each section having 30 points.

4.3.3.3　Scoring of CAVLT

The scoring program for CAVLT can be found on website

of Lextutor (2017). Following Laufer and Nation (1999), datas were closely checked and necessary revisions were made before they were put into the computer. Minor mistakes in spelling, i. e., mistakes that did not affect word recognition (such as "concieve" for "conceive"), were corrected. Grammatical mistakes were corrected as well. All other datas were kept unchanged and typed into the computer. The computer program then produced scores for CAVLT by hundred-marks. There were 6 scores for each participant, with 5 scores for the 5 sections in CAVLT, and a total score for the whole test.

Since in CAVLT grammar mistakes and minor spelling mistakes are corrected before scoring, the CAVLT is more of a test measuring the breadth of controlled active vocabulary, rather than measuring the depth of it (Laufer & Nation, 1999). From the hundred-mark score, the controlled active vocabulary size can be estimated. The test items at each section (except the academic word section) are sampled from 2,000 word frequency level, 3,000 word frequency level, 5,000 word frequency level, and 10,000 word frequency level, and each of these levels contains 1,000 word families. Therefore, if nine out of the 18 items in Section A are answered correctly, then the score of Section A is 50 points. The score indicates that 50% of the 1,000 word families at that frequency level may be known by the testee. The controlled active vocabulary size at that frequency level is therefore around 500 word families. In other words, there are around 500 word families at the level that are readily available for the testees' controlled productive use. The section of academic words contains items sampled from 836 words frequently used in academic texts. The size of a testee's academic controlled active vocabulary therefore can be estimated according to the percentage of correct answers in the section as well.

4.3.3.4 Scoring of Lex30 Test

According to Meara and Fitzpatrick (2000), the scoring of Lex30 is conducted by a software similar to Vocabprofile. In Lex30, associated words that belong to the Level 0 word list, i. e. , proper nouns, numbers, and high-frequency function words, get zero points. Associated words that belong to the Level 1 word list, i. e. , the first 1,000 frequent content words in English, are assigned zero point as well. Any association that does not belong to these two categories would obtain one point. Since there are in total 30 cues in the test, and testees are required to have 4 associations to each cue, the maximum score a testee can obtain is 120 points.

Before being entered into the computer for scoring, responses were processed. First, like in CAVLT, words with minor spelling errors that did not affect recognition (e. g. "concieve" for "conceive") were corrected. Words that had evident spelling mistakes were kept unchanged. Second, if one cue elicited a response but the response was written more than once by the testee, only one response was kept. All others were deleted, as the program would score the response repeatedly if it appears repeatedly. Third, following Meara and Fitzpatrick (2000), words with regular inflectional suffixes, including plural (e. g. apples, eggs), third person singular present tense (e. g. talks, runs), past tense (e. g. talked, ran), past participles (e. g. written, spoken), present progressive (e. g. working, running), comparative (e. g. better, bigger), superlative (e. g. most, best) and possessive (e. g. his, its), were lemmatised, and they were considered the same as their base forms. For example, the response word "digs" to the cue word "dig" would be lemmatised to be its base form "dig". Since the response "dig" was the same as its cue, it would score zero point. For another example, if the cue word "dig" elicited responses of "hole" and "holes", the responses of "hole" and "holes" would together score one point. This is because "holes" should be lemmatised as "hole", and "hole" belongs to the second 1,000 word frequency band. Meara and Fitzpatrick (2000), who designed the Lex30 test, holds that some affixes, usually those most frequent and regular derivational affixes, should be lemmatised to be base forms as well. These derivational affixes include -able, -er, -ish, etc. However, in this research the principle was not followed, due to the consideration that ESL learners may not have as much language instinct and grammar knowledge as native speakers do. Therefore, derivations that are frequent and regular to native speakers may not be so to ESL learners. For instance, knowing the word "hope" may not necessarily mean that an ESL learner would know the word "hopeful". Similarly, knowing the word "develop" may not mean that he knows "-ment" could be added to it to create the noun form "development". In this sense, lemmatising derivational suffixes may make ESL learners' vocabulary size underestimated. Owing to this consideration, derivations and irregular inflections were not lemmatised, and they were put into computer as valid data for scoring. It is believed that the data treatment can lead to a more objective measurement of the EFL learners' FAV. Meanwhile, it is admit that the treatment may result in higher Lex30 grades. However, since all the rounds of Lex30 test in this research adopt the same scoring standard, it does not affect the comparison of the scores, as well as the conclusion on the FAV development trend. The program to score Lex30 can be found at the website of Lognostics (2017).

4.3.3.5 Scoring of Writing Tasks

The computer program adopted in this research to score

testees' compositions was RANGE. Before the compositions were scored by RANGE, several steps were taken to process the data. First, although the testees were asked to write a composition of no less than 200 words, only the first 200 words from the main body of the text were taken out for analysis. This was based on the finding of Laufer and Nation (1995) that the LFP over 200 words tends to be stable, whereas that of less than 200 words does not. All the compositions were transcribed into Microsoft Word File, and like in CAVLT and Lex30, spelling errors that did not affect word recognition were corrected. Then words in every composition were counted by the Microsoft Word File. The first 200 words (not including the title) were taken out for further treatment. Due to the fact that a few testees' compositions were less than 200 words, these compositions were removed from valid data. As a result, 16 testees' compositions, which were 32 pieces in total, were left for final analysis. Second, pseudo words were deleted, so that RANGE would not count them as words of "not in the lists" and bring about wrong results. Words that were semantically wrong were deleted as well. It was due to the consideration that if a word is not used correctly in meaning, it should not be considered as known by the testee (Laufer & Nation, 1995). Additionally, to be consistent with the scoring standard of Lex30, proper nouns (e.g. Australia) were deleted, and they would not obtain points. This is consistent with the view of Laufer and Paribakht (1998) that proper nouns should not be regarded as a part of learners' vocabulary knowledge. Wrong derivations (e.g. "inhappy" for "unhappy") were deleted. It should be noted that Microsoft Word File only counts words that are correctly spelled. After the treatment, there were on average 201.4118 (SD=1.46026) tokens for each composition left for analysis in the first month, and 202. 4375 (SD＝1. 63172) tokens in the twelfth month. Then RANGE was run to conduct LFP calculation for each of the 32 compositions.

RANGE produces results in terms of tokens, types, and word families. The numbers and percentages of tokens may not be reliable for analysis, as tokens not only include the inflections and derivations, but also include all the repetitions of them. For example, if the word "runs" occurs three times in a text, then it is counted as three tokens. Therefore, the numbers and percentages of tokens at different frequency levels may make researchers draw unreliable conclusions on FAV's frequency distributions. The numbers and percentages of types and word families may not be suitable to be analysed directly either. With regard to types, the base forms (e. g. develop), inflections (e. g. developing) and derivations (e. g. development) are all considered to be different types. If inflections are regarded as different words from their base forms, the FAV size will be overestimated. Therefore, further treatment was conducted on the data to remove inflections as individual types. Based on the list of types presented in the results of RANGE, all inflections were transferred into base forms. Then together with their base forms, they were counted as 1 type. For example, if the list of types produced by RANGE showed that in the text there were types of "run" "runs" and "running", then "runs" and "running" were lemmatized to be "run", and together the three types were regarded to be one type. Similarly, if a text had types of "develops" and "developing", they were transferred to be "develop" and counted to be one type. The list of types of each composition was observed in this way, and extra types were manually deleted. Therefore, in this sub-study, the numbers and percentages of "types" refer to those after the treatment, not the original numbers and percentages of types calculated by RANGE.

The results of word families presented by RANGE need some manual treatment as well. As words of "not in the lists" do not belong to any of the three lists available in RANGE, the program is unable to calculate the numbers and percentages of word families that fall out of the 3 available word lists. Therefore, based on the types of "not in the lists" presented by RANGE, word families were counted by the student investigator. This manual processing was feasible, as there were a very limited number of types that belonged to "not in the lists" in each composition. This could be evidenced by the mean number of types being 5.3889 (SD=2.89297) in the first month, and the mean number of types being 5.5625 (SD=2.82769) in the twelfth month. Word families of "not in the lists" were counted, and then percentages of word families belonging to each of the 3 word lists in RANGE and "not in the lists" were calculated.

It is necessary to note that PVLT, CAVLT, Lex30 and LFP in writing tasks all measure testees' breadth of vocabulary rather than the depth of vocabulary. This is due to the fact that in these tests grammatical error is not a factor in scoring. It should also be noted that both Lex30 and LFP can only indicate FAV size indirectly. As is pointed out by Laufer (1998), it seems unlikely to devise a test that is able to measure how many words a person can produce, unless his FAV repertoire is very small. However, the limited function of Lex30 and LFP is enough for this study, as the purpose of the sub-study is to investigate whether FAV grows in a 12-month period of time, not to calculate exactly how many FAV words the testees have.

4.3.4 Data Analysis

Statistical Package for Social Science (SPSS) of version 20. 0 was adopted to conduct data analysis. All the scores of PVLT, CAVLT, Lex30, and LFP were entered into SPSS for statistical processing. The methods adopted in this sub-study included Paired-sample T test and Correlation Analysis. Paired-sample T test was used to compare passive vocabulary size, controlled active vocabulary size, and free active vocabulary size between the first-month tests and the twelfth-month tests. It should be noted that in LFP analysis, the number of types and word families obtained from writing are frequency data, and Chi-square is usually adopted to compare frequencies. However, Chi-square requires that the Expected N be more than 5 (the analysis factor, 2017). As in this research the relevant data could not meet this condition, Paired-sample T test was applied instead. In order to make T test appropriate to be used, frequencies were transferred into scores, in which one frequency was equal to one point. In addition to Paired-sample T test, Correlation Analysis was applied to investigate the relationship of passive vocabulary, controlled active vocabulary, and free active vocabulary.

4.4 Results

4.4.1 The Developmental Process of FAV in the 12-month Period of Time

The scores of Lex30 and LFP of types between the first month and the twelfth month were compared by Paired-sample

T test. The results are demonstrated in Table 4.2.

Table 4. 2 Comparison of Lex30 and LFP in Terms of Word Types between the First Month and the Twelfth Month

Test scores	Time to conduct the test	Number of subjects	Mean score	Standard deviation	t	df	p
Lex30	The first month	21	82.4762	9.88240	0.614	20	0.546
	The twelfth month	21	81.2857	10.03067			
Word types of the first 1,000 frequency level	The first month	16	92.7500	6.53707	3.306	15	0.005
	The twelfth month	16	84.8750	7.58837			
Word types of the second 1,000 frequency level	The first month	16	6.8750	2.70493	−0.075	15	0.941
	The twelfth month	16	6.9375	2.69490			
Word types of the Academic Word List	The first month	16	7.8125	3.74555	−1.544	15	0.143
	The twelfth month	16	9.6875	5.26268			
Word types of "not in the lists"	The first month	16	5.6250	3.51900	0.574	15	0.574
	The twelfth month	16	5.1250	2.24722			

Results of Paired-sample T Test indicate that there was no significant difference between the first month's Lex30 score and the twelfth month's Lex30 score ($t=0.614$, df$=20$, $p=0.546$, $p>0.05$). According to the scoring principle of Lex30, response words that do not belong to the first 1,000 frequent content words, together with high-frequency function words, proper nouns and numbers would obtain points. Therefore, the result indicates that testees' FAV beyond the first 1,000 frequent content words, high-frequency content words, proper nouns and numbers did not grow in the 12-month period of time.

LFP of types from writing tasks provides more information on FAV development. According to Table 4.2, word types in the first 1,000 frequency band decreased significantly in the 12-month period ($t=3.306$, df$=15$, $p=0.005$, $p<0.05$). However, there was no significant difference in words from the second 1,000 frequency band, academic words, and "not in the lists". This shows that testees' FAV in the second 1,000 frequency level, the academic level, and beyond did not increase in the 12-month period of time. The results of LFP in terms of word families are presented in Table 4.3.

Table 4.3 Comparison of LFP in Terms of Word Families between the First Month and the Twelfth Month

Test scores	Time to conduct the test	Number of subjects	Mean score	Standard deviation	t	df	p
Word families of the first 1,000 frequency level	The first month	16	82.8750	4.61700	3.088	15	0.007
	The twelfth month	16	77.4375	6.69297			
Word families of the second 1,000 frequency level	The first month	16	6.8125	2.71339	0.000	15	1.000
	The twelfth month	16	6.8125	2.76209			

Continued

Test scores	Time to conduct the test	Number of subjects	Mean score	Standard deviation	t	df	p
Word families of the Academic Word List	The first month	16	7.6250	3.51900	−1.316	15	0.208
	The twelfth month	16	9.2500	5.25991			
Word families of "not in the lists"	The first month	16	5.3125	3.40037	0.668	15	0.514
	The twelfth month	16	4.7500	2.08167			

In terms of percentages, in the first month the average percentage of types belonging to the first 1,000 frequency level was 82.4519%, to the second 1,000 frequency level was 5.0156%, to the academic words was 6.7806%, and to "not in the lists" was 4.8525%. In the twelfth month, the average percentage of types belonging to the first 1,000 frequency level was 80.5750%, to the second level was 6.3025%, to the academic words was 8.5819%, and to "not in the lists" was 4.5375%. In word families, the LFP distribution was similar. In the first month, the average percentage of word families in the first 1,000 frequency band was 81.0058% (SD=5.56919); in the second 1,000 frequency band was 6.6040% (SD=2.49476); in academic words was 7.3318% (SD=3.20586); and in "not in the lists" was 5.0583% (SD=3.01265). In the twelfth month, the average percentage of word families of the first 1,000 frequency band was 79.1893% (SD=6.2427); of the second 1,000 frequency band was 6.8991% (SD=2.49682); of the academic words was 9.1464% (SD=4.63597); of "not in the lists" was 4.7652% (SD=2.10334). No matter in terms of types or families, the average percentages of words belonging to the first 1,000 frequency level were around 80% in both the first-month test and the twelfth-month test. By contrast, the average percentage of words used by native speakers is around 70% (Cobb, 2003). It is indicated that even when L2 learners reach the upper-intermediate to advanced proficiency level, they still heavily depend on the very high frequency words to use. In addition, there is still a big gap between native speakers' FAV size and L2 learners' FAV size.

4.4.2 The Correlation of FAV with Passive Vocabulary and Controlled Active Vocabulary

In order to investigate the correlation of FAV with PV and CAV, the developmental process of PV and CAV was explored first (Table 4.4 and Table 4.5).

Table 4.4 Comparison of PVLT Scores between the First Month and the Twelfth Month

The test score	Time to conduct the test	Number of subjects	Mean score	Standard deviation	t	df	p
Total Score of PVLT	The first month	21	108.3333	10.42273	−4.811	20	0.000
	The twelfth month	21	116.9048	8.73444			
Score of Section A in PVLT(the 2,000 frequency level)	The first month	21	29.0952	0.99523	−1.482	20	0.154
	The twelfth month	21	29.5238	0.81358			

Continued

The test score	Time to conduct the test	Number of subjects	Mean score	Standard deviation	t	df	p
Score of Section B in PVLT (the 3,000 frequency level)	The first month	21	26.5714	1.98926	−3.325	20	0.003
	The twelfth month	21	27.5714	1.50238			
Score of Section C in PVLT (the 5,000 frequency level)	The first month	21	18.8095	4.74994	−7.469	20	0.000
	The twelfth month	21	23.0952	3.19225			
Score of Section D in PVLT (the 10,000 frequency level)	The first month	21	6.1429	5.46155	−1.356	20	0.190
	The twelfth month	21	7.8095	4.51242			
Score of Section E in PVLT (the academic words)	The first month	21	27.7143	2.32686	−2.449	20	0.024
	The twelfth month	21	28.9048	1.84132			

In Table 4.4, it can be seen that the receptive vocabulary grew significantly in the 12 months ($t = -4.811$, df $= 20$, $p = 0.000$, $p < 0.05$). With regard to different sections, only scores in Section A and Section D did not increase significantly. Scores in other sections, including Section B, Section C, and Section

E, got significant growth. In other words, receptive words at 2,000 and 10,000 frequency level did not get improvement, whereas receptive words at 3,000 level, 5,000 level, and academic level improved significantly.

Table 4.5 Comparison of CAVLT Scores between the First and the Twelfth Month

The test score	Time to conduct the test	Number of subjects	Mean score	Standard deviation	t	df	p
Total Score of CAVLT	The first month	21	230.4762	31.04290	−7.688	20	0.000
	The twelfth month	21	268.0000	33.04694			
Score of Section A in CAVLT (the 2,000 frequency level)	The first month	21	77.4762	9.92280	−2.528	20	0.020
	The twelfth month	21	82.6190	9.81568			
Score of Section B in CAVLT (the 3,000 frequency level)	The first month	21	62.3333	7.46548	−2.214	20	0.039
	The twelfth month	21	69.1429	13.37268			
Score of Section C in CAVLT (the 5,000 frequency level)	The first month	21	36.0000	13.53514	−4.492	20	0.000
	The twelfth month	21	47.1429	10.44646			

Continued

The test score	Time to conduct the test	Number of subjects	Mean score	Standard deviation	t	df	p
Score of Section D in CAVLT (the university words)	The first month	21	51.4286	9.61026	−2.138	20	0.045
	The twelfth month	21	55.9524	6.84453			
Score of Section E in CAVLT (the 10,000 frequency level)	The first month	21	3.2381	5.18560	−4.551	20	0.000
	The twelfth month	21	13.1429	12.04278			

Table 4.5 compares scores of CAVLT between the first month and the twelfth month. The table shows that CAVLT scores increased significantly in the 12-month period ($t = -7.688$, df $= 20$, $p = 0.000$, $p < 0.05$). With regard to scores in each section, all the sections' scores showed significant growth, including Section A ($t = -2.528$, df $= 20$, $p = 0.020$, $p < 0.05$), Section B ($t = -2.214$, df $= 20$, $p = 0.039$, $p < 0.05$), Section C ($t = -4.492$, df $= 20$, $p = 0.000$, $p < 0.05$), Section D ($t = -2.138$, df $= 20$, $p = 0.045$, $p < 0.05$) and Section E ($t = -4.511$, df $= 20$, $p = 0.000$, $p < 0.05$). It is indicative that testees' controlled active vocabulary at 2,000 frequency level, 3,000 frequency level, 5,000 frequency level, 10,000 frequency level, and academic level all grew significantly in the 12-month period of time.

From Table 4.4 and Table 4.5, it can be observed that the scores of PVLT and CAVLT decreased with the decrease of words' frequency levels. In the first month PVLT, the order of the mean scores in different sections was Section A (the 2,000 level, mean = 29. 0952, SD = 0. 9952) > Section B (the 3,000 level, mean = 26. 5714, SD = 1. 98926) > Section C (the 5,000 level, mean = 18. 8095, SD = 4. 74994) > Section D (the 10,000 level, mean = 6. 1429, SD = 5. 46155); in the twelfth month PV-LT, the order was Section A (the 2,000 level, mean = 29. 5238, SD = 0. 81358) > Section B (the 3,000 level, mean = 27. 5714, SD = 1. 50238) > Section C (the 5,000 level, mean = 23. 0952, SD = 3. 19225) > Section D (the 10,000 level, mean = 7. 8095, SD = 4. 51242). CAVLT in the first and twelfth month showed the same tendency. In the first month CAVLT, the order of mean scores in different sections was Section A (the 2,000 level, mean = 77. 4762, SD = 9. 92280) > Section B (the 3,000 level, mean = 62. 3333, SD = 7. 46548) > Section C (the 5000 level, mean = 36. 0000, SD = 13. 53514) > Section E (the 10,000 level, mean = 3. 2381, SD = 5. 18560); in the twelfth month CAVLT, the order was Section A (the 2,000 level, mean = 82. 6190, SD = 9. 81568) > Section B (the 3,000 level, mean = 69. 1429, SD = 13. 37268) > Section C (the 5,000 level, mean = 47. 1429, SD = 10. 44646) > Section E (the 10,000 level, mean = 13. 1429, SD = 12. 04278). This result is consistent with the view of Schmitt et al. (2001) that words are grasped in sequence, i. e. , more frequent words tend to be learned earlier, and less frequent words tend to be learned later.

Pearson Correlation was calculated for scores of Lex30, PVLT, and CAVLT. Results show that in the first month, Lex30 and PVLT were not significantly correlated ($r = 0. 374, p = 0.095, p > 0.05$), while Lex30 and CAVLT were significantly correlated at a median level ($r = 0.531, p < 0.013, p < 0.05$). Meanwhile, PVLT and CAVLT were significantly correlated, and the correlation reached median level ($r=0.512$, $p=0.018$, $p<0.05$). With regard to the correlation of Lex30 with different sections in PVLT and CAVLT, it turned out that Lex30 was only significantly correlated with Section B (the 3,000 frequency level) in CAVLT ($r=0.451$, $p=0.040$, $p<0.05$), but not correlated with other sections in PVLT and CAVLT. From this result, it could be concluded that Lex30 in the first month was generally not correlated with PVLT and CAVLT (except for Section B in CAVLT), but PVLT and CAVLT were significantly correlated with each other. In the twelfth month, Lex30 was not significantly correlated with either PVLT ($r=0.013$, $p=0.9567$, $p>0.05$), or CAVLT ($r=0.057$, $p=0.807$, $p>0.05$). However, PVLT and CAVLT were significantly correlated, and the correlation reached large level ($r=0.708$, $p=0.000$, $p<0.05$). No scores of individual sections in PVLT and CAVLT were correlated with scores of Lex30.

In sum, in this sub-study the testees' passive vocabulary and controlled active vocabulary kept growing, but free active vocabulary experienced stagnation in the 12-month period of time; the testees' passive vocabulary and controlled active vocabulary were highly correlated, but they were not correlated with free active vocabulary. The finding suggests that being able to recognise and spell a word does not necessarily mean being able to actively produce the word.

4.5　Discussion

4.5.1　The Developmental Process of FAV

A large amount of information on FAV's developmental process is obtained from this sub-study. First, it turns out that the Lex30 score did not change significantly in the 12-month period of time. According to the scoring standard of Lex30, only words beyond the first 1,000 frequent content words, high-frequency function words, proper nouns and numbers would get points. This means that in the 12 months, words beyond these categories did not grow significantly. Second, results by RANGE showed that in writing, word types at the first 1,000 frequency level decreased significantly, but word types at the second 1,000 frequency level, academic words and beyond did not increase significantly. It seems to be a good tendency that the testees tended to use less words belonging to the first 1,000 frequency band after 12 months. However, the whole picture is not as optimistic, as words beyond this level failed to have satisfactory growth. This result indicates that the improvement of the testees' repertoire of words in the second 1,000 frequency level and beyond is limited. The result on word families shows the same tendency: word families of the first 1,000 frequency level decreased significantly, whereas word families of the second 1,000 frequency level, academic words, and beyond did not increase significantly. It is indicative that although the testees tended to use fewer words from the first 1,000 most frequent words, they failed to use more words from other frequencies after 12 months. If a text comprises primarily the most basic vocabulary, the expression in writing will be limited and not authentic enough.

Some findings in this sub-study can be compared with those in previous research. First, different from this sub-study, Laufer (1991) found that participants' academic words got significant growth. The participants in Laufer's (1991) study were year-one university students from English department. According to Laufer (1991), they were required to have a large amount of writing on language and literature in the first year. In this sub-study, the participants were the year-three to year-four university students from English major. In the year of the sub-study, the participants were required to have some writing practice as well. For example, they needed to complete a piece of academic thesis of around 5,000 words for graduation. The thesis was under a teacher's supervision, and the whole process included revisions for at least three times according to the supervisor's feedback. In addition, they had a compulsory unit of writing, which took 2 hours each week and lasted for one semester. In this unit writing practice was conducted. However, even with these writing practices, the academic words did not improve. The different results of the two studies may be primarily owing to the fact that the participants in the two studies were at different learning stages. The input and output activities may promote academic words' growth more easily at low and inter-mediate proficiency levels than at upper-intermediate to advanced levels, as the abundant input and output seem not to work as efficiently as before. Second, this result is consistent with that of Laufer (1998). In Laufer's (1998) research, participants' FAV seemed to "fossilize" even when their passive vocabulary and controlled active vocabulary increased.

In sum, the results of Lex30 test and LFP in this sub-study provide a relatively comprehensive picture on FAV's develop-mental process in a 12-month period of time. During this period, words (no matter in terms of types or families) at various levels seemed to experience stagnation.

4. 5. 2   The Relationship of FAV with Passive Vocabulary and Controlled Active Vocabulary

To investigate the relationship between different types of

vocabulary knowledge, it is necessary to investigate the developmental process of receptive vocabulary and controlled active vocabulary at first. In the 12-month period of time, the testees' passive vocabulary and controlled active vocabulary grew significantly. With regard to passive vocabulary, except for words in the 2,000 level and in the 10,000 level, words of all other levels increased significantly. These included the 3,000 level, the 5,000 level, and the academic words. The reason why words from the 2,000 frequency level did not get significant growth may be that the high-frequency words had been grasped well to upper-intermediate to advanced ESL learners. This can be evidenced by the very high mean score of Section A in the first-month PVLT test (mean=29.095, SD=0.99523), and that in the twelfth-month PVLT test (mean=29.523, SD=0.81358). The total score of each section in PVLT was 30 points. Therefore, the mean scores of Section A show that most of words from this level had been grasped receptively, and there was almost no more space for further development. The lack of growth for words in the 10,000 frequency level may be due to the fact that this is a very low frequency level, and learners may not have many chances to encounter these words in their study. Therefore, the score in the 10,000 level did not change significantly, and it maintained low. It can be evidenced by the mean score in the first-month PVLT test (mean=6.1429, SD=5.46155) and that in the twelfth-month test (mean=7.8095, SD=4.51242). The increase of words at the 3,000 and 5,000 level in PVLT indicates that the testees' capability to read authentic English texts had improved (Schmitt et al., 2001); the increase of academic words in PVLT test shows that their ability to read English academic text improved after 12 months as well. With regard to the controlled active vocabulary, words at all frequency levels developed significantly. This indicates that in the 12 months of time, the testees not only could recognise more words, but also could spell more words. Additionally, the Pearson Correlation analysis shows that testees' PV and CAV were significantly correlated with each other in both the first-month test and the twelfth-month test. However, FAV seems not to have a close relationship with receptive vocabulary and controlled active vocabulary, as it turns out that FAV was not significantly correlated with receptive vocabulary in the first and twelfth month, and with controlled active vocabulary in the twelfth month. Although FAV was correlated with controlled active vocabulary in the first month, further analysis shows that it was only correlated with Section C, not with any other sections in CAVLT. In other words, in the first month spelling seemed to be correlated with vocabulary production, but this correlation was rather limited.

The sub-study thus answers the second proposed question as well. FAV is not correlated with passive vocabulary, and FAV is generally not correlated with controlled active vocabulary either. However, passive vocabulary and controlled active vocabulary seem to be closely correlated with each other. In addition, both passive and controlled active vocabulary grew significantly in the 12 months. It is indicative that at least in upper-intermediate to advanced proficiency stage, the development of ESL learners' recognition and spelling capability does not promote their FAV growth. This finding is consistent with Laufer's (1998) finding that FAV does not grow with the growth of passive and controlled active vocabulary. In Laufer (1998), two groups of subjects participated in the study. One group was consisted of 26 16-year-old 10th graders in Israel, who had been learning English for six years. The other groups were 22 17-year-old students in the 11th grade in Israel, who had been studying English for seven years. Just like the Chinese subjects in this sub-study, English was a foreign language in Israel, and there was no English environment in their everyday life. These participants primarily obtained the English input from formal classes. By comparing FAV beyond the first 2,000 frequency level, Laufer (1998) found that there was no significant difference between the two groups in FAV size. And Laufer (1998) discovered that the 11th graders' passive vocabulary and controlled active vocabulary were significantly higher than those of 10th graders. Based on findings in Laufer (1998) and this research, it may be concluded that the FAV threshold tends to occur periodically, whereas passive vocabulary and controlled active vocabulary tend to develop in a more linear way.

However, the finding seems to be contrary to Meara and Fitzpatrick's (2000) finding that the larger the receptive vocabulary is, the more the FAV will be. Taken a closer observation, it may be seen that the reliability of Meara and Fitzpatrick's (2000) study seems to be questionable. In the study, the variable of L2 proficiency may not be well controlled. The participants were 46 adult learners at different proficiency levels. The proficiency level seems to be an important factor affecting results of vocabulary tests. Therefore, the conclusion of Meara and Fitzpatrick (2000) may not be convincing as the variable of proficiency is not controlled.

This sub-study not only proves the Threshold Hypothesis proposed by Laufer (1991), but also obtains more information on the FAV threshold phenomenon. First, the threshold seems to be long-lasting, since in the 12 long months of the sub-study FAV did not grow. Second, the stagnation of FAV seems to be more serious than our expectations: it is widespread, almost occurring at all frequency levels, and even at the frequency level as high as the second 1,000 frequency band. Third, the FAV threshold phenomenon seems to be "stubborn", as in the 12 months passive and controlled active vocabulary kept growing, but FAV was not promoted by the development of the two. Fourth, combined with results of other research, it can be concluded that FAV threshold may occur periodically and at various proficiency stages.

These features of FAV threshold phenomenon provide some pedagogical implications to ESL learners. First, teachers should be conscious that the FAV threshold phenomenon may occur, especially when ESL learners reach upper-intermediate to advanced proficiency level. Knowing the existence of the threshold may be the first step to tackle the problem. Second, teachers should be conscious that the threshold may be a serious problem in ESL learning: it is long-lasting, it occurs widely, and it occurs at most frequency levels. Third, the efficiency of traditional teaching and learning methods to tackle the problem seems to be limited. Although it may easily lead people to think that strengthening word recognition and spelling will help promote FAV development, the results of this sub-study indicate that at least when students reach upper-intermediate to advanced level of L2 proficiency, it is not the case. In other words, teachers should keep in mind that promoting FAV growth by strengthening passive and controlled active vocabulary may not be an efficient effort.

4. 6 Conclusion

This chapter has reported the findings of a 12-month longitudinal sub-study to explore the developmental process of FAV,
and its relationship with PV and CAV. The findings have answered
the proposed research questions. It was found that among a group
of upper-intermediate to advanced ESL learners, FAV stagnated
in the 12-month period of time. It was not correlated with either PV
or CAV. Both PV and CAV kept growing in the 12-month period,
but FAV did not. Several features were detected in the FAV
developmental process. First, the stagnation of FAV seems to be
long-lasting, since the sub-study lasted for 12 months and found
no growth in FAV. Second, the stagnation of FAV seems to be
"stubborn", as it not only lasted for a long time, but also was not
related with the growth of other types of vocabulary. Third, the
FAV threshold tends to occur widely, as it happened at most
frequency levels. This chapter empirically supports the Active
Vocabulary Threshold Hypothesis raised by Laufer (1991), and
obtains more information on the threshold phenomenon. In the
following chapters, more quantitative and qualitative research
will be carried out to investigate factors that may cause the
threshold phenomenon.

Chapter 5   Comparison of Lexical Network between Frequently and Seldom Produced Words

5.1   Introduction

As it has been found in Chapter 4, not all receptive words could smoothly develop into productive words; some of them stagnate in the process, and fail to become productive. In order to explore the reasons for the stagnation, it is necessary to examine the mental representation of receptive and productive words, and investigate whether there are differences between the two. Unfortunately, it is difficult to pick receptive and productive words from learners' mental lexicon. This is because the mental lexicon is like a dark box and cannot be examined directly. Even if a word is never used by a person in the past, researchers should be cautious to conclude that the word is not a productive word. There is still possibility that the word will be retrieved and produced in a specific circumstance. The alternative idea of this sub-study is that although receptive and productive words cannot be directly picked out, words that are frequently produced by L2 learners, and words that are seldom or almost never used by them may be picked in some way. If a word is a high-frequency word in authentic English texts and have no cultural strangeness, it can be postulated that the word is frequently needed in similar L2 contexts as well. Therefore, if both a group of frequently produced words (FPW) and seldom produced words (SPW) are high-frequency words in authentic English texts, and if learners are familiar with both of them, the reason why one group is used frequently by the learners and why the other groups are not an interesting issue. The difference between the two groups of words in mental representation may shed some light on the lexical network construction procedure in FAV development.

This chapter attempts to investigate the issue posed above. It first raises research questions, then proposes research methods, including the research instruments, data collection procedures, and data analysis methods. At the end of the chapter, results of the sub-study are reported and discussed, and conclusions are presented.

5.2　Research Questions

The primary question in this chapter is: What are the differences (if any) of the mental lexicon organisation between frequently produced words and seldom produced words? In order to be more manageable, the general question is broken into three sub-questions:

(1) Do semantic nodes and non-semantic nodes distribute differently in FPW and SPW? What are the differences (if any)?

(2) Do different types of semantic nodes distribute differently in FPW and SPW? What are the differences (if any)?

(3) Do different types of non-semantic nodes distribute differently in FPW and SPW? What are the differences (if any)?

5.3   Research Method

This section presents major components of the research method adopted in this sub-study, including instruments, procedures of data collection, data preparation, and data analysis. The background information for participants participating in this sub-study has been provided in Chapter 3.

5.3.1   Instruments

Four instruments were adopted in this sub-study. The instruments included two Vocabulary Knowledge Scale (VKS) tests and two word association tests. These tests are introduced in this section.

5.3.1.1   Vocabulary Knowledge Scale Test

It has been repeatedly found that familiarity of words has a significant effect on the response pattern (Entwisle, 1966; Namei, 2004; Wolter, 2001; Zareva & Brent, 2012). To control this extraneous variable, this sub-research adopted Wesche and Paribakht's (1996) Vocabulary Knowledge Scale (VKS) test to measure testees' familiarity level to candidate stimulus words in word association tests. In the test, five scales were given after a target word was presented:

Ⅰ. I don't remember having seen this word before.

Ⅱ. I have seen this word before but I don't know what it means.

Ⅲ. I have seen this word before and I think it means

_____. (synonym or translation)

Ⅳ. I know this word. It means _____. (synonym or translation)

Ⅴ. I can use this word in a sentence, e. g. : _____. (write a sentence)

Scores corresponding to choice Ⅰ,Ⅱ,Ⅲ,Ⅳ and Ⅴ were 0,1,2,3, and 4 respectively. However, as has been pointed out in Section 2.3.2.2, the testee's choice of the scale did not necessarily mean that they would get the corresponding score; it also depended on what they filled in the following blanks. For example, if the testee chose "Ⅲ" but gave a wrong synonym or translation in the following blank, he would not get a score of 2, but 1 instead; if the testee chose "Ⅳ" but gave a wrong synonym or translation in the following blank, he would not get a score of 3, but only 1. In sum, it was not only the scale testees chose, but also their answer to the blank would decide the score they could get. The VKS tests and the word association tests used in this sub-research are presented in Appendix F and Appendix G.

It should be noted that with the tested word being provided, the familiarity level measured by VKS test only covers recognition and controlled production of the tested word. As the target word has been given in the test, free active production of the word is not tested. In other words, the word tested to have high familiarity level by VKS test can possibly be FPW or SPW.

5.3.1.2 Word Association Test

Based on the research aim of this sub-study, which was to compare lexical organizations of SPW and FPW, this sub-study adopted word association tests as the research instrument. In word association tests, there are a number of factors affecting testees' reaction pattern. These factors include whether the stimulus words are cognates in testees' native language (Fitzpatrick & Izura, 2011; Wolter, 2001), whether they tend to trigger set responses (Fitzpatrick et al., 2015), stimulus words' lexical class (Clark, 1995; de Groot, 1992; Deese, 1962; Fitzpatrick et al., 2015; Källkvist, 1999; Lotto & de Groot, 1998; Nissen & Henriksen, 2006; Sökmen, 1993), cultural strangeness (Carolyn et al., 2004; Chow et al., 1987; Son et al., 2014), concreteness (de Groot, 1989, 1993; Fitzpatrick et al., 2015; Kolers, 1963; D. L. Nelson & Schreiber, 1992; van Hell & de Groot, 1998), and familiarity (Entwisle, 1966; Namei, 2004; Wolter, 2001; Zareva & Brent, 2012). Therefore, in order to ensure the validity and reliability of the sub-research, these variables need to be effectively controlled.

To achieve this goal, several measures have been taken. First, the General Service List (GSL) was referenced from the website of Lextutor (2017). From its second 1,000 most frequent word band, pairs of words containing similar meanings were picked out. The exclusion of the first 1,000 band in word selection was due to the consideration that words from that frequency level tend to elicit dominant responses, which may conceal the characteristics of lexical representations (Wolter, 2001). Limiting the selection to the second 1,000 most frequent words ensured that participants could recognise, and in most cases were familiar, with the cues (Wolter, 2001). In addition, having the same frequency meant the participants had similar chances to encounter these words in English texts in reading and listening.

Second, the selection criteria were: one word in the pair is frequently used by ESL students on college level, whereas the other word in the pair, even though having similar meanings and from the same frequency band, is seldom or never used. In this step, 13 pairs of words were selected. Due to the fact that these pairs of words shared similar meanings and were chosen from the same band, it could be ascertained that they were of the similar frequency, concreteness, and most likely, they were of the same primary lexical class. However, it should be noted that in this stage the word selection was based on the researcher's subjective judgement. Although the researcher in this study has had a number of years' ESL teaching experience at universities, the judgement was subjective, and objective standards were needed.

Therefore, in the next step, *The Spoken and Written English Corpus of Chinese Learners* (2.0) by Wen, Wang and Liang (2009) was referenced. The corpus collected 6,579 spoken and written compositions done by Chinese university students, from both English and other majors. Each word from the 13 selected pairs was searched in the corpus with the use of the software AntConc3.3.5w. The software counted the target words' frequency of occurrences in the corpus. Based on the results, two pairs of words were removed, and 11 pairs were kept for further selection. All the remaining 11 pairs shared the feature that one word in each pair appeared for a number of times (496 times on average) in the corpus, whereas the other one almost never appeared (0 time on average). This indicated that one word from each selected word pair was frequently used by Chinese university students, but the other word was not. This step was more objective than ESL teachers' subjective judgement by teaching experience. It further ensured that the selected words were suitable for the sub-study.

Third, a pilot study was conducted. 11 students in the university, who were in the same year level and from the same major as the formal participants, participated in this sub-study. In the

pilot study, Wesche and Paribakht's (1996) VKS test was administered. According to the results, words to which some students
showed low familiarity were excluded. Words having more than
one frequently used meanings were removed as well. For example, it
was found that the word "bold" had two frequently used meanings, one was "brave", and the other was "darker and thicker
for font". Therefore, the candidate word "bold" was excluded
from the cues. The reason to remove these words was to avoid
confusions in response categorisation. After the selection, 5
pairs of words were left to be stimulus words. Due to the fact that
the participants in the pilot study were in the same year level and
in the same major of the university, they were considered to be
at roughly the same English proficiency level, i. e., upper-intermediate to advanced level, as the formal testees in this sub-study
were. Additionally, the selected words were all high-frequency
words. Therefore, it was well based to assume that the formal
testees were familiar with those cue words as well. However,
even with these considerations, VKS tests would still be conducted in the formal sub-study. If some words turned out to have
low familiarity, they would be removed from data analysis.

Although efforts had been made in FPW and SPW selection,
other intervening variables still existed. It was possible that there
were individuals who could not produce the words as others did,
and it was possible that there were individuals who frequently
used the words that were not produced by most of the L2 learners
in similar proficiency levels. However, it was believed that
this possibility was low. First, the researcher had been teaching
ESL in China for over ten years. Therefore, the researcher had
rich experience on the students' interlanguage of English in China.
Second, the corpus adopted in this sub-study collected more than

6,500 speaking and writing texts by Chinese L2 learners from public universities. These students shared with the participants the age, native language, and language environment in China. In addition, they all experienced standard elementary and middle school education, and then passed the national college entrance examination in China, which was a requirement for higher education. After entering college, the standard national syllabus was followed in college teaching. Therefore, the corpus can represent the general English usage patterns of L2 learners in universities in China.

The five pairs of selected words covered nouns, adjectives, verbs, and adverbials. Among them, there were three pairs of abstract words and two pairs of concrete words. The level of concreteness was judged by the concreteness scale of P. Zhang (2010a), which had been introduced in Chapter 2. None of the selected words was cognates of Chinese, neither were they culturally strange to the testees. None of them was very short words or very long words, i.e., words that were less than three letters long or words that were more than ten letters long. The key information on the selected stimulus words is demonstrated in Table 5.1 and Table 5.2.

Table 5.1　Key Information on Selected FPW

FPW	Word class	concreteness
afraid	*adj.*	abstract
damage	*v.*	abstract
happy	*adj.*	abstract
quickly	*adv.*	concrete
soil	*n.*	concrete

Continued

SPW	Word class	concreteness
cowardly	*adj* .	abstract
wreck	*v* .	abstract
amused	*adj* .	abstract
hastily	*adv* .	concrete
clay	*n* .	concrete

5.3.2　Data Collection Procedures

5.3.2.1　Pilot Study

Before the formal data collection, a pilot study was carried out. In the pilot study, 11 year-three English-major students, who were studying in the same university as formal testees were asked to do the VKS test and word association tests. There were several purposes of the pilot study. The first purpose was to help researchers find suitable stimulus words for the formal sub-study. The second purpose was to ascertain that the test requirements and test items were clear enough to the testees. The third purpose was to help researchers find the appropriate length of time for formal tests. According to the results of the pilot study, ten words were selected as cue words. Based on the students' feedback obtained in the pilot study, minor changes were made to make test requirements clearer to testees. First, to avoid misunderstandings and confusions, the test instructions were provided in Chinese. Second, more details were provided in the instruction. In the word association section, testees were told that there was no limit on the type of association, and they were asked to write down any association that came into their minds when they encountered the cue words. In the vocabulary knowledge scale section, testees were reminded to fill in the blanks if their choice was Ⅲ, Ⅳ, or Ⅴ. In addition, an example on how to fill in the blanks was provided. In both the word association section and the vocabulary knowledge scale section, testees were reminded not to use dictionaries when they did the tests. Based on the length of time spent in the pilot tests, it was decided that in the formal sub-study each VKS test would take two minutes, and each word association test would take one and a half minutes.

5.3.2.2 Formal Data Collection

The formal data collection was conducted in May and June, 2015. The reason to choose this time to collect data was due to the consideration that usually subjects were in the mid semester at that time; therefore, the results could reflect their normal performance. Before the datas were collected, the student investigator orally explained the requirements for VKS test and word association test, and written instructions on those tests were presented to testees as well. Moreover, the testees were encouraged to ask questions on the test format and requirement until there was no doubts and confusions. After ascertaining that all subjects had understood the test format and requirements correctly, the formal tests were conducted. Since the stimulus words in the SPW group and FPW group shared similar meanings, the tests were conducted at two different times to avoid reminding effects. The interval between the tests was one month, so that the first VKS and association test would have little influence on the second one. Meanwhile, the interval time was not long enough for the testees to have a significant change in their vocabulary size and L2 proficiency. The first VKS and word association test was for SPW, and the second was for FPW. Both tests were conducted out of class. To avoid audio or oral mistakes, word association tests adopted look-and-write pattern, in which the participants were asked to instantly write down three words that came to their mind as soon as they saw the prompt word. Guided by the pilot study, the student investigator told testees not to change the answers that they had already written down; if they could not make any association when encountering the prompt word, they should just leave the blank empty. In addition, they were told that there was no "right" or "wrong" answers to the prompts. Dictionaries were forbidden in both VKS and word association tests.

It should be noted that the "chain phenomenon", in which testees' response was not a reaction to the stimulus word, but rather a reaction to the former response that they gave in the test, appeared in some research such as P. Zhang (2011), and Nissen and Henriksen (2006). To avoid this phenomenon, some researchers (e. g. P. Zhang, 2011) chose to only analyse the first response. Some other researchers (e. g. Nissen & Henriksen, 2006) chose to consider chained response as a valid response in analysis, and classed it as non-semantic response. It may not be advocated in this sub-study, however, that a chained response be considered as valid for analysis. A chained response is a reaction elicited by the response before it, not a reaction to the prompt word. It therefore offers little information on the prompt's lexical connection in mental lexicon. Moreover, in this sub-study the chain phenomenon only occurred occasionally. In FPW group, there were four chained responses, accounting for 1.33% of the total responses; in SPW group, there were five responses of this type, accounting for 1.67% of all responses. Therefore, the occurrence of chain phenomenon in this sub-study was rare and could be neglected. Moreover, observing three responses, instead of only one, may help researchers draw a more comprehensive picture of the word's lexical organisation (Schmitt, 1998). Taking all these factors into consideration, it was proposed in this sub-study that three responses to each stimulus word be observed and analysed; chained responses would be discarded as invalid data, and they would not be used in analysis.

5.3.3 Data Preparation

5.3.3.1 Selection of Valid Data

After the subjects finished all the tests, the test papers were collected. Then several steps were taken to select valid data. First, the test papers were sorted into two groups, one was SPW group, and the other was FPW group. Each group contained a VKS and a word association test. Second, data done by the subjects who failed to participate in both times were removed. Only data by the subjects who had participated in both times, i. e., one time for SPW, and the other time for FPW, were kept. Third, the test papers suspected to be done carelessly, such as those having a number of empty blanks, were discarded as well. After this selection procedure, 20 subjects' datas were left for final analysis, resulting in 600 responses in word association tests.

5.3.3.2 Scoring the VKS Tests

The subjects' VKS tests were graded according to the scoring standard set up by Wesche and Paribakht (1996). If the subjects' choice was Ⅰ or Ⅱ, they would get a score of 0 or 1 respectively.

If subjects' choice was Ⅲ, Ⅳ, or Ⅴ, their answer to the blank needed to be checked as well. If the answer to the blank was correct, a score of 2,3,or 4 would be given to choice Ⅲ, Ⅳ,and Ⅴ respectively. However, if a subject chose Ⅲ or Ⅳ, but gave a wrong synonym or translation for the target word, then he could only get 1 point; if he chose Ⅳ, but the sentence he composed was correct in word meaning but incorrect in grammar, he would get 2 points; if he chose Ⅳ, but wrote a sentence with wrong meaning for the target word, he could only get 1 point.

5.3.3.3   Scoring the Word Association Tests

Each response needed to be categorized before the test was scored. Categorization was conducted according to the revised categorization framework introduced in Chapter 2. After the classification, the frequency of occurrences for each type of response by every subject was counted. One occurrence would be given 1 point; therefore, the frequency of occurrences was equal to the points being obtained.

5.3.4   Data Analysis

The software used for statistical data analysis was Statistical Package for Social Science (SPSS), and the version of the software was 20.0. All scores of VKS and word association tests by the selected 20 subjects were entered into SPSS for statistical processing. Statistical processing methods in this sub-study included descriptive analysis, Paired-sample T test, and One-way Repeated Measures ANOVA. Descriptive Statistics were applied to portray a general picture of the subjects' familiarity with the target words, and to offer researchers descriptive information on the subjects' response scores in word association tests. Paired-sample T test was adopted to compare familiarities between SPW and FPW group, and to compare response scores between the two groups. Paired-sample T test was used to compare scores of different response types within SPW and FPW group as well. In cases where more than two types of responses needed to be compared, One-way Repeated Measures ANOVA was adopted. It should be noted that usually Chi-square is applied to compare frequencies between two or more groups. However, as has been pointed out in Chapter 4, when Chi-square is used, it is expected that the sample size be above 150, since the value of Chi-square is significantly affected by sample size; in addition, it is suggested that the Expected N should be more than 5 (The analysis factor, 2017). As in this sub-research these two conditions cannot be met, Paired-sample T test and One-way Repeated Measures ANOVA were applied instead of Chi-square test. In order to use Paired-sample T test and One-way Repeated Measures ANOVA, the data were given further treatment. Frequencies of responses were transferred into scores, in which one occurrence was equal to one point. Since in word association tests subjects were asked to write down three responses to each of the five stimulus words, there was a total of 15 points for each subject.

5.4　Results

The results yielded by SPSS were reported in this section. The Paired-sample T test showed that there was no significant difference in the familiarity between SPW and FPW ($t = -1.000$, df $= 19$, $p > 0.05$). In addition, the mean familiarity scores of SPW and FPW were 24.250 (SD $= 0.96655$) and 24.450 (SD $= 0.99868$)

respectively, indicating that subjects were familiar with both SPW and FPW.

5.4.1　Semantic and Non-semantic Distribution of SPW and FPW

To answer the first question posed in Section 5.2, mean scores of semantic and non-semantic responses were compared by Paired-sample T test, as displayed in Table 5.3 and Table 5.4.

Table 5.3　Comparison of Semantic and Non-semantic Responses in FPW and SPW

Word type	Response type	Number of subjects	Mean score	Standard deviation	t	df	p
FPW	Semantic	20	12.050	1.791	11.949	19	0.000
	Non-semantic	20	2.750	1.713			
SPW	Semantic	20	8.550	2.089	2.440	19	0.025
	Non-semantic	20	6.200	2.238			

Note: Each subject's full score was 15 points

Table 5.3 demonstrates that FPWs' semantic responses were significantly higher than their non-semantic responses ($p=0.000<0.05$). Meanwhile, semantic responses accounted for 81.4% of all responses in FPW group, and non-semantic responses accounted for 18.6%, indicating that FPW's lexical network was dominated by semantic links. With regard to SPW, semantic responses significantly outnumbered non-semantic responses as well ($p<0.05$). The percentage of semantic responses was 58%, and the percentage of non-semantic responses was 42%. This result indicated that although SPW's semantic connections outnumbered non-semantic connections, the advantage of semantic links in

SPW was not as evident as that in FPW, as was revealed by the percentage of semantic and non-semantic responses. Past research has found that semantic links dominated in L1 mental lexicon. For example, Wolter (2001) found that semantic links accounted for 92.7% in L1 mental lexicon, and P. Zhang (2010b) discovered that L1 testees' semantic responses reached 86.0% of all responses; Dong and Zhang (2011) examined responses in Edinburgh Association Thesaurus (EAT), which could be downloaded from the website of EAT (2015). In the thesaurus, each cue word was made associations by 100 native speakers. Dong and Zhang (2011) found that stimulus words' first most frequent responses were all semantic responses. Referencing these findings, it could be concluded that with regard to semantic and non-semantic distribution in lexical network, L2 FPW seems to be more similar to L1 words than L2 SPW do.

Table 5.4   Comparison of Semantic and Non-semantic
Responses between FPW and SPW

Response type	Word type	Number of subjects	Mean score	Standard deviation	t	df	p
Semantic	FPW	20	12.05	1.791	−5.552	19	0.000
	SPW	20	8.55	2.089			
Non-semantic	FPW	20	2.75	1.713	5.368	19	0.000
	SPW	20	6.20	2.238			

Note: Each subject's full score was 15 points

As displayed in Table 5.4, the semantic responses of FPW were significantly higher than those of SPW ($p = 0.000 < 0.05$); the non-semantic responses of FPW, on the other hand, were significantly lower than those of SPW ($p = 0.000 < 0.05$).

5.4.2   Distribution of Different Types of Semantic Nodes in SPW and FPW

In order to explore the distribution of different types of semantic nodes in FPW and SPW, Paired-sample T test and One-way Repeated Measures ANOVA were adopted, as demonstrated in Table 5.5 and Table 5.6.

Table 5.5   Descriptive Statistics for Different Types of Semantic Responses in FPW and SPW

Word type	Response type	Number of subjects	Mean score	Standard deviation
FPW	Paradigmatic	20	8.900	1.071
	Syntagmatic	20	2.050	2.489
	Encyclopaedia	20	1.100	1.234
SPW	Paradigmatic	20	6.150	2.346
	Syntagmatic	20	0.800	0.768
	Encyclopaedia	20	1.600	1.789

Note: Each subject's full score was 15 points

An One-way Repeated Measures ANOVA was conducted to compare response scores of paradigmatic, syntagmatic, and encyclopaedia associations in both SPW and FPW. The means and standard deviations were presented in Table 5.5. As for FPW, there was a significant effect of response type (Wilks' Lambda$=0.104, F [2,18]=77.366, p<0.01$, multivariate partial eta squared$=.896$). With regard to SPW, there was a significant effect of response type as well (Wilks' Lambda$=0.130, F [2,18]=60.439, p<0.01$, multivariate partial eta squared$=0.870$).

This result indicated that the amount of paradigmatic, syntagmatic and encyclopaedia links were significantly different in both SPW and FPW.

In the FPW group, paradigmatic responses accounted for 73.86% of semantic responses, syntagmatic responses accounted for 17.01%, and encyclopaedia responses accounted for 9.13%. Ranking of the three types of responses from high to low was paradigmatic>syntagmatic>encyclopaedia. In the SPW group, paradigmatic responses accounted for 71.93% of semantic response, syntagmatic response was 9.36%, and encyclopaedia response was 18.71%. Ranking of the three types from high to low was paradigmatic > encyclopaedia > syntagmatic. This result was consistent with the findings of Zareva and Brent (2012) and Zareva (2007). Zareva and Brent (2012) and Zareva (2007) found that to advanced L2 learners or to words with high familiarity, paradigmatic connections would outnumber syntagmatic connections. This result also suggested that no matter to FPW or to SPW, paradigmatic responses would play a dominant role, accounting for more than 70% in semantic links; in addition, paradigmatic nodes' proportion from SPW to FPW was stable. Another finding was that the lexical structure of the two groups was different. In the FPW group, the testees showed a preference for paradigmatic and syntagmatic responses, whereas in the SPW group they showed a preference for paradigmatic and encyclopaedia responses. Therefore, from SPW to FPW the importance of syntagmatic nodes tended to elevate, whereas the importance of encyclopaedia nodes tended to decline.

Table 5. 6   Comparison of Different Types of Semantic
Responses between FPW and SPW

Response type	Word type	Number of subjects	Mean score	Standard deviation	t	df	p
Syntagmatic	FPW	20	2.050	1.234	−3.263	19	0.004
	SPW	20	0.800	0.768			
Paradigmatic	FPW	20	8.900	2.490	−3.832	19	0.001
	SPW	20	6.150	2.346			
Encyclopaedia	FPW	20	1.100	1.071	1.157	19	0.262
	SPW	20	1.600	1.789			

Note: Each subject's full score was 15 points

To compare the semantic organisation between the SPW
and FPW, different types of semantic reactions, including syntagmatic, paradigmatic, and encyclopaedia responses were compared. Table 5. 6 exhibits that paradigmatic responses in FPW
group were significantly higher than those in the SPW group
($p=0.001<0.05$); syntagmatic responses in FPW group were
significantly higher than those in SPW group as well ($p=0.004<
0.05$). As for encyclopaedia responses, the two word groups did
not show significant difference ($p=0.262>0.05$). Based on
the statistics in Table 5. 5 and Table 5. 6, it could be concluded
that from the SPW group to the FPW group paradigmatic and
syntagmatic responses experienced significant increase, whereas
the encyclopaedia responses did not; meanwhile, the proportion
of syntagmatic responses in semantic connections tended to increase,
whereas encyclopaedia responses tended to decrease. To have a
closer observation, different types of paradigmatic and syntagmatic reactions were investigated. Table 5. 7 provides results of
Descriptive Statistics for different types of paradigmatic responses

in FPW and SPW.

Table 5.7　Descriptive Statistics for Different Types of
Paradigmatic Responses in FPW and SPW

Word type	Response type	Number of subjects	Mean score	Standard deviation
FPW	Synonym	20	6.750	2.268
	Antonym	20	0.700	0.801
	Hyponym	20	0.000	0.000
	Meronym	20	0.000	0.000
	Coordinate	20	0.850	0.988
	Ingredient	20	0.600	0.598
SPW	Synonym	20	3.800	1.673
	Antonym	20	0.200	0.523
	Hyponym	20	0.000	0.000
	Meronym	20	0.000	0.000
	Coordinate	20	1.150	0.988
	Ingredient	20	1.000	0.725

Note: Each subject's full score was 15 points

An One-way Repeated Measures ANOVA test was conducted to compare scores of different types of paradigmatic responses in both SPW and FPW. The means and standard deviations are presented in Table 5.7. With regard to FPW, there was a significant effect of response type (Wilks' Lambda$=0.063$, $F[4,16]=59.561$, $p<0.01$, multivariate partial eta squared$=0.937$). With regard to SPW, there was a significant effect of response type as well (Wilks' Lambda$=0.118$, $F[4,16]=29.911$, $p<0.01$, multivariate partial eta squared$=0.882$).

Table 5.7 exhibits that in FPW synonym had the highest rate of occurrence, accounting for 75.84% of all paradigmatic links; coordinate (9.55%) came the second, followed by anto-nym (7.87%) and ingredient (6.74%); the last two categories were hyponym and meronym, both had no occurrence at all. With regard to SPW, the order was somewhat similar, with synonym (61.7%) being the largest category, followed by coordinate (18.70%), ingredient (16.26%) and antonym (3.25%); hyponym and meronym were the last two categories, accounting for 0% of all paradigmatic links. This result revealed the evident advantage of synonym links in both FPW and SPW, which sup-ported the conclusion made by Liu et al. (2012) that synonym played an important role in L2 mental lexicon. Table 5.8 provides the comparison of different types of paradigmatic responses between FPW and SPW.

Table 5.8   Comparison of Different Types of Paradigmatic Responses between FPW and SPW

Response type	Word type	Number of subjects	Mean score	Standard deviation	t	df	p
Synonym	FPW	20	6.750	2.268	-4.914	19	0.000
	SPW	20	3.800	1.673			
Antonym	FPW	20	0.700	0.801	-2.236	19	0.038
	SPW	20	0.200	0.523			
Hyponym	FPW	20	0	0			
	SPW	20	0	0			
Meronym	FPW	20	0	0			
	SPW	20	0	0			
Coordinate	FPW	20	0.850	0.988	1.371	19	0.186
	SPW	20	1.150	0.988			
Ingredient	FPW	20	0.600	0.598	1.902	19	0.072
	SPW	20	1.000	0.725			

Note: Each subject's full score was 15 points

As it has been discussed in Chapter 2, paradigmatic category is further classed into hyponym (e. g. animal→cat; chair→furniture), meronym (e. g. hand→body), antonym (e. g. cold→hot), synonym (e. g. sad→upset), ingredient (e. g. china→clay), and coordinate (e. g. cat→dog). Responses of these types between the FPW group and the SPW group were compared, which was demonstrated in Table 5. 8. Results showed that there were no hyponym or meronym connections. Even the stimulus word "soil", which may have more potential to trigger hyponym or meronym responses, did not elicit these two types of reaction. This may suggest that hyponym and meronym do not play significant roles in L2 lexical network construction. With regard to other types of paradigmatic connections, synonym ($p=0.000<0.05$) and antonym ($p=0.038<0.05$) in the FPW group were significantly higher than those in the SPW group.

The findings from Table 5. 7 and Table 5. 8 suggested that from SPW to FPW the number of synonym and antonym nodes tended to grow; the percentage of both synonym and antonym in paradigmatic responses tended to rise. However, they rose at different degrees, with synonym by 14.05%, and antonym by 4.62%; ingredient and coordinate nodes did not have significant increase in number, but both of them declined in percentage in paradigmatic responses, with ingredient declining by 9.52%, and coordinate by 9.15%. Therefore, different types of nodes seemed to change in different directions and at different degrees: some nodes tended to grow in percentage, while some tended to decline; some tended to increase in number, while some did not. The comparison of different types of syntagmatic responses in FPW and SPW is presented in Table 5. 9.

Table 5. 9   Comparison of Different Types of Syntagmatic Responses in FPW and SPW

Word type	Response type	Number of subjects	Mean score	Standard deviation	t	df	p
FPW	Compound/chunk	20	0.100	0.308	−5.663	19	0.000
	Syntactic	20	1.950	1.317			
SPW	Compound/chunk	20	0.000	0.000	−4.660	19	0.000
	Syntactic	20	0.800	0.768			

Table 5.9 suggests that different types of syntagmatic responses were significantly different in response amount in both SPW and FPW. Syntactic nodes were dominant in both FPW and SPW, accounting for 96.269% of syntagmatic connections in the SPW group, and 95.082% in the FPW group. Syntactic nodes are evidently important for word production, since words are usually produced in sentences, and syntactic principle is a critical factor to construct sentences (Tallerman, 2015). Moreover, when language users do not have adequate syntactic knowledge of the target word, they may consciously or unconsciously avoid using the word in order to prevent making mistakes. In terms of compound/ chunk, the percentage of compound/chunk was small, with 4.918% in FPW, and 3.731% in SPW. The cue word "afraid" was selected to be observed individually, due to the consideration that "afraid" may have more potential to elicit compound/chunk response than other cues in this sub-study. This was because the set phrase "afraid of" was of high frequency in English usage. However, only 2 participants produced the response "of" to the cue "afraid". It is believed by some researchers (e. g. Zareva & Brent, 2012) that compound/chunk links are inevitable parts in an efficient lexical network. However, results of this sub-study failed to confirm

this view. It might result from the feature of the prompt words adopted in this sub-study, as these words did not compose rich compounds or chunks with other words. Therefore, the issue may need further investigations. The comparison of different types of syntagmatic responses between FPW and SPW is presented in Table 5.10.

Table 5.10   Comparison of Different Types of Syntagmatic Responses between FPW and SPW

Response type	Word type	Number of subjects	Mean score	Standard deviation	t	df	p
Compound/ chunk	FPW	20	0.100	0.308	−1.453	19	0.163
	SPW	20	0.000	0.000			
Syntactic	FPW	20	1.950	1.317	−2.881	19	0.010
	SPW	20	0.800	0.768			

Table 5.10 showed that the number of syntagmatic nodes in FPW were significantly higher than that of those in SPW ($p < 0.05$), but there was no significant difference in compound/chunk nodes between the two groups. The number of syntactic nodes had a significant increase in SPW-to-FPW process, but the number of compound/chunk nodes did not.

5.4.3   Distribution of Different Types of Non-Semantic Nodes in SPW and FPW

The comparison of different types of non-semantic responses between FPW and SPW is presented in Table 5.11.

Table 5. 11   Comparison of Different Types of Non-semantic
Responses between FPW and SPW

Response type	Word type	Number of subjects	Mean score	Stand deviation	t	df	p
Phonological-formal	FPW	20	2.100	1.410	−5.080	19	0.000
	SPW	20	4.500	1.821			
Pseudo word	FPW	20	0.200	0.523	2.027	19	0.057
	SPW	20	0.600	0.821			
No response	FPW	20	0.100	0.308	2.483	19	0.023
	SPW	20	0.800	1.196			
Unclassifiable	FPW	20	0.350	1.137	−0.224	19	0.825
	SPW	20	0.300	0.470			
Translation	FPW	20	0.000	0.000			
	SPW	20	0.000	0.000			

Note: Each subject's full score was 15 points

Table 5.11 shows that there was no "translation" response in both the SPW and FPW groups. It seemed that the testees did not try to search for corresponding words in L1 mental lexicon when they encountered the cues, which may indicate that testees' L2 mental lexicon was not dependant on L1 mental lexicon. In addition, Table 5. 11 shows that the "pseudo word" responses were sparse as well. The pseudo word links in the SPW group accounted for 4. 07% of all responses, and in the FPW group accounted for 1. 35%. The phonological-formal responses in the SPW group were significantly higher than those in the FPW group, and "no responses" in the SPW group were significantly higher than those in the FPW group. Other types of nodes did not have significant differences between the two groups. "No response" in the FPW group accounted for 0. 68% of all responses, and in the SPW group accounted for 5.42%, indicating that both FPW and SPW had set up rich nodes in lexical network. However, "no response" nodes in SPW were significantly higher than those in FPW, which implied that FPW's lexical network was denser than SPW's, and it had less empty points in the network. The number of pseudo words declined significantly, and its percentage in non-semantic connections declined significantly as well, suggesting that in SPW-to-FPW process the invalid wrong connections tended to decrease. The Descriptive Statistics for different types of non-semantic responses in FPW and SPW is provided in Table 5.12.

Table 5.12 Descriptive Statistics for Different Types of Non-semantic Responses in FPW and SPW

Word type	Response type	Number of subjects	Mean score	Standard deviation
FPW	No response	20	0.100	0.308
	Unclassifiable	20	0.350	1.137
	Phonological-formal	20	2.100	1.410
	Pseudo word	20	0.200	0.523
	Translation	20	0.000	0.000
SPW	No response	20	0.800	1.196
	Unclassifiable	20	0.300	0.470
	Phonological-formal	20	4.500	1.821
	Pseudo word	20	0.600	0.820
	Translation	20	0.000	0.000

Note: Each subject's full score was 15 points

An One-way Repeated Measures ANOVA test was conducted to compare scores of different types of non-semantic responses in both the SPW and FPW. The means and standard deviations were presented in Table 5.12. With regard to FPW, there was a significant effect of response type (Wilks' Lambda = 0.248, $F [4,16]=12.147, p<0.01$, multivariate partial eta squared=0.752). With regard to SPW, there was a significant effect of response type as well (Wilks' Lambda = 0.089, $F [(4,16]=40.732, p<0.01$, multivariate partial eta squared = 0.911). Ranking of those responses in the SPW group from high to low was phonological-formal (72.58%) > no response (12.90%) > pseudo word (9.68%)>unclassifiable(4.84%)>translation(0%), and ranking of the FPW was phonological(76.36%)>unclassifiable (12.73%)> pseudo word (7.27%) > no response (3.64%) > translation (0%). In terms of percentage, phonological-formal responses were dominant, with 72.58% of non-semantic connections in SPW, and 76.36% in FPW. This means that in the SPW-to-FPW process, the number of phonological-formal responses declined, but their percentage increased. The number of "no response" declined significantly, and its percentage declined as well.

5.4.4   Qualitative Data Analysis

Qualitative analysis was conducted as a supplement to quantitative analysis. All participants' responses were examined, so that some features could be detected. Through the examination it was found that in both the SPW and FPW groups, there were few responses that were obviously influenced by subjects' mother language, no matter in culture (e.g. spring → festival), or in expression (e.g. eat → vinegar). This may somewhat correspond with the phenomenon of zero translation response in both SPW and FPW group, which indicated that to upper-intermediate to advanced L2 learners or to words with high familiarity, the L2 mental lexicon is stored independently from the L1 mental lexicon.

The second feature detected was that for both SPW and FPW, most "pseudo word" responses were not fake words created without any reasons; rather, most pseudo words were created with semantic or phonological-formal relations with the cues. For example, the pseudo word "timous" may most likely be created to mean "timorous", and it was semantically related to the cue word "cowardly"; "wreckle" was made by some testees, which was phonologically or formally related to the cue word "wreck"; "hostly" was created because it was phonologically or formally similar to the cue "hastily". This phenomenon may imply that the testees had grasped a certain amount of linguistic and semantic knowledge on the target language, and with the knowledge they endeavoured to add nodes in their lexical network when there were empty positions.

5.5   Discussion

The results of VKS and word association tests are presented in Section 5.4. In this following section, these results are given further analysis and discussion, aiming to answer the three research questions proposed in Section 5.2. The final goal of answering these questions is to find explanations for the threshold phenomenon from cognitive perspective. The cognitive factors that may motivate SPW-to-FPW development are discussed as well.

5.5.1   Differences of Lexical Representation between SPW and FPW

The results of this sub-study answered the three research sub-questions proposed in section 5.2. It was found that there were a number of differences in the testees' mental representations between SPW and FPW.

First, the semantic and non-semantic distribution was different. FPW was found to have significantly more semantic nodes than SPW did, and had significantly fewer non-semantic nodes than SPW did.

In terms of the proportion of semantic and non-semantic links in lexical network, semantic nodes accounted for the majority in FPW, and non-semantic nodes constituted only a small part.

By contrast, in SPW, although semantic nodes outnumbered non-semantic nodes, the advantage of semantic connections was not as evident as that in FPW. This could be reflected by the fact that both semantic and non-semantic connections accounted for nearly 50% in the lexical network.

Second, the two types of words' semantic distributions were different. FPW's paradigmatic and syntagmatic nodes significantly outnumbered those of SPW, but there was no significant difference in encyclopedia nodes between these two groups. Ranking of these responses in FPW from high to low was paradigmatic>syntagmatic>encyclopedia; ranking in SPW from high to low was paradigmatic>encyclopedia>syntagmatic. In addition, the proportion of syntagmatic and encyclopedia nodes in semantic connections between the two types of words was different. In FPW, the syntagmatic connections accounted for 17.01% of semantic connections, and in SPW, they accounted for 9.36%; the encyclopedia connection in FPW accounted for 9.13%, and in SPW it accounted for 18.71%. Moreover, both paradigmatic and syntagmatic distributions between FPW and SPW were different. In terms of paradigmatic distribution, the number of synonym and antonym nodes in FPW was significantly higher than those in SPW. Ingredient nodes in FPW were significantly less than those in SPW. In terms of syntagmatic distribution, there were significantly more syntactic nodes in FPW than those in SPW.

Third, the non-semantic distribution in SPW and FPW was different. FPW had significantly less phonological-formal and "no response" nodes than SPW did. With regards to the percentage, phonological-formal nodes' percentage in non-semantic connections tended to increase from the SPW group to the FPW group, although the amount of it tended to decrease. By contrast, both the amount and percentage of "no response" tended to decrease in the SPW-to-FPW process.

From the comparison, it could be concluded that the lexical networks of SPW and FPW were organised differently in many aspects, and some features reflected in the comparison was worth paying attention to.

First, the tendency of "semantisation" in the SPW-to-FPW process seems to be salient. In SPW-to-FPW process, semantic nodes tend to increase until they become dominant, and non-semantic nodes tend to decrease until they lose their dominance in the lexical network. This adjustment seems to be helpful for word production. More semantic nodes in a word web may mean that there are more semantic paths available, which could lead language users to the target word when the word is needed in speaking or writing. Moreover, there are less non-semantic nodes, which block the access to the target word in word-searching process. Therefore, the target word will be accessed and retrieved more easily with the adjustment.

Second, in the SPW-to-FPW process, different types of nodes tend to develop at different rates and even in different directions. This feature can be reflected in a number of aspects. For example, paradigmatic, syntagmatic and encyclopedia nodes tend to grow at different degrees. Paradigmatic nodes grow to different extents, showing salient advantage over other types of semantic nodes. Syntagmatic nodes grow to a great extent as well, both in number and in percentage of semantic links. Encyclopedia nodes do not increase in number, and their percentage in semantic links decline. This imbalanced change results in the change of inner semantic distribution, where syntagmatic nodes surpass encyclopedia nodes in both number and percentage. The semantic distribution changed from paradigmatic > encyclopedia > syntagmatic in SPW to paradigmatic > syntagmatic > encyclopedia in FPW. It is believed in this sub-research that this change is helpful for word production. According to the definition by Nissen and Henriksen (2006), syntagmatic responses are those that have syntactic or compound/chunk relations with the prompt word, and meanwhile they are semantically related to the prompt. Encyclopedia nodes are concerned with the prompt word's world knowledge, including cultural, social knowledge and personal experiences. Therefore, in the SPW stage, when words cannot be produced but can be recognized and comprehended correctly, encyclopedia connections seem to be more important than syntagmatic connections. This is because the target word may not need much grammar or compound/chunk information for comprehension, but need encyclopedia information to have a deeper and more comprehensive understanding of the word. However, in the FPW stage, the situation seems to be reversed. Syntagmatic knowledge becomes significant, as sentence construction needs syntactic and sometimes compound/chunk knowledge. In speaking and writing people usually produce words in sequence, such as in phrases or sentences, rather than produce isolated words that are unrelated to each other (Meara & Fitzpatrick, 2000). Without enough syntagmatic nodes in the lexical network, production of the target word in contexts will be difficult. By contrast, encyclopedia knowledge may not facilitate word production to the same degree. Therefore, in the FPW stage syntagmatic nodes seem to play a more important role than encyclopedia nodes do; the growth of syntagmatic nodes helps motivate word production.

It was noticed that the phenomenon of "syntagmatic-paradigmatic shift" did not occur in this sub-study. A number of previous studies (e. g. Ervin, 1961; Fu et al. , 2009; Namei, 2004; Söderman, 1993) detected that there is a "syntagmatic-paradigmatic shift" in both L1 and L2 mental lexicon development. These studies found that with the development of mental lexicon, paradigmatic nodes tend to keep increasing, whereas syntagmatic nodes tend to keep decreasing. The notion that there is a paradigmatic-syntagmatic shift in L2 mental lexicon development seems to have been widely accepted now (Khazaeenezhad & Alibabaee, 2013; Namei, 2004; Piper & Leicester, 1980; Söderman, 1993; Wolter, 2001). However, the shift failed to occur in this sub-research, since both paradigmatic and syntagmatic nodes' amount and percentage grew in SPW-to-FPW process.

Reasons for the inconsistent results need to be investigated. Upon examining previous research more closely, it was found that almost all those studies adopted testees' age or language proficiency level as independent variables (e.g. Fu et al.,2009; Namei,2004;Söderman,1993). For instance,Namei (2004) conducted a cross-sectional research to compare word associations by children of different ages. His study found the phenomenon of syntagmatic-paradigmatic shift. However,it may be too hasty to conclude from the study that the shift is a result of the progress of word acquisition. Rather,the shift may have resulted from testees' enlarging vocabulary size or world knowledge when their age or language proficiency progresses. Fu et al. (2009) conducted a longitudinal study to investigate mental lexicon development. In her study,40 words that testees were unfamiliar with were selected to be target words. Forty sophomores in English major participated in the study,and they were asked to do word association tests for three times during a three-month period. The study found a slight "syntagmatic-paradigmatic shift" tendency. The original goal of the research was to observe the mental lexicon change in individual words' acquisition development. However, since the study lasted for three months, the informants' L2 proficiency and word knowledge may also develop in this period. Additionally,the target words' acquisition level or familiarity level seemed to be only judged by the researcher's subjective assumption that in the three months those words developed. No measuring instrument was adopted to ensure whether they truly developed or not,and to what degrees they had developed. A slight "syntagmatic-paradigmatic shift" was discovered in the study, but the slight degree may have resulted from the short duration of three months,since in three months informants' L2 proficiency and world knowledge may only develop at a limited degree. Namei (2004), Zareva (2007),and Zareva and Brent (2012) also believed that the growth of age and language proficiency would make informants elicit more paradigmatic reactions, since age difference may cause difference in testees' world knowledge, and L2 proficiency difference may cause difference in testees' vocabulary size. Therefore, the conclusion could not confirm that syntagmatic-paradigmatic shift does exist in words' acquisition development. That is to say, the notion that there is a paradigmatic-syntagmatic shift in words' acquisition progress in fact has never been confirmed by previous research. However, conclusions of those researches sometimes seem to mislead people that there is a syntagmatic-paradigmatic shift in word acquisition development (e. g. Wolter, 2001). People tend to overlook the fact that those studies indicating the shift adopted age or language proficiency, not word acquisition level, as the independent variable. In fact, the syntagmatic-paradigmatic shift has nothing to do with the individual words' mental lexicon development. The misunderstanding may have negative effects, because it may make ESL teachers think that in vocabulary teaching they should focus more on paradigmatic nodes, rather than on syntagmatic nodes. This teaching principle may not be effective.

In addition, it seems that even the method of adopting age or language proficiency level as the independent variable is problematic. One of the evidences reflecting the problem is that a number of relevant studies ended in illogical results. For example, S. Zhang (2004) investigated some advanced Chinese ESL learners, and found that these learners produced a great deal of phonological responses. Söderman (1993) discovered that advanced ESL learners produced numerous phonological responses, but beginners produced a number of paradigmatic responses. Namei's (2004) finding is similar in that even the most advanced L1 and L2 speakers have phonological and syntagmatic reactions, whereas even the very beginning L1 and L2 users have a great deal of paradigmatic reactions. Söderman (1993) and Namei (2004) therefore pointed out that no matter in which proficiency level, there are always words that are unknown, partially known, or well known; each word would experience a sequence of development from being unknown to well known, and the sequence is not affected by language proficiency. In other words, it is the word's acquisition level, rather than proficiency level, that would determine response patterns. In research adopting language proficiency as the independent variable, conclusions may be completely different if the selected words have different acquisition levels. Similarly, studies adopting age as the independent variable may have the same validity problem as well. No matter in which age level, there are always words that are unknown, partially known, or well known; each word would experience a sequence of development from being unknown to well known, and the sequence is not affected by age, if the factor of cognitive ability in age is excluded. In other words, it is the word's acquisition level, rather than age, that would determine response patterns. In research adopting age as the independent variable, conclusions may be completely different if the selected words have different acquisition levels.

In this sub-study, word acquisition levels were adopted as the independent variable, which was named as "familiarity" and measured by VKS test. The variables of age and language proficiency were controlled, since the testees were of similar proficiency and age. It is believed that the sub-study's validity is comparatively satisfactory. The "syntagmatic-paradigmatic shift" was not found in this sub-study. Therefore, it seems reliable to conclude that at least in the SPW-to-FPW stage, both paradigmatic and syntagmatic nodes keep increasing, and no paradigmatic-syntagmatic shift would occur.

The feature of the nodes' imbalanced development is reflected in the different types of paradigmatic responses as well. In the paradigmatic responses, synonym got prior growth, and it was the largest type of response in paradigmatic connections. Antonym experienced significant growth as well, although it only accounted for a small proportion in paradigmatic connections. All other types of paradigmatic responses did not grow significantly. According to the Spreading-activation Model by Collins and Loftus (1975), the more properties two nodes share, the more related and connected they are to each other. Since synonym contains similar or identical meaning as the stimulus word does, it may be the closest type of node to the stimulus. Therefore, the prior development of synonym may reflect a tendency of building "shortcuts" in network construction in the SPW-to-FPW process. This tendency is helpful for word production, since more synonym connections may assist target words to be accessed and retrieved more quickly and easily. The feature of imbalanced development can be evidenced by the prior growth of syntactic nodes, and the significant decrease in phonological-formal nodes and pseudo word nodes.

The third feature is that lexical connections tend to get stronger in the SPW-to-FPW process. This feature can be reflected in a number of aspects. For example, in the SPW-to-FPW process, paradigmatic and syntagmatic connections had significant growth, but encyclopedia nodes stagnated in development. As it has been pointed out, encyclopedia response (e. g. Antarctica→ ozone hole) is related to testees' word knowledge. Although this type of response is semantic, it seems not as closely related to stimulus words as paradigmatic and syntagmatic nodes do. The semantic distance between the stimulus word and its encyclopedia response is comparatively distant, and the connection between them is loose. Therefore, the phenomenon that paradigmatic and syntagmatic got prior development may indicate that the lexical network tends to get stronger in the SPW-to-FPW process. The change in non-semantic connections can also demonstrate this feature. In non-semantic connections, the proportion of phonological-formal response kept rising, although the amount of it was shrinking. Other types of response either declined in percentage, or did not change in percentage. Compared with other types of non-semantic response, phonological-formal response is more related to the cue word, since it is phonologically or formally similar to the cue. Other non-semantic response, such as non-classifiable, pseudo word and "no response", have no common properties in any aspect with the cue. Therefore, the increasing proportion of phonological-formal nodes in non-semantic connections suggests that non-semantic network tend to get stronger and tighter, although its size tends to shrink. Additionally, the increase of semantic nodes and the decrease of non-semantic nodes demonstrate this feature as well.

However, it may be necessary to clarify that the decrease of some types of nodes does not necessarily mean they disappear from the word web.

Since the word association tests only asked testees to give the first three reactions to the cue, only the central area of the network was observed in this sub-study. Therefore, the decrease of some types of nodes may not mean that those nodes have been "wiped out" from the word web, but rather they remain their presence but are not at the center of the word web any more. For example, when the target word is SPW with high familiarity, there are numerous encyclopedia nodes around the target word. These nodes offer the language user adequate social, cultural or personal information on it, and they help the language user have an in-depth comprehension of the word. When the target word develops to be FPW, the encyclopedia nodes are still in the network, but great deals of them move to less important positions, and their original positions are taken by syntagmatic nodes. According to Laufer and Goldstein (2004) and Meara and Fitzpatrick (2000), the sequence of word development is to become receptive first, and on this basis to develop into productive ones. Therefore, in the productive stage, nodes that function at the receptive stage are still functioning, but nodes that are more important for word production are integrated into the network.

Similarly, in the early acquisition stage, the phonological-formal nodes may be dominant in its lexical network, as reported by Fu et al. (2009). Fu et al. (2009) ound that setting up phonological-formal connections fwith other words might be the first step in word acquisition. With further development, more semantic nodes are integrated into the web, and they replace phonological-formal nodes in the central positions. However, it does not mean that the phonological-formal nodes disappear from the network, but rather they move to less important positions. In other words, they do not play a role as important as before in word activation and retrieval. Their functions are still there, which is to offer the language user the target words' spelling and pronunciation information.

5.5.2   The Lexical Construction Procedure in SPW-to-FPW Process

The results of this sub-study have shed some light on how the lexical network is constructed in SPW-to-FPW process. When a word can be recognized with high familiarity, but is not ready to be frequently produced, almost half of its nodes in its lexical network are non-semantic. These non-semantic nodes become "barriers" when L2 users try to access and retrieve the word's meanings from mental lexicon. The other half of nodes are semantic. Most of the semantic nodes at this stage are paradigmatic and encyclopedic. These paradigmatic and syntagmatic nodes can offer L2 users information on the target word from various perspectives, especially on synonyms, antonyms, social and cultural knowledge, grammatical knowledge, and collocatioal knowledge. Therefore, the word not only can be correctly recognized, but also can be well comprehended by the language user. At this stage, there are not as many syntagmatic nodes as paradigmatic and encyclopedic nodes; therefore, the lexical network does not have adequate paths for L2 users to retrieve the target words' syntactic or compound/chunk information for production.

With further development, semantic nodes keep growing, and non-semantic nodes keep shrinking, until semantic nodes obtain salient advantage over non-semantic ones, and they become the majority in the lexical network. At this stage, not only does the size of semantic connections get enlarged, but also the inner structure of semantic connections changes as well. Paradigmatic and syntagmatic nodes get significant growth, but encyclopedia nodes do not. The result of this change is that the syntagmatic nodes surpass the encyclopedia nodes and become the second biggest type of response. In paradigmatic connections, synonyms get prior development and become the majority in paradigmatic connections. Therefore, when target words are needed in oral or written expression, a large number of paradigmatic nodes (especially synonyms) and adequate encyclopedia nodes would offer numerous channels for target words to be reached and retrieved. Meanwhile, a great deal of syntagmatic (especially syntactic) nodes are accessed and activated, making the target word ready to be produced in oral and written contexts.

In sum, this part of study detected three features in the SPW-to-FPW process. The first feature is that lexical network tends to get semantised; the second feature is that different types of nodes tend to change at different speeds and in different directions (increasing or decreasing); the third feature is that connections of lexical network tend to get stronger and tighter. According to the Spreading-activation Model, mental lexicon is organised as a network of nodes; the nodes are connected with each other at "different distance, strength, and spreading-activation levels" (Liu et al., 2012). In other words, links in lexical network have different accessibility, such as strength and travelling time (Collins & Quillian, 1969, 1972). The results of this sub-study, to some extent, confirm the hypothesis of the Spreading-activation Model in that at least in the SPW-to-FPW stage, the lexical network tends to develop in the way that nodes become more easily accessed, activated, and retrieved. Therefore, some words' stagnation in the SPW-to-FPW development may be attributed to some problems in lexical network construction. It may lie in the inadequate semantisation, i. e. , the inadequate growth of semantic nodes, especially synonym, antonym, and syntactic nodes. Therefore, in the SPW-to-FPW development, semantic construction seems to be important, and great importance should be attached to synonym, antonym and syntactic nodes in particular.

It may be necessary to reiterate that the conclusion from this sub-study does not mean that some other types of nodes are not important. Rather, those nodes have their own functions in lexical development. For instance, encyclopedia nodes can help language users obtain in-depth comprehension for the target word, and phonological-formal nodes can assist language users to grasp spelling and pronunciation of the word. The conclusion of this sub-study just means that at the stage when the target word has become SPW with high familiarity, numerous encyclopedia and phonological-formal nodes have already been built and integrated in the lexical network. Learners have grasped the words' form and pronunciation, and have had an in-depth comprehension of the word. In this stage these nodes have completed their mission and withdrawn to less important positions in the lexical network. Therefore, these types of nodes should still be built and strengthened in vocabulary teaching and learning, but at earlier stages. In the stage when SPW aim to develop into FPW, more focus should be given to synonym, syntactic and antonym nodes. It seems that at different word acquisition stages, there are different types of nodes that need to be focused on.

5.5.3 Pedagogical Implications

Based on the results of this sub-study, some suggestions are proposed on ESL vocabulary teaching and learning.

Firsy, semantisation is necessary in the SPW-to-FPW development. Therefore, after the target words become SPW with high familiarity, semantic building should be given adequate attention in ESL teaching and learning; more semantic nodes should be integrated in mental lexicon. This goal may be achieved by semantic input and output. The semantic input activities may include intensive reading, extensive reading, listening, etc. The semantic output activities may include speaking and writing. That is to say, adequate quantity of reading, listening, speaking, and writing should be ensured. Adequate activities in these areas may be the first step to motivate SPW-to-FPW development.

Second, semantisation alone may not be enough. The results of this sub-study indicate that some types of nodes seem to play more important roles than the others in the SPW-to-FPW process. These nodes include synonym and syntactic nodes. Antonym nodes play a somewhat positive role as well. In other words, not only the amount of input and output is significant, what to input and output is important as well.

Therefore, after SPW have reached high familiarity, more attention should be focused on the building of synonym, syntactic and antonym nodes. This sub-research found that there are several activities that may be helpful in building synonym nodes. For instance, paraphrase may be an efficient way, since paraphrasing involves target words being substituted by words of similar meanings. Other activities include rewriting and retelling, which ask students to have oral or written restatement. Brainstorm can be used as well (it can also be used to collect antonyms), where students are asked to collect synonyms of a target word as many as possible.

With regard to syntactic nodes, several tasks may be helpful. After words become SPW with high familiarity, adequate grammar input should be offered by teachers. For example, if the target word is a transitional verb, the objects that can be followed, the subjects that can be used before it, and the adverbials that can co-exist with the verb should be provided as well. Sentences which can demonstrate grammatical features of the target word could be given as examples. Moreover, various types of grammatical practices are encouraged to be carried out, such as matching (which asks students to connect the target word with its correct usage), True or False (which asks students to judge whether the word is used correctly in a sentence), and filling in the blanks (which asks students to use the target word with correct syntactic forms). In addition to input of grammar, output of grammar should be encouraged. This part of study recommended that students be asked to make sentences with the target words. If syntactic mistakes occur in the sentence, feedback should be provided in time, and mistakes should be corrected. With these measures, syntactic nodes may obtain more chances to be built in lexical network, and those nodes that already exist may get more chances to get strengthened and become closer to the target word.

Students' consciousness seems to be necessary as well. They should be advised to be more conscious on semantic construction. They should be suggested to pay enough attention to the target words when they encounter those words in contexts, and to consciously use them in speaking and writing. In addition to the methods suggested in this sub-study, there may be other teaching and learning methods that can facilitate lexical construction. Teachers and learners are advised to design different activities based on the principles detected from this sub-study to promote FAV development.

5. 6 Conclusion

This chapter compared lexical network representation between SPW and FPW. The results indicate that the two types of words' representations differ in numerous aspects, including semantic and non-semantic distribution, semantic distribution, and non-semantic distribution. Three features are revealed from the results. First, the lexical network tends to be semantised in SPW-to-FPW development. Second, nodes of different types develop at different extents and directions; some types of nodes seem to play more important roles than others in SPW-to-FPW process. Third, connections in lexical network tend to get stronger and tighter in the process. The results of this sub-study to some degree confirm the hypothesis of the Spreading-activation Model that nodes tend to be more easily accessed, activated, and retrieved in lexical network development. Based on the conclusion, it is proposed that one of the chief reasons for the threshold phenomenon is that some SPW with high familiarity do not get adequate semantisation in the SPW-to-FPW development. In particular, synonym, antonym and syntactic nodes' inadequate growth may play a critical role for the stagnation.

In this chapter the word association sub-study is presented. The purpose of the sub-study is to explore the mental lexicon construction procedure in SPW-to-FPW process, and to detect effective ways to promote FAV development. In the next chapter, the qualitative sub-study of interview is presented. The purpose of the sub-study is to find possible factors in learning and teaching that may affect FAV development, and to find possible ways to facilitate FAV development.

Chapter 6   Interview

6. 1   Introduction

This chapter reports on the investigation of students' consciousness on free active vocabulary (FAV) development, teachers' guidance on free active vocabulary learning, the effective learning strategies students adopt (if any) to enlarge FAV storage, and the effective teaching strategies (if any) teachers adopt to assist students' FAV development. The aim of the sub-study is to find possible factors in learning and teaching that may affect FAV development, and to find possible ways to facilitate FAV development. The chapter first poses the aspects around which interview questions were designed, then presents research method, including instruments, data collection, data preparation and data analysis. At the end of the chapter, results are reported and discussed, and conclusions are made.

6. 2   Aspects of Interview Questions

The interview questions were designed surrounding four aspects:
(1) Students' awareness of FAV in L2 study.
(2) Learning strategies (if any) adopted to improve FAV.
(3) Teachers' guidance on FAV learning.

（4）Teaching strategies（if any）that may help promote students' FAV development.

6.3　Research Method

This section presents major components of the research method adopted in the sub-study, including instruments, procedure of data collection, data preparation, and data analysis. The participants of the interview have been introduced in Chapter 3.

6.3.1　Instrument

The instrument adopted in the sub-study is a face-to-face interview. Questions in the interview are designed in four aspects, which are presented in Table 6.1. It should be noted that in the formal interview, extra questions may be added when necessary, so that more detailed information on the relevant topic can be obtained.

Table 6.1　Aspects and Corresponding Questions in the Interview

Aspects	Corresponding questions
Aspect One: Students' consciousness of FAV in L2 study	1. Have you ever had difficulties in searching for suitable words to express the meaning you want to express in L2 writing or speaking? 2. What are the difficulties (if any)? 3. Do you know free active vocabulary? Or do you know this type of vocabulary knowledge, even if you do not know the terminology of it? 4. Have you ever attempted to improve your free active vocabulary size in L2 study?

Continued

Aspects	Corresponding questions
Aspect Two: Learning strategies adopted to enlarge FAV	1. Have you ever taken some measures to enlarge FAV size? 2. What are the measures (if any)? 3. Do you think these measures are effective?
Aspect Three: Teachers' guidance on FAV in L2 teaching	1. Have your teachers told you that FAV is important? 2. Are there many teachers who did so? 3. Have any teachers given you any suggestions on how to enlarge FAV? 4. What suggestions did they give you (if any)?
Aspect Four: Teaching strategies that may help students' FAV development	1. Do you think some teaching strategies are helpful in FAV acquisition? 2. What are they (if any)?

6.3.2　Data Collection Procedure

6.3.2.1　Pilot Study

A pilot study was conducted before the formal interview. Five year-three students who were studying in the same major and from the same university took part in it. Interview questions were presented, and feedback was collected. The pilot study aimed to ensure that the interview questions were clear enough to interviewees, and to check whether it was necessary to design additional questions in the formal interview. It also aimed to find the suitable length of time to conduct the interview. The interviewees' answers and feedback showed that the designed questions were clear to interviewees. However, it was found that some students did not know the terminology of free active vocabulary, but they in fact knew that there was this type of vocabulary knowledge. Therefore to avoid drawing wrong conclusions, an explanation on what is free active vocabulary was to be provided to the interviewees, and a follow-up question was added to the original question of "Do you know free active vocabulary?". The added question was "Do you know that there is this type of vocabulary knowledge, even if you don't know the term 'free active vocabulary'?" The pilot study showed that the time needed for each interview was around 5 to 7 minutes.

6.3.2.2　Formal Data Collection

The formal data was collected in June, 2016. It was considered to be a suitable time to collect the data, as at the end of the four-year university study, students would have enough spare time to participate in the interview. In addition, it was a time when they were able to have a comprehensive reflection of the learning and teaching activities in the past four years. Before the data collection, the student investigator asked the interviewees to answer interview questions as detailed as possible. They were also encouraged to raise questions if they had any doubts on the interview questions. Then the interview started. Each student was interviewed separately, so that their answers would not be affected by other interviewees. The entire process was recorded.

6.3.3　Data Preparation

Interviews were audio recorded. Then the recordings were played and checked by the student investigator to ensure that the interviewees answered the questions seriously. If details were given in the interviewees' answers, it was believed that the interviewees answered the questions seriously. It turned out that all the interviewees did the interview with a serious attitude, and therefore all the datas were valid. Then the recordings were transcribed by the student investigator for further analysis. In order to protect privacy, the interviewees were kept anonymous, and they were coded as Interviewee A, Interviewee B, and Interviewee C.

6.4 Results and Discussion

Transcription of the recording consists of approximately 3, 260 words in total. The student investigators read the transcription sentence by sentence, and then had the transcription encoded, arranged, and categorised. The interview results are reported and discussed in this section.

When being asked "Have you ever felt difficulties in searching for suitable words to express the meaning you want to express in writing or speaking?", the interviewees' answers were almost the same. They reported having difficulties in seeking for the right words to use in writing and speaking. Specifically, the students' challenge primarily lied in the fact that sometimes their effort in searching for the most accurate word failed. Interviewee A felt unsure sometimes about the precision of the candidate words in writing, or sometimes he could not find an exact word to express what he wanted to express. In this condition, he had to use a substitute instead. This led to the loss of accuracy in his writing. Interviewee B had the same concern. She said:

"I definitely feel the difficulty. As a senior student, I start to have job interviews. In some of the interviews, the interviewers would require me to have oral communication (in English) with them. Sometimes I feel my vocabulary is rather limited ... The word that I use is not precise, but I cannot find the precise one." (Interview B)

Interviewee C told the investigator that she suffered from this trouble frequently:

"I think words have both general meaning and specific meaning, but in many cases I only know the general meaning. Thus, in a specific circumstance, I may not be able to find the specific word, and thereby have to use a general word to replace it."

The student then gave an example. Once she wanted to express "the 'American dream' contains different potential meanings in different times", but she could not find a suitable word to express "potential meaning", such as "connotation" or "implication". Thus she had to use the word "meaning" instead. She said this problem often occurred. Moreover, she told the investigator that the difficulty she faced was not in choosing the right word among options. The trouble seemed to be even worse: she could not think of optional words at all. She had to use a basic, general word, as it was the only one that could come into her mind. This difficulty corresponds with the statement by Swain (2000): "Learners may notice that they do not know how to express precisely the meaning they wish to convey at the very moment of attempting to produce it ... they notice, so to speak, a 'hole' in their interlanguage." This problem may result in the loss of important information the student wants to convey in writing and speaking.

It can be inferred from the interview that the difficulty in FAV usage is common even among upper-intermediate to advanced students. These students' difficulty is primarily in retrieval, rather than in the selection of the right word among retrieved words. Findings in Chapter 5 may shed some light on the retrieval difficulty. As is concluded in Chapter 5, the lexical network is organised differently between frequently produced words (FPW) and seldom produced words (SPW). The semantic nodes of FPW tend to outnumber those of SPW, whereas non-semantic nodes of SPW tend to outnumber those of FPW. With regard to proportion, semantic links account for the majority in FPW, but in SPW they do not. Taking a closer look, it can be seen that FPW's paradigmatic and syntagmatic links are significantly more than SPW's. Within paradigmatic links, FPW has significantly more synonym and antonym nodes than SPW does. Within syntagmatic links, FPW has significantly more syntactic nodes than SPW do. The investigation in Chapter 5 also found that there is difference between FPW and SPW in the number of non-semantic links. There are significantly less phonological-formal and no-response nodes in FPW than in SPW. The finding seems to indicate that SPW may not have enough semantic nodes, but too many non-semantic nodes in their lexical network. Specifically, SPW may not have adequate synonym, antonym, and syntactic nodes, but have too many phonological-formal and non-response nodes around them. The lexical representation sheds some light on reasons for the retrieval difficulty. Those SPW may not have enough semantic paths to be reached in lexical network, but have too many non-semantic paths to block the retrieval. In addition, the lack of syntactic links makes it hard to be produced in context, as grammatical knowledge is an inevitable factor in sentence creation.

The next set of questions is on students' consciousness of FAV in L2 study. All the interviewees indicated their awareness of FAV. However, when they were asked whether they had made effort to enlarge FAV storage in L2 study, two of them answered that they only took "some" effort to it. For example, interviewee B reflected that for a period of time she tried to enlarge FAV, but gave up later. This indicates that some students know the existence of FAV, and have attempted to improve it, but the attempt seems to be inadequate, as they may give up after a while.

Effective learning strategies in FAV development were then investigated. Two interviewees reflected that taking deliberate "output" practice was helpful to them. For example, Interviewee A reflected that he tried to pay extra attention to the target word, and then forced himself to produce the word. When he encountered a new word in study, he would deliberately create chances to use the word in writing or speaking. Interviewee B stated a similar strategy. In reading, if some new words attracted her attention, the student would put them down in a notebook. If these words were encountered for a second time, she would pay more attention to it, and attempted to apply these words in writing. She said the purpose of this activity was to help these words be transferred from receptive to productive. The student stressed that if the word was not used, it would be forgotten with time passing by.

Analysing the context and putting down example sentences were deemed to play positive roles as well. Interviewee C told the investigator that in reading, when she first encountered a new word that drew her notice, she would put down the word. If she encountered the word again, she would pay more attention to it, and considered why it was used in this context. By this method she would learn how to use the word. If she noticed that a word appeared frequently, she would look it up in a dictionary, and then copied the example sentences to her notebook. The reason to do this was because these examples might be helpful for her writing.

In the interview one phenomenon attracted the investigator's attention: the students seemed to be sensitive to word frequency in FAV acquisition. Two interviewees stated that usually if they only encountered the word once, they might notice it, but would not consider how to use it. Only when they met the word repeatedly would they try to output it by themselves. This tendency may imply that word frequency is considered to be important by students. If a word appears frequently, they will think that the word is worthwhile to be transferred into FAV; if a word does not appear frequently, they tend not to think so, and thereby will not make efforts to develop it into FAV. This finding corresponds with the finding in the 12-month longitudinal sub-study that words are usually acquired in order. More frequently used words are usually learned before less frequently used ones (Schmitt et al., 2001). The suggestion is that repeated occurrence of the target words may be helpful for FAV development. In texts or lectures, teachers are advised to deliberately increase the occurrences of the target word, so that students' attention can be attracted. This measure may have an indirect positive effect on FAV development.

The interviewees described some other strategies that they felt effective as well. One strategy was collecting synonyms. Interviewee C introduced this method, and she thought it was very helpful to her. She said at lower proficiency level, words encountered were mostly basic words. With further study, more synonyms were encountered in intensive and extensive reading. The interviewee deemed that collecting synonyms was helpful to writing. In this way various words could be used, therefore the writing would not be as plain as water. The student pointed out that if only the most basic words were applied, quality of the writing would be similar to that of middle school students.

Another strategy being reported was to make use of "context". Interviewee A told the student investigator that he often looked for authentic reading materials, such as those in foreign English magazines. If he encountered a new word in these reading materials, he would try to figure out the meaning of the word in the context. Then he would know that it was appropriate to use the word in this type of context. When he met a similar circumstance, he would know that it was proper to use this word in it. The interviewee reported that this learning strategy worked for him.

The Output Hypothesis by Swain (1985, 1995) can be used to explain why this strategy is effective. The Output Hypothesis states that although comprehensible input is essential in second language acquisition, solely having input is not enough. Comprehensible output is essential as well. The hypothesis holds that language production, no matter in spoken form or written form, would elicit language learning/acquisition to occur (Swain, 1985). According to Swain (1985), being "pushed" not only means to make learners convey a message, but also to convey it precisely, coherently, and appropriately. He believes that the act of "pushing" would force ESL learners to make more mental effort in study, thus process the language more deeply. Swain's (1985) Output Hypothesis is originally on general second language acquisition, rather than specifically on vocabulary or FAV acquisition. However, some scholars found this theory was relevant to L2 FAV learning as well, and therefore they applied this theory to L2 FAV study. For instance, Laufer (1998) holds that if L2 learners are not pushed to use L2 words, the words may never be activated, and they may only remain in passive vocabulary. Henriksen (1999) believes as well that pushed output helps promote receptive words to develop into productive words. Empirical studies have been conducted. Ellis and He (1999) found learners with output practice improved significantly in both receptive and productive vocabulary (FAV in this case) learning. The experiment by Fuente and José (2002) showed that negotiation of input plus pushed output resulted in more L2 target words' production than negotiation of input without pushed output. The experiment by Arash (2016) reveals that when L2 learners are given chances to produce the target words, their performance of word production is better than the performance when they are not given the chance. Arash (2016) therefore concluded that pushed output can improve L2 word production.

It may be necessary to note that the pushed output in this study refers to the pushed "semantic" output, rather than pushed "formal" output, as the output of forms does not do much for the words' semantic construction. Barcroft (2006) administered an experiment to check the effect of forced output of forms on vocabulary learning. In his study, subjects attempted to learn a group of L2 words by viewing word-picture pairs. In the process, the participants were asked to copy half of the target words, but not to do so for the other half of the target words. The productive vocabulary knowledge was tested after the treatment. Subjects were required to write down words after viewing relevant pictures. It is deemed in this study that the activity of picture-word writing to some extent assesses subjects' FAV, since the test does not provide any hint on the words' spelling or pronunciation to subjects. The subjects had to "freely and actively" produce the word when they saw the picture. Results of this study reveal that the no-copying group significantly outperformed the copying group in FAV learning. The implication of the study, according to Barcroft (2006), is that the forced output without access to meaning would have negative effects on vocabulary (FAV in this case) learning, as learners have to spare processing resource to encode forms of the words.

Although Krashen (1998), who proposed the Input Hypothesis, doubts the significance of output in second language acquisition (SLA), this sub-study seems to support the opposite view that output does play a positive role in SLA, specifically in FAV acquisition in this case. When students try to create sentences with the target word, they are "pushing" themselves beyond their current level of word use, as they force themselves to use a word that they never used before. They tend to make more mental effort in this condition than when they solely receive input of the word from the teacher. This may be the reason why the pushed output activity can work effectively for FAV development.

All the effective learning strategies reported by the interviewees can be explained by theories of Depth of Processing, Task-induced Involvement, and findings in mental lexicon. The Theory of Depth of Processing is proposed by Craik and Lockhart (1972). According to the theory, the depth at which a piece of information is processed is an important factor in memorization: the deeper the processing is, the better the memorization will be (Craik & Lockhart, 1972). For example, trying to memorize a word out of context and trying to memorize a word in context may involve different depth of processing: memorizing the word in context involves more meaning analysis than memorizing it out of context, and therefore it may bring better results (Yue, 2008). The shallow depth of processing might primarily be on sensory levels, such as visual or acoustic processing; deeper processing might primarily be on meaning analysis and structure analysis

(Craik & Lockhart, 1972). The strategies of making sentences, referring to a dictionary, taking notes on word meanings, putting down example sentences, analysing the context, and collecting synonyms may all result in a deep processing on the target word. Therefore, these learning methods work effectively for FAV development.

Another theory is Task-induced Involvement Theory, proposed by Laufer and Hulstijn (2001). Laufer and Hulstijn (2001) hold that different tasks tend to elicit different amounts of cognitive involvement load. The cognitive involvement includes three aspects: need, search, and evaluation. Different tasks contain different loads of involvement in the three aspects, thus result in various acquisition results. For instance, in the study by Duan and Yan (2004), experimented words were presented to participants in different ways. The participants of Group 1 read an article with target words and then did multiple-choice tasks, in which correct meanings for the target words should be chosen. Each of the tasks had more than one correct answer. The participants of Group 2 read the same article with the target words, and then did multiple-choice tasks for correct word meanings as well, but each task had only one correct answer. Group 3 read the article with the target words, and the word meanings were given to them directly. The three tasks contained different levels of involvement. The first task elicited all the three involvements. There was "need" to seek the word meanings, "search" to look for the correct choices of word meanings, and "evaluation" to judge whether the choices were correct or not. The second task elicited all the three involvements as well, but the amount of "search" and "evaluation" was most likely smaller than that in the first task. It was because in the second task only one correct choice needed to be selected and evaluated. By contrast, in the first task two or more than two correct choices needed to be found, therefore it needed more effort in "search" and "evaluation". The study showed that the first task resulted in the best word acquisition outcome, the second task came next, and the third one resulted in the least acquisition. The study verified the Task-induced Involvement Theory.

In fact, the Theory of Depth of Processing and Task-induced Involvement are related to each other, as the Task-induced Involvement is developed on the basis of Theory of Depth of Processing (Yue, 2008). The weakness of the Theory of Depth of Processing is that the "depth" cannot be quantified and measured. By contrast, the Task-induced Involvement overcomes this weakness, as the theory makes the amount of involvement possible to be measured and evaluated by investigating whether the task contains "need", "search", and "evaluation". Therefore, the Task-induced Involvement makes relevant empirical studies feasible to be conducted (Yue, 2008).

Moreover, it is found that the effectiveness of the learning strategies can find explanations in mental lexicon construction. As is reflected in previous paragraphs, frequently produced words have a rich connection of semantic nodes. The strategies of analysing context, looking for word meaning in dictionaries, putting down example sentences, and collecting synonyms all help set up semantic nodes in the lexical network. The construction plays a positive role in transferring the target words into FAV.

The next series of questions aim to investigate teachers' guidance on FAV learning and the effective teaching strategies they adopted to assist students' FAV development. When being asked whether their teachers had told them the importance of

FAV, all the interviewees answered yes. However, they recalled that only one teacher teaching them *Intensive Reading* in the third year did so. This indicates that many teachers may not be conscious of the significance of FAV; even if they have the consciousness, they may not take any action to help students improve FAV. The guidance that students can obtain from teachers, therefore, is limited. In addition, teachers may lack knowledge on how to help students effectively, as the literature review reflected that the relevant research is rather limited. This condition makes students unable to get adequate guidance from teachers.

The lack of strategy guidance can be evidenced from the interview. When the investigator asked the interviewees whether their teachers had given them suggestions on how to improve FAV, two of them reported no specific methods recommended by their teachers. Only one interviewee reflected that the Intensive Reading teacher suggested them to put down new words in notebooks, and to deliberately use them in writing. The teacher told them that this was a method used by one of her former students, who had good writing capability.

It was found that few teaching strategies had been adopted to enlarge students' FAV. However, the interviewees described some teaching strategies that aimed for other purposes but played a positive role in FAV acquisition. For instance, two interviewees recalled that some teachers often provided them with synonyms of the target words. For instance, one of them reflected that once in class when students were studying the words "strength" and "weakness", the teacher provided them synonyms of "advantage" and "disadvantage", "merit" and "demerit". In this way, not only were the target words learned, but also their synonyms were learned as well.

One of the teachers took a step further. Instead of solely providing synonyms, the teacher conducted "negotiation" to students. According to Arash (2016), "negotiation" means to negotiate the meaning of the word, such as to clarify, confirm, or repeat the word meaning to students. The study by Arash (2016) shows that input of word meaning with negotiation leads to greater FAV gains than input of word meaning without negotiation. Another study testifies the positive effect of both negotiation and pushed output. The research by Teng (2015) shows that extensive reading with negotiation and pushed output activities prompt more FAV gains than solely extensive reading does. In this sub-study, the interviewee said:

"Maybe because the teacher majors in literature, she has a precise understanding of words. Most teachers would only provide us with a general explanation on a target word, or just give us a translation or an example sentence with it. But she would analyse why this word is used properly here, and why the word is a good choice. She often does so."

This method goes one step further than offering synonyms, translations, or examples, as it gives students detailed information on the words' connotations, and a deeper analysis on the words' context. In other words, it provides students with "negotiations" of the word. Negotiation helps students have a deeper processing on the word. Negotiation may help students set up semantic network in mental lexicon as well. When students encounter a proper circumstance, the word will be more easily reached and retrieved from their mental lexicon. This may be the reason why negotiation can help students in FAV development.

6. 5   Conclusion

The interviews in this chapter obtain information in the four aspects proposed in Section 6.2. The first aspect is students' consciousness to FAV in L2 study. It shows that students know FAV, and the awareness is most likely aroused by the difficulty they encounter in word production. Being aware of FAV's significance, they have taken some effort trying to enlarge it in study. However, students' effort may not be adequate, as the number of strategies they use is rather limited, and they may give up the effort later. In summary, students may know the concept of FAV, but their effort to improve FAV may not be enough.

The second aspect is on effective learning strategies students adopt for FAV development. It is reflected that students do take some measures trying to enlarge their FAV size. The strategies that they feel effective include making sentences with the word, taking notes of the word's meaning, putting down example sentences, attempting to use the word in proper context, and collecting synonyms. A problem was revealed from the interview. The number of strategies adopted is limited, as each interviewee only reported one or two strategies, and confirmed later that those strategies were all that they used. The inadequacy in strategy use may be one factor for FAV stagnation.

The third aspect is teachers' guidance of FAV learning. Regrettably, the interview indicates that many teachers may not be aware of the significance of FAV; even if some of them know it, they fail to give adequate guidance to students on FAV learning. In the interview it was reflected that almost no teachers, except for one Intensive Reading teacher, had ever mentioned FAV to students. In addition, few suggestions had been given to the interviewees on how to enlarge FAV storage.

The fourth aspect is effective teaching strategies that may help students in FAV development. The interview shows that the guidance provided by teachers on FAV development is not adequate. However, some teaching methods were found by interviewees to be helpful to FAV development, although they were not adopted for this purpose. These methods include providing synonyms, negotiating word meanings, analysing contexts, arousing students' attention to target words, etc. Some effective teaching strategies overlap with students' learning strategies. Like the effectiveness of learning strategies, the effectiveness of these teaching strategies can be theoretically explained by the Depth of Processing Theory, Task-induced Involvement Theory, and findings from the mental lexicon sub-study.

Some problems are detected from the interview. The first problem is that students lack proper guidance in FAV development. The interview shows that many teachers almost never mention FAV in teaching, let alone provide students with instructions and suggestions on how to improve it. Moreover, few teaching strategies are adopted to help promote students' FAV development. However, it may be hasty to blame this neglect on teachers, as research in this field is rather limited, and it cannot give teachers enough guidance yet. Although researchers have detected the FAV threshold phenomenon in L2 study, there is a limited number of studies, especially empirical ones, on how to tackle this problem. Even if teachers feel the great necessity to help students enlarge their FAV, they can find little reference to give them valuable suggestions. Therefore, relevant research is in dire need. On the students' side, realizing the significance of FAV, they have to "grope" for effective learning methods by themselves. The effectiveness of their trials thus mostly depends on luck. Some strategies may turn out to be helpful, some may not; some may be helpful, but may only be helpful to a specific person, rather than having a universal value.

The second problem is that although the interview shows that students know FAV, their effort to improve FAV seems not adequate. The inadequacy can be reflected by two aspects. Firstly, the number of strategies they use is rather limited. Each interviewee only reported one or two strategies that they felt effective. Secondly, some students may make effort to enlarge FAV, but tend to give up later. This may be because without teachers' guidance, students tend to get discouraged or forget to keep doing it.

Findings of the interview shed some light on ways to enlarge FAV. On the learning side, students not only need to know the significance of FAV, but also need to know useful strategies to tackle the problem. The interview shows that pushed-output activities, such as making sentences with the target word, may help. In addition, collecting synonyms, analysing context, taking notes of example sentences, paying extra attention to the target word may help as well. Continuous effort should also be made, rather than non-sustained efforts, as achieving significant FAV growth may need a long process. On the teaching side, teachers should realize the significance of FAV in L2 study. They should remind students to keep paying attention to FAV development. They should give students suggestions and guidance on how to tackle the stagnation problem. Moreover, teachers should adopt effective teaching strategies to assist students. The interview shows that helpful teaching strategies include negotiation, context analysis, synonym collection, and drawing students' attention to target words. It can be seen that some of the effective teaching strategies overlap with the effective learning strategies.

However, it should be noted that the effectiveness of those strategies is based on the interviewees' subjective judgment, not evidenced by empirical studies yet. Effective learning and teaching strategies not only should be guided by experience and theories, but also need to be tested by empirical studies. Therefore, it is recommended that more empirical research be conducted to verify the effectiveness of these strategies. It is believed that with quantitative support the conclusion will be more convincing and instructive to FAV learning.

Chapter 7 Documentary Analysis

7.1 Introduction

As English is a foreign language in China, formal class in-struction is a major source from which students obtain English training. Therefore, the course structure plays a significant part in L2 learning. This chapter investigates the discipline-related courses students took in the period of the 12-month longitudinal sub-study. The aim of this sub-study is to investigate whether there are factors in course structure that may affect students' free active vocabulary (FAV) development. The chapter first poses research questions, then presents research method, including data collection, data preparation and data analysis. At the end of the chapter, results are reported and discussed, and conclusions are made.

7.2 Research Questions

This part of research continues to explore the following question:

• What are the possible factors in teaching that may affect FAV development?

7.3　Research Method

7.3.1　Data Collection

As the 12-month longitudinal sub-study started in May, 2015 and ended in May, 2016, the participants of the sub-study went through three semesters during the period. Therefore, the course structure in the three semesters was collected. The course structure included all the units students took in the three semesters and the number of hours per week for each unit.

7.3.2　Data Preparation

After the course structure data were collected, the non-discipline-related units, such as Politics, were removed, as they were not related to English language study. The discipline-related units that were not related to English language study, such as Japanese as a Second Foreign Language, were excluded as well. After the treatment, only those units related to English language were left for final analysis.

7.4　Results and Discussion

The units for final analysis are presented in Table 7.1.

Table 7. 1   Discipline-related Units

Semester	Time	Units	Hours per week
Semester 1	May,2015—July, 2015	*Intensive Reading*	4
		Introduction to Linguistics	2
		British Literature and Anthology	2
		English Pedagogy	2
		Theory and Practice of Translation	2
		Phonemics	2
		Research Methods in English Teaching	2
		Selected Reading in English Essays	2
Semester 2	September, 2015—January, 2016	*Introduction to Linguistics*	2
		American Literature and Anthology	2
		Theory and Practice of Translation	2
		Selected British and American Newspaper Reading	2
		English Pedagogy	2
		English Academic Thesis Writing	2
Semester 3	February,2016— May,2016	*Undergraduate Thesis*	2

It is observed that in Semester 1 and Semester 2, the courses were concentrated on English training. According to *The Syllabus of English Courses for College English Majors* by Chinese Ministry of Education（2000）in China, the discipline-related units for English major fall into three types. The first type is of professional skills, such as units for writing, reading, listening, *etc*. The second type is of professional knowledge, such as units on linguistics, literature, *etc*. The third type is professional-oriented, such as units on English teaching, business negotiation in English, *etc*. It is observed that the courses in the three semesters cover all the three types of units. For example, *Intensive Reading* and *Theory and Practice of Translation* are units of professional skills; *Introduction to Linguistics*, *British Literature and Anthology*, and *Phonemics* belong to units of professional knowledge; *English Pedagogy* and *Research Methods in English Teaching* are professional-oriented units.

It is also observed that there are only 3 units for output training. These units include *English Academic Thesis Writing*, *Undergraduate Thesis Writing*, and *Theory and Practice of Translation*. According to the requirement of *The Syllabus of English Courses for College English Majors*, one of the major aims of *Theory and Practice of Translation* is that through the unit students will be able to translate different types of essays between L1 and L2. In the unit, a great deal of translation practice is conducted, and the translated work is discussed and evaluated by the teacher and students. *The Undergraduate Thesis Writing* is another unit for output training. The entire unit takes about six months, involving several steps. First, students will be asked to choose an academic topic that they wish to write about. The topic should be related to linguistics and applied linguistics, literature, culture, or translation. They should choose a teacher to be their supervisor according to the topic. Then students will meet their supervisor and discuss the appropriateness of the chosen topic. Usually when the topics are decided, a department meeting will be held, where the appropriateness of the topics are further examined and discussed. After that the research proposal will be made. Then the outline of the thesis will be written by students. The draft of the outline will be revised by the supervisor for at least three times, until it becomes satisfactory. Second, thesis writing of about 5,000 words is conducted. The draft of the writing is again revised by the supervisor for at least three times, until it becomes satisfactory. When the thesis is completed, the defence will be administered in school. If students pass the thesis defence, the final version of the paper, together with all the drafts of outlines and thesis writings, will be submitted to school for storage. Another unit for output training is *English Academic Thesis Writing*. It is a unit teaching students how to write an academic thesis in English. Usually in the unit the writing practice will be conducted, and the work will be checked and evaluated by the teacher. These units are considered to be output-focused, as the teaching and training of writing constitutes a major part in all the three units.

It seems that the number of units for output training is in a salient disadvantage in the course structure. There are in total 15 discipline-related units, but among them there are only 3 units for output training. Meanwhile, the participants of the longitudinal sub-study received a large amount of L2 input from classroom instruction. As the participants are senior students in their last year of university study, the input covers a variety of professional topics. This feature can be reflected from *The Syllabus of English Courses for College English Majors*. For example, according to the syllabus, the aim of *Selected British and American Newspaper Reading* is that students will be able to read British and American newspapers and magazines. The syllabus requires that the teaching material of the unit should cover a wide variety of topics, and reach a certain level of difficulty. The teaching material should include comments on current events, editorials, political comments, special news reports, *etc.*, from British and American mainstream newspapers and magazines. The topics should cover society, politics, economy, wars, environment, people, international relations, science and technology, *etc.* For another example, the syllabus stated that the aim of *British Literature and Anthology* is to foster students' capability to read, appreciate and understand the original English works, and to grasp basic knowledge and skills to have literature critiques. With regard to *Introduction to Linguistics*, the syllabus points out that its purpose is to let students know human beings' great achievements in language research, and to enhance students' understandings of languages' significant value to society, humanity, economy, science and technology, and personal cultivation. The syllabus requires that the unit should cover topics such as language and mind, structure of language, origin of language, language and brain, language transition, *etc*.

Being a regular public university, the university in this study follows the syllabus in course design and teaching material selection. As the syllabus requires that the discipline-related units for seniors should reach upper-intermediate to advanced L2 proficiency level, it is rational to postulate that the input students receive from these units contains a large amount of words beyond the first 1,000 most frequent words. In other words, students have numerous chances to encounter vocabulary that are beyond the first 1,000 most frequent words from the input of these units. However, the longitudinal sub-study in Chapter 4 shows that no significant FAV growth occurred during the 12-month period of time.

Krashen (1982) proposed Input Hypothesis in second language acquisition (SLA). The Input Hypothesis holds that we acquire language "only when we understand language that contains structure that is a little beyond where we are now" (Krashen, 1982). At the beginning the hypothesis was on general SLA. In 1989, Krashen extended it to L2 vocabulary acquisition, claiming that L2 input, such as reading and listening, would facilitate incidental vocabulary acquisition. He referenced a considerable number of empirical studies to support this view. From these studies of incidental vocabulary acquisition, Krashen concluded that "comprehensible input alone can do the entire job for vocabulary and nearly the entire job for spelling" (Krashen, 1989). It is noticed that Krashen (1989) only mentioned the effect of comprehensive input on passive vocabulary (PV) and controlled active vocabulary (CAV) since in the studies referenced by Krashen (1989) only words' recognition and spelling was tested. Therefore no FAV was examined and discussed by Krashen (1989). It seems that the effect of comprehensible input on FAV acquisition is a neglected point in relevant research.

In recent years, some studies have been conducted to investigate the effect of different types of comprehensible input on "productive vocabulary" development. However, these studies need to be referenced cautiously, as the "productive vocabulary" in these studies are measured in different ways and may reflect different types of vocabulary knowledge. For example, in Pietila and Merikivi (2014) and Laufer and Nation (1999), Controlled Productive Vocabulary Test was adopted to assess students' vocabulary size. In Hazrat and Hessamy (2013), researchers tested the target words by asking testees to fill in the blanks of given sentences. In each blank, the first letter of the target word was provided, so that the non-target words that fit the context can be avoided. Soleimani and Mahmoudabadi (2014) examined the impact of input and output tasks on "productive vocabulary", but the "productive vocabulary" was measured by asking testees to make sentences with the given target words. Therefore, all of these studies in fact measure some other aspects of "productive vocabulary" rather than FAV.

Excluding these studies, a few studies are left that investigate the impact of input on FAV acquisition. Arash (2016) examined the effects of three types of input on productive vocabulary development. The three types include non-negotiated pre-modified input, negotiation of input without output, and negotiation plus output. To test "productive vocabulary", testees were provided with images of the target words. Then they were asked questions on the images. The purpose of this activity was to invoke the testees to speak out the words. Whether the target words could be produced or not completely depended on the testee himself. Therefore, it was believed that the test in this study examined testees' FAV. Arash (2016) found all the three types of input facilitate FAV gains. Teng (2015) investigated impacts of extensive reading and extensive reading plus explicit vocabulary learning on "productive vocabulary" acquisition. In the test, the participants were asked to fill in the blanks of given sentences. It is believed that this test assessed FAV as well, as there was no hint of spelling or pronunciation of the target words in the test. Testees had to depend on themselves to retrieve and use the target words in the context. Results of the research indicated that both extensive reading and extensive reading plus explicit vocabulary learning considerably facilitated FAV development.

Both the two studies seem to prove that comprehensible input helps in FAV development. However, the documentary analysis in this sub-study seems to lead us to a different conclusion that comprehensible input is not facilitative, or at least not adequately facilitative to FAV development, as after large input for 12 months the FAV did not show significant increase. In other words, the sub-study tends to indicate that a large amount of comprehensible input fails to promote significant FAV growth. Different from FAV, the longitudinal sub-study in Chapter 4 shows that participants' passive vocabulary （PV） and controlled active vocabulary （CAV） kept growing in the 12 months. This result to some extent backs up Krashen's (1989) view, as the large amount of comprehensible input seems to facilitate the development of word recognition and spelling. Students' FAV, which was not mentioned by Krashen （1989）, seems not to have benefited from the large amount of comprehensible input.

This sub-study therefore yields results different from previous studies. A large amount of input did not result in a significant growth in FAV. Taken a closer look, it is found that the different outcomes may be attributed to participants' different L2 proficiency levels. It should be noted that the L2 proficiency of lower interme-diate, intermediate, higher/upper intermediate and advanced levels are often used arbitrarily by researchers, and it seems that there is no set standards yet for proficiency evaluation. The arbitrariness sometimes causes confusions, and makes it difficult to have comparisons across studies. Therefore, it is necessary to examine participants' background information even if their L2 proficiencies have been tagged by researchers. Teng （2015） described his participants as "lower-intermediate" L2 learners. In his study, subjects were freshmen majoring in Business English. Their ages ranged from 18 to 20 years old. The mean score of the Vocabulary Size Test designed by Nation and Beglar (2007) was 21. 36. The researcher therefore concluded that the subjects' English proficiency was lower-intermediate. Although subjects in this study did not take the same vocabulary size test as those in Teng (2015) did, it is postulated that they are of higher L2 profi-ciency level, as they are senior English-major students who have had concentrated professional English training for three to four years. That is to say, subjects in Teng （2015） may not have reached the stage where FAV threshold occurs yet, and that is possibly the reason why comprehensible input yielded positive results in Teng's (2015) study, but did not do so in this sub-study. It is therefore postulated that comprehensible input plays a positive role in FAV progress before FAV threshold occurs; when learners' L2 proficiency reaches a certain level and FAV stagnation occurs, even a large amount of comprehensible input does not help. In other words, comprehensible input may not be an effective factor to tackle FAV stagnation. Another study by Arash (2016) cannot be analysed and compared in this case, as no background information on the participants' proficiency is provided by the researcher.

It should be noted that the conclusion does not necessarily mean that input is not helpful at all to FAV acquisition. Although no significant FAV growth is detected in the 12-month longitudinal sub-study, no significant regression is detected either. The large amount of input may do some work in preventing FAV from regressing, since frequent input can remind participants of the words by providing them with chances to encounter those words repeatedly. When FAV size reaches a certain level, a large amount of input may be helpful to keep FAV at the level, but not helpful enough to invoke further growth. Other factors may be needed to achieve this goal.

It seems that the output-training units are not substantially facilitative to FAV development as well. There are three output-training units in the course structure. As the longitudinal sub-study shows, no significant FAV gains occurred during the 12-month period. It seems that the output-training units did not work efficiently either. However, it may be hasty to conclude that just like input, output does not help in FAV growth. Compared with other units, the units for output training are in a salient disadvantage, as they only account for 20% of the whole course structure. Therefore, the insignificant role of output-training units in FAV development may be attributed to the inadequacy of them. As is shown in Chapter 6, pushed output was found by interviewees to be helpful to FAV development. Therefore, the limited number of output-training units may imply that more of them should be added to the current course structure.

It is only postulated that inadequate pushed output is one of the possible factors for FAV stagnation. The postulation needs to be further testified by empirical studies. If it is true, then the appropriate amount of pushed output needs to be investigated by empirical studies as well.

Incidental acquisition seems not to be an efficient factor in FAV development. The interviews in Chapter 6 show that many teachers do not provide guidance in FAV development, and almost no teaching strategies have been adopted to specifically facilitate it. It can be concluded then that there is little intentional FAV teaching in these units. If any FAV is obtained in classes, it is most likely acquired incidentally. However, the amount of FAV acquired incidentally may be rather limited, as no significant growth of FAV is detected in the 12-month longitudinal sub-study.

It seems that few previous studies have investigated incidental FAV acquisition. The only one that can be found was conducted by Yue, Dai, and Zhang (2012). Yue et al. (2012) compared effects of semantic processing and form processing on incidental vocabulary acquisition. In the study, the task of semantic processing was to translate the target words into L1, and then to match them with their L2 paraphrases; the task of form processing was to count the numbers of letters in the target words, and then to find letter combinations that match the given pronunciations. The study found that both the two types of processing significantly facilitated participants' incidental acquisition of PV and CAV. However, the study detected no considerable progress in FAV, which is a higher level of knowledge than PV and CAV. Both the study by Yue et al. (2012) and this sub-study indicate that the amount of FAV acquired incidentally is rather limited. And as is found in Chapter 6, attention to target words plays a positive role in FAV learning. Based on these findings, it seems rational to postulate that intentional learning may be more effective than incidental acquisition in FAV development. Therefore, more intentional learning should be conducted for FAV development. In other words, FAV should be developed more consciously and deliberately, rather than unconsciously and incidentally.

7.5 Conclusion

This sub-study answered the proposed questions. There are some factors in the course design that may help promote FAV progress. The first factor is pushed output. To invoke constant increase of FAV, more output-training units may need to be integrated into the current course structure, or more activities that promote output may need to be integrated in teaching and learning. The second factor is intentional teaching and learning. Intentional teaching and learning seem to be necessary to promote FAV growth.

There are some factors that are detected not to be as powerful as expected. The first one is comprehensible input. With a large amount of input, no significant growth of FAV was detected. The second factor is incidental acquisition. The amount of FAV acquired incidentally seems to be limited. Therefore, comprehensible input and incidental acquisition may not be suitable tools to tackle FAV threshold phenomenon.

Chapter 8 Discussions, Findings, Implications and Recommendations

8.1 Introduction

In light of the previous chapters, this chapter examines whether the five research objectives have been addressed and achieved through the research. Based on the analysis of results, discussions were made, and five major findings pertaining to the research objectives were uncovered. Discussions are also made in this chapter to examine whether the research questions have been answered satisfactorily. It was found that some findings are supported by previous literature; some findings, by contrast, are different or even opposite to arguments in past studies. This chapter first presents findings pertaining to the research objectives and research questions. It then discusses the theoretical and pedagogical implications of the findings. Lastly, recommendations for free active vocabulary (FAV) development are provided.

8.2 Discussion

This section provides a general discussion on the results of this research. There are in total four sub-studies in this research, namely, the 12-month longitudinal sub-study, the word association sub-study, the interview and the documentary analysis. The four sub-studies work together to provide researchers with a more comprehensive view on L2 FAV development, in particular, the threshold phenomenon in FAV development. They also provide a more comprehensive view on the reasons for the occurrence of the threshold phenomenon, and the ways to tackle the problem.

The 12-month longitudinal sub-study shows that the Lex30 score did not change significantly over the 12-month period of time. According to the scoring standard of Lex30 test, only words beyond the first 1,000 frequent content words, high-frequency function words, proper nouns, and numbers would obtain points. Therefore, the result of Lex30 test indicates that, in the 12 months of the longitudinal sub-study students' FAV beyond these categories failed to grow. The test of writing in the longitudinal sub-study yields similar results. The Lexical Frequency Profile (LFP) by RANGE shows that in writing, words (no matter in terms of word types or word families) that are beyond the first 1,000 frequency level failed to increase significantly. Therefore, both the Lex30 test and the writing test indicate that FAV experienced stagnation in the 12-month longitudinal sub-study.

With regards to the relationship of FAV with passive vocabulary and controlled active vocabulary, the 12-month longitudinal sub-study shows that the participants' passive vocabulary and controlled active vocabulary grew significantly. In other words, the participants could recognize and spell more words in the 12-month L2 learning. The sub-study also shows that in both the first month and the twelfth month, the PV and CAV are significantly correlated with each other. By contrast, FAV is not closely related with PV and CAV, as it is not significantly correlated with PV in the first and the twelfth month, and it is not significantly correlated with CAV in the twelfth month. It is only partially correlated with CAV in the first month. The results in this sub-study are consistent with the cross-sectional study by Laufer (1998). In Laufer (1998), there were two groups of participants. One group of participants were 26 16-year-old 10th graders in Israel who had been learning English as a foreign language for six years; the other group of participants were 22 17-year old students in the 11th grade in Israel, who had been studying English as a foreign language for seven years. Just like the participants in this sub-study, Laufer's (1998) participants primarily obtained English training from formal English classes. Laufer (1998) found that the two groups' FAV beyond the first 2,000 frequency level were not significantly different; by contrast, the PV and CAV of the 11th graders were significantly higher than those of the 10th graders. Both the study by Laufer (1998) and this sub-study tend to indicate that L2 learners' FAV tend to stagnate in its development, whereas PV and CAV tend to develop in a more linear way. In other words, when learners' English reaches intermediate, upper-intermediate and advanced proficiency levels, their capability to recognize and spell words does not help promote FAV growth significantly. The results of Laufer's (1998) study indicate that FAV development may involve a more complicated process, and the development of PA and CAV may not be adequate to promote FAV growth.

Then the associations of a group of frequently produced words (FPW) and a group of seldom produced words (SPW) were compared. The comparison shows that there are more semantic nodes in FPW than in SPW; the semantic nodes constitute the majority of links in the lexical network of FPW, but this is not the case in SPW.In terms of the non-semantic nodes,the condition is different: the SPW contains significantly more non-semantic nodes than the FPW. Also, within the SPW, both the semantic nodes and non-semantic nodes account for about 50% in the lexical network. Within the semantic connections, it is found that the number of paradigmatic, syntagmatic, and encyclopaedia nodes are different. There are significantly more paradigmatic and syntagmatic connections in FPW than in SPW. In addition, syntagmatic connections account for a bigger proportion in FPW than in SPW,as it is 17.01% of semantic connections in FPW,but 9.36% in SPW. The encyclopedia nodes in FPW account for 9.13% in FPW,but its proportion in SPW is bigger,accounting for 18.71%. The paradigmatic connections are different as well.In FPW,there are more synonyms and antonyms then in SPW.By contrast,there are more syntactic nodes in FPW than in SPW. In terms of non-semantic nodes, the distribution in SPW and FPW is different as well. FPW has significantly less phonological-formal nodes and "no response" nodes than SPW had.The results of the word association sub-study may indicate that the organization of the lexical network plays an important role in FAV development. The lexical network of FPW seems to be more semantised than SPW. Being more semantic may mean that the words can be accessed and retrieved more easily when the words are needed in expressions. In addition, the structure of the semantic connection in FPW seems to be more "appropriate" than that is in SPW,as semantic nodes that have shorter semantic distance to the target word tend to outnumber other semantic nodes.

The different features of the lexical network of FPW and SPW can shed some light on network construction to help promote FAV development. It seems that from SPW to FPW, the lexical network tend to get more and more semantic. As semantic nodes provide semantic paths in word access and retrieval, the tendency may be helpful for words' access and retrieval when language users need it in context. In addition, the semantic connection in the lexical network tends to get stronger and tighter, as nodes which are more closely related to the target word grew significantly. The two tendencies are consistent with the Spreading-activation Model proposed by Collins and Loftus (1975), which assumes that lexical network develops in the direction that words are more easily accessed, activated, and retrieved. Based on the results of the word association sub-study in this research, it is assumed that some words may not get adequate semantic construction in the lexical network, and within the semantic connection the network is not adequately constructed to be stronger and tighter. Therefore, these words fail to become FPW.

In order to detect other possible reasons in addition to the cognitive reasons for the threshold phenomenon, interviews and documentary analysis were conducted. Interviews were also conducted to investigate effective learning and teaching strategies for FAV growth. The interview questions include students' consciousness of FAV in L2 study, learning strategies the learners adopted to enlarge FAV, teachers' guidance on FAV in L2 teaching, and teaching strategies that teachers adopted to help promote students' FAV development. When being asked whether they ever met difficulties in searching for suitable words to express the meaning they wanted to express, all the interviewees answered "Yes". They reported that they often had difficulties in searching for the most accurate word to use. In many cases they knew the word that they could retrieve was not the most accurate one, but they had to use the word,as they could not think of the most needed one.Thus some important information or subtle feelings may be lost in the context. The retrieval difficulty may find explanations from the word association sub-study. It was found in the word association sub-study that SPW has less semantic nodes then FPW,but more non-semantic nodes than FPW. Therefore,when the target word is needed in context,the SPW is more difficult to be accessed and retrieved. As the difficulties in FAV usage are widely felt by the students,most of them reported that they knew the existence of this type of vocabulary knowledge, although they may not know the terminology of FAV.

The effective learning strategies to assist FAV development were also asked. The strategies reported by interviewees include making sentences,referring to a dictionary,taking notes on the word's meanings,analyzing contexts,putting down example sentences,collecting synonyms,memorizing authentic context for the target word. The effectiveness of these learning strategies are also consistent with the findings of the word association sub-study. It was found that all the strategies can help the semantic network construction of the target word in mental lexicon. Some of them also help the semantic network become stronger and shorter,such as the strategy of synonym collection. Constructing the lexical network in this direction may help words develop into FAV.

A group of questions were asked to investigate teachers' guidance on FAV learning and the effective teaching strategies that teachers adopted for FAV development. It seems that the guidance that learners could get from the teachers is rather limited, as in the four years' study,only one teacher told them that FAV is important. The student participants also reflected that very few suggestions were provided by their teachers; and almost no teaching strategies were adopted to promote FAV growth. This may be due to that fact that teachers are not conscious of the importance of FAV; or even if they are conscious of it, they lack adequate strategies to help learners with FAV development. However, it may not be appropriate to solely blame teachers for this deficiency. As relevant research is far from adequate, teachers may not have enough resources to obtain guidance and information on this issue.

Some teaching strategies that are not adopted for FAV development but are thought to be effective are reported by interviewees. These strategies are providing synonyms of the target word to learners and negotiating the meanings of the target word with learners. The effectiveness of negotiation is supported by the empirical studies of Arash (2016) and Teng (2015). It is noticed that both synonym provision and negotiation can help construct and strengthen the semantic network of the target word, and thus they help make the word easier to be accessed, activated, and retrieved. The documentary analysis was adopted to investigate the possible reasons for FAV stagnation as well. By studying the course structure, it is found that units for output training were rather limited, as there were only 3 units for output training. These units are *English Academic Thesis Writing*, *Undergraduate Thesis Writing*, and *Theory and Practice of Translation*. Output practice is a significant part in these units. However, it is found that compared with other units, the output-training units are in a salient disadvantage. The output-training units only account for 20% in the course structure. According to the Output Hypothesis by Swain (1985, 1995), language production elicits language learning. Laufer (1998) and Henriksen (1999) pointed out that output can promote FAV acquisition; the word may remain passive and never be activated if learners are not pushed to produce the word. The empirical studies by Arash (2016) and Fuente and José (2002) show that pushed output plays a positive role in FAV development. This conclusion is consistent with what the interviewees reflected in the interview. In the interview the interviewees reported that they feel the output practice of the target word helps FAV development. From these results it is speculated that the inadequacy of output-focused units is one of the factors for FAV stagnation, and more such units should be integrated into the current course structure.

8.3   Major Findings

8.3.1   Findings to Research Objective One: the Developmental Process of FAV

The first research objective of this study is to investigate the developmental process of FAV when L2 learners reach upper-intermediate to advanced L2 proficiency level. This objective was addressed by the 12-month longitudinal sub-study. The following questions in relation to the research objective were asked:

• What is the development pattern of FAV when L2 learners reach upper-intermediate to advanced proficiency level?

• If the threshold phenomenon occurs in the FAV development, what are the features of the threshold phenomenon?

The 12-month longitudinal sub-study was conducted to answer the two research questions. It tracked the development of FAV during a 12-month period, and found that the FAV did not grow in a linear way; instead, it stagnated during that period. It thus empirically supports the Active Vocabulary Threshold Hypothesis raised by Laufer (1991).

The research has answered the second research question as well. Several features were demonstrated in the FAV developmental process. First, the stagnation of FAV seems to be long-lasting, since the sub-study lasted for 12 months and saw no growth in FAV. Second, the stagnation of FAV seems to be "stubborn", as it not only lasted for a long time, but also was not correlated with the growth of other types of vocabulary. Third, the FAV threshold tends to occur widely, as in the sub-study it emerged at most word frequency levels. The sub-study shows that words (no matter in terms of types or families) of the first 1,000 frequency level decreased significantly, whereas words of the second 1,000 frequency level, academic words and beyond did not increase significantly. This tendency is problematic, as according to Schmitt *et al*. (2001), the most frequent 2,000 words are usually for basic everyday communication, and words beyond 2,000 are more for authentic texts. Learners' LFP in this sub-study indicates that they tended to use much more basic words than NSs do. As pointed out by Cobb (2003), "over-use of basic vocabulary indicates, of course, under-use of other richer, more precise, and more varied vocabulary". This may account for the sense of vagueness felt by readers who have English as their native language in advanced L2 learners' writings (Cobb, 2003). Not only the NSs, the interview in this research shows that L2 learners themselves also feel their writing sometimes is "as plain as water". Therefore, even upper-intermediate to advanced L2 learners have a long way to go in FAV development.

In sum, the results of the longitudinal sub-study provide a comprehensive picture on FAV's developmental process in a 12-month period. During this period, words (no matter in terms of types or families) at most frequency levels experienced stagnation. Several features were captured from the sub-study as well, which are explained in Chapter 4.

8. 3. 2   Findings to Research Objective Two: the Relationship between FAV and Other Types of Vocabulary Knowledge

The second research objective is to investigate the relationship between FAV and passive vocabulary (PV), and the relationship between FAV and controlled active vocabulary (CAV). There are four research questions for the research objective:

• What is the developmental process of PV when L2 learners reach upper-intermediate to advanced L2 proficiency level?

• What is the relationship between FAV and PV?

• What is the developmental process of CAV when L2 learners reach upper-intermediate to advanced L2 proficiency level?

• What is the relationship between FAV and CAV?

The longitudinal sub-study has answered these research questions. It not only tracked the developmental process of FAV, but also tracked the developmental process of PV and CAV in the 12-month period of time. It turns out that during the period, both testees' PV and CAV grew significantly. With regard to PV, except words in the 2,000 level and in the 10,000 level, words of all other frequency levels increased significantly. These included the 3,000 level, the 5,000 level, and the academic words. The reason why words from the 2,000 frequency level did not have significant growth may be that the high-frequency words had already been grasped well by the upper-intermediate to advanced ESL learners, and there was almost no more space for further increase. The lack of growth for words in the 10,000 frequency level may be due to the fact that it is a very low frequency level. In other words, the chances to use words in the 10,000 frequency level are slim. Therefore, learners may not have many chances to encounter these words in their study. For this reason, scores in the 10,000 level did not change significantly and maintained low. With regard to CAV, words at all frequency levels developed significantly. This indicates that in the 12-month period, the testees not only could recognise more words, but also could spell more words. By contrast, FAV did not grow significantly in that period. It indicates that in upper-intermediate to advanced proficiency stage, FAV does not grow with the growth of PV and CAV. The result is different from Laufer's (1998) speculation that a larger PV size may indicate a larger FAV size. This sub-study shows that this may not be the case, at least when L2 learners reach upper-intermediate to advanced proficiency level. The gap between PV and FAV, and between CAV and FAV in fact becomes larger.

8.3.3 Findings to Research Objective Three: the Lexical Network Construction in FAV Development

The third research objective is to explore how lexical network is constructed in the process of FAV development. As people's mental lexicon is like a "dark box", the procedure of network building cannot be observed directly. Therefore, the lexical organizations of two types of vocabulary are compared. One is vocabulary that is seldom produced, or highly unlikely to be produced by learners in writing and speaking; the other is vocabulary that is frequently produced, or is highly likely to be produced by learners in writing and speaking. It is assumed that if words develop from SPW to FPW, then the difference between the two in lexical organisation may shed some light on the network construction procedure in the process. Based on the research objective, one research question is proposed:

• What are the differences (if any) of the mental lexicon organisation between frequently produced words and seldom produced words?

The third research objective is addressed via word association tests. The word association tests found that there were a number of differences in the lexical organisation of the two types of vocabulary.

First, the semantic and non-semantic distribution in the network is different. FPW turned out to have significantly more semantic nodes than SPW, and have significantly fewer non-semantic nodes than SPW. In terms of the proportion of semantic and non-semantic nodes in the network, semantic nodes of FPW were dominant in the network, while non-semantic nodes only constitute a small part in the network. By contrast, in SPW, although semantic nodes outnumber non-semantic nodes, the advantage of semantic nodes is not as evident.

Second, the semantic distribution is different. The number of paradigmatic and syntagmatic nodes of FPW is significantly higher than that of SPW, but there is no significant difference in the number of encyclopaedia nodes between the two types of words. The ranking of semantic nodes in FPW is paradigmatic＞syntagmatic＞encyclopaedia; the ranking of semantic nodes in SPW is paradigmatic＞encyclopaedia＞syntagmatic.

Thirdly, the non-semantic distribution is different. FPW have less phonological-formal and "no response" nodes than SPW do. The percentages of phonological-formal nodes in non-semantic connections are different as well. The percentage tends to be higher in SPW than in FPW. Both the number and percentage of "no response" nodes tend to decrease in the process of SPW-to-FPW development.

Based on the results of this sub-study, the lexical construction procedure in FAV development can be portrayed. When a word can be recognized easily, but are highly unlikely to be produced, almost half of its nodes in its lexical network are non-semantic. These non-semantic nodes become a hindrance when L2 users try to access and retrieve the word from mental lexicon. The other half of the nodes are semantic nodes. Most of the semantic nodes at this stage are paradigmatic and encyclopaedic nodes. These paradigmatic and syntagmatic nodes can offer L2 users information on the target word in various perspectives, especially in synonyms, antonyms, social and cultural knowledge, grammar, and collocations. Therefore, the word not only can be correctly recognized, but also can be well comprehended by the language user. At this stage, there are not as many syntagmatic nodes as paradigmatic and encyclopaedic nodes; therefore, the lexical network does not provide the learners with adequate paths to retrieve the target words' syntactic or compound/chunk information for production in context. With further development, semantic nodes tend to grow, and non-semantic nodes tend to shrink, until semantic nodes obtain salient advantage over non-semantic nodes and become dominant in the lexical network. At this stage, not only the size of semantic connections gets enlarged, the inner structure of semantic connections changes as well. Paradigmatic and syntagmatic nodes get significant growth, but encyclopaedia nodes do not. The result of this change is that the syntagmatic nodes surpass the encyclopaedia nodes and become the second biggest type of response. In paradigmatic connections, synonyms get prior development and become the majority in paradigmatic connections. Therefore, when target words are needed in oral or written expression, a large number of paradigmatic nodes (especially synonyms) and adequate encyclopaedia nodes would offer numerous channels for target words to be reached and retrieved. Meanwhile, a great deal of syntagmatic (especially syntactic) nodes are accessed and activated as well, making the target word ready to be produced in oral and written contexts.

In sum, the word association sub-study captured three possible features in FAV development. The first feature is that the lexical network tends to get semantised; the second feature is that different types of nodes tend to change at different speeds and in different directions (increasing or decreasing); the third feature is that the connections of the lexical network tend to get stronger and tighter. It is postulated that in L2 learning some words may not obtain enough network construction towards these directions; therefore, they fail to further develop into FAV.

8.3.4　Findings to Research Objective Four: Possible Factors Related to FAV Stagnation

The fourth research objective is to find possible factors in teaching and learning that may affect FAV development. Based on the research objective, two questions are designed:

- What are the possible factors in teaching that may affect FAV development?

- What are the possible factors in learning that may affect FAV development?

Findings from the interview and documentary analysis can help answer the two questions. On the teaching side, the first factor that may be related to FAV stagnation is that teachers seem not to attach great importance to FAV in teaching. Most teachers of the interviewees almost never mentioned FAV in class, let alone provided students with guidance on how to improve it. Therefore, realising the significance of FAV, students had to "grope" for effective learning methods by themselves. In most cases, the effectiveness of their trials depended on luck. Some strategies may turn out to be helpful, some may not; some may be helpful, but were only helpful to a specific person, not having a universal value.

The second factor in teaching is that little effort is made to help promote students' FAV development. The interview reveals that few teaching strategies were adopted to facilitate students' FAV development. However, it may be hasty to completely put the blame on teachers, as research in this field is rather limited, and it cannot give teachers sufficient guidance. Although researchers have detected the FAV threshold phenomenon in L2 study, such as Laufer (1991), Gu and Li (2013), Huang (2012), Lu (2008) and Y. Zhao (2011), there is a limited number of studies, especially empirical ones, to investigate how to tackle this problem. Even if teachers feel the great necessity to help students enlarge FAV, they can find little reference for valuable suggestions. Therefore, relevant research is in dire need.

The third factor in teaching is detected from documentary analysis. It was observed that in the 12 months of longitudinal sub-study, only a few units were on L2 output. These units included *English Academic Thesis Writing*, *Undergraduate Thesis Writing*, and *Theory and Practice of Translation*. Compared with other units in the course structure, it seems that the number of units on output was in a salient disadvantage. Therefore, the limited number of units on output may be a factor for FAV stagnation, as in this condition L2 learners cannot get enough systematic output training in class.

Meanwhile, the course structure shows that the English-major students in the longitudinal sub-study received condensed English training, and the units covered a wide range of English-related topics, such as *British and American Literature*, *Linguistics*, *Intensive Reading*, etc. Therefore, it is postulated that students received a large amount of L2 input in that period of time. However, the FAV stagnation in the period indicates that the large amount of comprehensible input failed to promote significant FAV growth. In other words, when L2 learners have reached upper-intermediate to advanced L2 proficiency level, large comprehensible input may not be an effective way to tackle FAV stagnation.

It should be noted that the conclusion does not necessarily mean that input is not helpful at all in FAV acquisition. Although no significant FAV growth was detected in the 12-month longitudinal sub-study, no significant regression was detected, either. The large amount of input may do some work in preventing FAV from regressing, since frequent input can have students encounter the words repeatedly, and thereby it has a reminding effect. When FAV size reaches a certain level, a large amount of input may help FAV maintain at the level, but may not help it have further growth.

On the learning side, several possible factors for FAV stagnation are detected as well. The first factor is insufficient effort. The interview shows that although students knew FAV, their effort to improve FAV seemed to be insufficient. The inadequacy can be reflected by two aspects. First, the number of strategies they used is rather limited. Each interviewee only reported one or two strategies. Second, although some students endeavoured to improve FAV, they gave up later. This may be because without teachers' guidance, students tended to get discouraged or forget to keep doing it.

Insufficient intentional teaching and learning of FAV may be another factor for the stagnation. The interview shows that most teachers never reminded students to pay attention to FAV development, and almost no teaching strategies had been adopted to specifically facilitate this. Therefore, there is little intentional FAV teaching in class. On the students' side, learning strategies adopted for FAV learning are quite limited as well. Meanwhile, in the interview the students reflected that attention to target words plays a positive role in FAV learning. Based on these findings, it seems rational to postulate that more intentional teaching and learning is needed to promote FAV growth.

8.3.5 Findings to Research Objective Five: Effective Strategies to Tackle the Threshold Phenomenon

The fifth research objective is to find effective ways to tackle the FAV threshold phenomenon. The research question is:

• What are the effective strategies (if any) to tackle FAV threshold phenomenon?

Some strategies were detected from the interview. On the learning side, the interview shows that making sentences with the target word, taking notes on the target word, putting down example sentences, and collecting synonyms of the word are effective strategies. On the teaching side, providing synonyms of the word to students, negotiating word meanings, analysing contexts, and encouraging students to make sentences with the target word could be helpful. Arousing students' attention to the target word is helpful as well, as it may elicit students to have intentional learning on the word. It is noticed that some teaching and learning strategies overlap with each other.

8. 4   Implications

8. 4. 1   Theoretical Implications

The 12-month longitudinal sub-study in this research proved the existence of FAV threshold phenomenon. It also supports Laufer's (1991) view that FAV does not develop with PV and CAV. Moreover, the research has a further development on Laufer's (1991) FAV threshold hypothesis, as several features are captured in the phenomenon. First, when L2 learners are at upper-intermediate to advanced proficiency level, their FAV tends to stagnate at various word frequency levels. Except for words from the first 1,000 frequency level, words from the second 1,000 frequency level, academic words, and beyond all stagnate. Second, when L2 learners reach upper-intermediate to advanced proficiency level, FAV threshold tends to be long-lasting, since in the 12 months of sub-study FAV did not grow. Third, FAV threshold seems to be "stubborn". This feature can be demonstrated by the fact that through a concentrated L2 learning for 12 months, learners' PV and CAV got significant growth, but FAV did not.

In addition to the development on FAV threshold hypothesis, the research helps researchers and ESL teachers obtain a better understanding of L2 mental lexicon. As far as it is known, little research has attempted to explore learners' mental lexicon change in the process when words with high familiarity develop into FAV. Additionally, little is known on how lexical organisation interacts with memory search and retrieval in word production. It is indicated by this research that FAV development may involve readjustment in lexical organisation. There are three tendencies in the readjustment. The first tendency is that the lexical organisation tends to get semantised; the second tendency is that different types of nodes tend to change at different speeds and in different directions (increasing or decreasing); the third tendency is that the lexical network connections tend to get stronger and tighter. The three tendencies show that in FAV development, the lexical network tends to develop in a way that the target word becomes more easily accessed, activated, and retrieved. This research therefore to some extent fills in the gap in literature.

8.4.2 Pedagogical Implications

Some pedagogical implications can be made from the research.

First, teachers should be conscious of the existence of FAV threshold phenomenon. This may be the first step to tackle the stagnation problem. To raise the awareness, more research should be conducted in this area, so that teachers can get more chances to read studies on the phenomenon. Meanwhile, the issue should be integrated into textbooks and training courses for ESL teachers. More discussions on the topic are suggested to be conducted on the Internet, and more materials on L2 FAV learning should be posted on the Internet, so that teachers can get more access to know the issue.

Second, teachers not only need to know the phenomenon, but also need to have a better understanding of it. For example, teachers should know that FAV stagnation tends to occur widely at various word frequency levels. Teachers should also be awared that when L2 learners reach upper-intermediate to advanced proficiency level, a larger PV and CAV size may not substantially help the growth of FAV. In other words, when learners reach upper-intermediate to advanced proficiency level, promoting FAV growth by strengthening PV and CAV may not be an effective effort. Teachers should inform students of the phenomenon as well, including its features. Suggestions and guidance should be provided. For example, teachers are suggested to provide learners with effective learning strategies, such as collecting synonyms, making sentences with the target word, taking notes on the target word's meanings, discussing word meanings with others, and paying more attention to the target word. The software RANGE can be introduced to students, so that students can monitor their FAV in writing by using it. Test tools of Passive Vocabulary Levels Test, Controlled Active Vocabulary Test, and Lex30 test are suggested to be introduced to students as well, so that they can monitor their development of receptive vocabulary, controlled active vocabulary and free active vocabulary by doing these tests. On the learning side, the implication is similar. Students should be aware of the FAV threshold phenomenon, and have a better understanding of it.

Third, the study reveals that some strategies may be helpful to tackle the problem. As is discussed in Section 8.2.5, strategies such as making sentences with the target word, negotiating word meanings, collecting synonyms of the target word, and taking notes on the word's meanings may facilitate FAV development. In addition, persistent efforts should also be made, as FAV growth appears to be a long, slow process. With regard to the course design, more units training learners' L2 output should be integrated into the courses. Meanwhile, more output-oriented activities should be conducted in classes.

The principles behind the effective strategies are suggested to be provided to students as well, so that they can have a better understanding of why these strategies work. These principles include: first, when words have been grasped with high familiarity, strategies should be adopted to facilitate the semantisation in mental lexicon construction; second, the network construction of synonym and syntactic nodes should be paid specific attention to. And it is encouraging to see that based on this research, some new findings have been made (e.g. Yue & Fan, 2019; Yue & Wang, 2019).

8.5　Recommendations

Section 8.3.2 presents pedagogical implications obtained from the research. However, as reflected in the interview, these strategies seem to be far from enough. More teaching and learning tactics need to be adopted to promote FAV growth. Therefore, based on the principles concluded from this research, some tactics are recommended in this section.

8.5.1　Tactics to Strengthen Network Building

The first principle implied by the research is that teachers and learners should pay sufficient attention to network building in mental lexicon. When learners can recognise a target word with high familiarity, two directions should be followed in mental lexicon network building. The first one is semantisation. More semantic nodes should be integrated in the target word's network. To achieve this goal, it is recommended that traditional presentation style of the new words in textbooks be changed. Usually new words are listed in an alphabetic order in textbooks. In the list, the words' pronunciations, lexical classes, and word meanings are provided as well. This presentation pattern offers little help in semantic network building, as it represents words in an isolated way. In order to overcome this weakness, it is suggested that new words are not presented individually. Instead, words should be presented in clusters, with other words that are semantically related to them. For example, in a lesson the new words for students to learn are "rice" "cook" "country", and "remote". Traditionally, the words would be listed in an alphabetic order as "cook" "country" "remote", and "rice". Student will have to encounter these words in a way that they are isolated with each other. However, if the words are clustered semantically, they will be presented in two groups. One is "cook" and "rice", and the other is "remote" and "country". This presentation will be more helpful in students' semantic network building of the words. In addition, not only word meanings should be provided in the presentation, various example sentences should be provided as well. For example, when the new word "cook" is presented, various examples of the word such as "cook the meal" "cooking class" "She likes cooking." can be provided. Word chunks or collocations, if they appear in the text, are also suggested to be given. For example, if "give" is a new word, and "given away" is used in the text, the collocation of "give away" and its example sentences should be presented in the vocabulary list as well. Moreover, target words should be designed to appear repeatedly in texts, as repetition is likely to be facilitative in FAV learning. Meanwhile, teachers should help students form good learning habits. When looking up a new word in textbooks or dictionaries, students should not only seek word meanings, but also check the word's semantic properties, such as its contexts, collocations, and synonyms. These tactics may facilitate the semantic network building.

Another suggestion for semantic network building is negotiation. As reflected in the interview, word negotiations by teachers are facilitative to FAV learning. Negotiations by students may be helpful as well, as the empirical study by Arash (2016) reveals that L2 learners can benefit from negotiations between themselves, or with teachers. Through word negotiations, such as clarification, confirmation or repetition of word meanings, more semantic nodes that are closely connected with the word will be integrated into the network. Therefore, in addition to word negotiations by teachers, students should be encouraged to have negotiations by themselves as well. Teachers can provide students with opportunities to conduct word negotiations on the target words. An activity, for example, is that students collaborate in groups to write a composition on a given topic. In the process, group members work together to collect proper words for the writing. Whether the selected words are appropriate or not will be discussed. Dictionaries and the Internet are encouraged to be used in the process. In the end, the teacher will join their discussion and help them with word choice.

The second direction in network building is that paradigmatic and syntagmatic nodes should be strengthened. Among these nodes the synonym and syntactic nodes should be strengthened in particular. Several activities are recommended in building synonym nodes. The first one is paraphrase. In paraphrase, students are pushed to collect words of similar meanings to explain the target words. Rewriting and retelling are helpful as well. In rewriting and retelling, students are asked to use other words to express the same meaning. Brainstorming can also be used. In brainstorming, students are asked to work together and collect synonyms of a target word as many as possible.

With regard to building syntactic nodes, several tasks are recommended. After words can be recognized with high familiarity, adequate grammar input should be provided by the teacher. Grammatical knowledge should be provided, and example sentences that can demonstrate the grammatical features of the target word should be given as well. Then various types of grammatical practice are encouraged to be carried out. For example, in the "matching" exercise, students would be asked to connect the target word with its correct usage. In "true or false", students would be asked to judge whether the word is used correctly or not in a sentence. In "filling in the blanks", students would be asked to use the target word with a correct syntactic form. In addition to input, output of grammar should be encouraged as well. This study recommends that students be asked to create sentences with the target words. If syntactic mistakes occur in the sentence, feedback should be offered in time, and mistakes should be corrected. With these measures, syntactic nodes may obtain more chances to be built in lexical network, and those syntactic nodes that have already existed may get strengthened and become closer to the target word in the network.

8.5.2　Tactics to Strengthen Intentional FAV Learning

The second principle implied by the research is that intentional learning may work more efficiently than incidental learning in FAV development. Therefore, more intentional learning should be integrated. It is recommended that more pushed output activities be conducted, as in pushed output, students are "forced" to produce the target words intentionally. In addition to sentence-making, gap-filling is another pushed-output activity. In the gap-filling exercise, proper context is provided to students, and they are required to fill in the gap with suitable words. After the exercise is completed, feedback and explanations from the teacher should be given. This tactic is supported by the findings of Arash (2016) that if words are pushed to be produced and then feedback is given from the teacher, students' ability to produce the words would progress to a great extent. It is believed that pushed-output activities not only help students set up paradigmatic and syntagmatic connections in mental lexicon, but also make students more confident to use the target word. With confidence students will not avoid using those words in writing and speaking.

Another recommendation is that a unit on FAV development be designed and integrated into the current course structure. With further and deeper research, the development pattern of FAV and the threshold phenomenon will be better understood by ESL researchers and educators. This will provide foundation to design a unit for FAV development. The unit will provide students with a systematic training of FAV. Multiple strategies will be adopted in class; words from the second 1,000 frequency level, academic words and beyond will be the target words to be trained, as words from these frequency levels tend to stagnate. As FAV development seems to be a slow, time-consuming process, the ideal condition would be that the unit be provided in every academic year as an optional unit for ESL learners with a good command of English to take.

The last suggestion in intentional FAV learning is that teachers adopt the tool RANGE to check students' LFP in writing. By comparing students' LFP with that of native speakers, students' word production capability in each word frequency level can be estimated, and the improvement will be better directed. Students should be taught to use RANGE by themselves as well, so that they can have self-management in FAV development. By applying the software, students can monitor their LFP in writing by themselves. In this way, student will be more conscious about their weaknesses in word production, and they will be more targeted in FAV learning. For example, if RANGE shows that someone's academic words in an argumentative writing is very low, then the student can work more on the academic words and try to elevate the percentage of that part of words in his writing.

8. 6   Conclusion

This chapter has provided an overall reflection of the findings in relation to the research objectives and questions in this study. Based on the findings, the research objectives have been achieved, and questions have been answered. The chapter then discusses the theoretical and pedagogical implications of the research, which is followed by recommendations on strategies that may help to tackle FAV threshold phenomenon.

Chapter 9　Conclusion

9.1　Introduction

This chapter is a conclusion of the research. It gives an overview of the research, including a reflection on the research journey, a summary of the major findings, and a discussion on the significance of the research. Then it looks into the possible directions for future research.

9.2　The Research Journey

As stated in the Introduction Chapter, the initial inspiration of the study was derived from the student researcher's own teaching experience. In her eight-year ESL teaching career, the researcher found that her English-major students, including those senior students who had been studying English as a second language for over ten years, were confined to the most common, unnuanced words in writing. The overuse of the most common, unnuanced words always made students' writing vague, and caused difficulties in expressing different moods and connotations. This problem triggered her interest in having a deeper investigation in L2 free active vocabulary (FAV) acquisition. Then the student investigator did literature reading on the topic, which confirmed that the problem she encountered has also been experienced by others. It seems that there is a big gap between native speakers (NSs) and ESL learners in the FAV size. The literature reading further sparked her interest to explore this issue, and finally the formal research was conducted.

The research aimed to have a deeper understanding of FAV acquisition and to find possible ways to tackle the FAV threshold phenomenon if it occurred. It had five objectives. The first objective was to track the developmental process of FAV. The second objective was to investigate the relationship between FAV and passive vocabulary (PV), and the relationship between FAV and controlled active vocabulary (CAV). The third objective was to explore how lexical network was constructed in the process of FAV development. The fourth objective was to find possible factors in teaching and learning that may affect FAV development. The fifth objective was to find effective ways to tackle the FAV threshold phenomenon, if it did occur in the research.

To achieve the research objectives, several sub-studies were carried out. First, a 12-month longitudinal sub-study was conducted. In the first month, the participants were asked to complete a series of tests, including the Passive Vocabulary Levels Test, the Controlled Active Vocabulary Levels Test, and the Lex30 test for free active vocabulary. A composition of no less than 200 words was collected as well, to measure the testees' free active vocabulary in contexts. In the 12th month, the tests and composition were conducted again. Then results in the first month and the 12th month were compared. The purpose of the sub-study was to examine learners' FAV development pattern in the 12-month period of time. Another purpose of the sub-study was to investigate the relationship between

FAV and PV, and the relationship between FAV and CAV.

During the same period as the longitudinal study, the second sub-study was conducted as well. In this second sub-study two types of tests were conducted, one was Vocabulary Knowledge Scale test, and the other was word association test. The Vocabulary Knowledge Scale test was in a Likert-scale form, and it was adopted to measure testees' familiarity with the target words. The word association tests were adopted to examine the lexical organisation of the target words. There were two types of words, one was words that were highly likely to be produced by upper-intermediate to advanced L2 learners, and the other was words that were highly unlikely to be produced by them. Both these two types of words were high-frequency words used by native speakers. The Vocabulary Knowledge Scale test indicated that the testees were highly familiar with both of the two types of target words. Then the lexical organizations of the two types of words were compared. The purpose of the sub-study was to investigate the change of lexical organization in FAV development.

The first and second sub-studies adopted quantitative approaches. The third and fourth sub-studies adopted qualitative approaches. After the longitudinal sub-study was completed, three senior students from the department were interviewed. The interview questions were designed from four aspects. The first aspect was on students' consciousness on FAV learning; the second aspect was on the learning strategies (if any) students adopted in FAV learning; the third aspect was on whether teachers have attached importance to FAV in teaching; and the fourth aspect was on effective teaching strategies (if any) to facilitate students' FAV development. Surrounding these aspects 14 questions were designed. When the interview was formally conducted, each interviewee was interviewed individually,so that they would not be influenced by others. Each interview took around five to seven minutes. The purpose of the interview was to detect possible factors for FAV stagnation,and to detect effective strategies to promote FAV development.

Originally, the research involved the three independent sub-studies stated above. However, with further honing on the research plan,it was found that class instruction was a significant part in ESL learning,and should not be ignored in the investigation. Therefore, another sub-study was integrated into the original plan.The added sub-study was documentary analysis.In the sub-study, the course structure in the period of the 12-month longitudinal sub-study was collected.Then the units were examined and ana- lysed. *The Syllabus of English Courses for College English Majors in China* was examined and analysed as well. The purpose of the sub-study was to find possible factors in course design that may affect FAV development. And again,with the development of the research,it was strongly felt that an even longer longitudinal sub-study,together with the investigation of the courses students took in the period, was necessary. Therefore these two sub- studies were supplemented to the research.They are introduced in Chapter 10.

In general,all the sub-studies were conducted smoothly,and all the research objectives have been achieved. Moreover, the entire research project was completed within a reasonable time frame. In terms of the data,as both quantitative and qualitative methods were adopted in the research,there was a triangulation of the data source. The research instruments were fully justified by prior studies and theories,and by the carefully designed pilot study. The careful selection of the participants ensured the gen- eralizability of the research findings. The data analysis was conducted by using professional tools, including AntConc, RANGE and SPSS. In sum, every care has been made for the completion of the research project.

9. 3 Summary of the Major Findings

This research uncovered five significant findings pertaining to the research objectives. A brief summary of the findings will be presented in this section.

First, it is found that the FAV threshold phenomenon exists when L2 learners reach upper-intermediate to advanced L2 proficiency level. Three features were captured in the threshold phenomenon. The first feature is that the threshold phenomenon is long-lasting; the second feature is that the threshold phenomenon is "stubborn", as it does not grow with the growth of PV and CAV; the third feature is that the FAV threshold tends to occur widely, as it occurs at most of the word frequency levels.

Second, it is found that both PV and CAV keep growing when L2 learners reach upper-intermediate to advanced proficiency level; FAV is not significantly correlated with PV and CAV at this stage, and the gap between PV and FAV, and between CAV and FAV become larger.

Third, there are three tendencies in lexical network construction when a word is developing into FAV. The first tendency is that the word's lexical network tends to be semantised; the second tendency is that some types of nodes tend to increase in the process, while other types of nodes tend to decrease; and they change at different speeds. The third tendency is that the connections of the lexical network tend to get stronger and tighter. In summary, the lexical network tends to develop in a way that the word becomes easier to be accessed, activated, and retrieved.

Fourth, it is found that there are possible factors for FAV stagnation in both ESL teaching and learning. In teaching, the first factor is that teachers seem not to have attached great importance to FAV in classroom instruction. The second factor is that little effort has been made to facilitate students in FAV development. The third factor is that there are inadequate units for output training in the curriculum. In learning, there are several possible factors for FAV stagnation as well. The first factor is that students' effort to improve FAV may not be enough, as the strategies students adopted were rather limited; sometimes the effort was not persistent, as it was given up later. The second factor is that there is insufficient intentional learning in FAV study.

Fifth, some effective teaching and learning strategies are detected from the research. The learning strategies include sentence making with the target word, note-taking on the target word, putting down example sentences, collecting synonyms, etc. The effective teaching strategies include providing synonyms of the target word, negotiating word meanings, analysing the word's contexts, encouraging students to make sentences with the word, and raising students' attention to the word. In general, the proposed research objectives have been fulfilled, and the research questions have been answered. The implications of the research have been discussed in Chapter 8.

9. 4　Significance of the Research

As pointed out in the chapter of Introduction, little prior research has adopted a long-time longitudinal study to track the developmental process of FAV, let alone to track the growth of

FAV, PV and CAV simultaneously. In this research, a longitudinal sub-study lasting for 12 months was carried out, and the research unfolded the FAV threshold in the 12-month period of time. Therefore, the sub-study provides a vigorous evidence and a robust support for Laufer's (1998) FAV threshold hypothesis. Additionally, it uncovered more details on the phenomenon, which helps ESL teachers and researchers obtain a better understanding of it.

The research also explored the change of mental lexicon in FAV development. In addition to seeking external reasons in teaching and learning for the FAV threshold phenomenon, this research attempted to investigate the inner mechanism in FAV development. The word association sub-study investigated the lexical network of words that were highly likely to be produced by upper-intermediate to advanced L2 learners, and words that were highly unlikely to be produced by them. Then the lexical organizations of the two were compared. It is assumed that the difference between the two may shed some light on how the network in mental lexicon is constructed when words develop into FAV. Some possible tendencies in the process were discovered, and the sub-study may provide a kick-off for further research in this direction.

Another devotion of this research is that it broadens the research view on FAV study. The school courses offer a major source for L2 learners to receive ESL instruction, but it had been seldom integrated in FAV research. By observing the units learners took at the time of the longitudinal sub-study, some possible drawbacks in course design were detected. Lastly, by interviewing the learners, more first-hand data were obtained to explore students' attitude to FAV learning, their strategy use, and teachers' teaching on FAV.

In general, the research provides robust evidence for FAV threshold hypothesis. It also broadens the view to investigate FAV threshold phenomenon to mental lexicon and course design. Moreover, the research may bring a positive impact on FAV learning and teaching, as it raises more attention to the threshold issue, offers ESL teachers and learners more guidance in FAV development, and help them understand, predict, and tackle the problem more efficiently.

9.5　Possible Directions for Future Research

Although the research has achieved the proposed objectives and answered the research questions, it was found that there are still numerous unanswered questions on FAV threshold phenomenon. More studies are needed to have an even deeper insight into the phenomenon. Moreover, it is acknowledged that limitations exist in this research. It is therefore hoped that future research can answer the questions and overcome the limitations.

Although a part of the research is a 12-month longitudinal sub-study, it is strongly felt that an even longer longitudinal study is in dire need. The outcome of this longitudinal sub-study reveals that in the 12 months of time learners' FAV did not grow. Then questions emerge: When does the threshold start to occur? Does the threshold occur periodically, or does it occur once and stay there permanently? In other words, is the threshold temporary and periodical, or is it eternal? The longitudinal sub-study in this research only followed upper-intermediate to advanced L2 learners for 12 months. A more ideal condition would be that the researcher follows a group of participants throughout the four-year English-major study at a university, and if possible, keeps following the participants who continue with their Master's and PhD study. This will provide a more comprehensive picture on FAV development.

Another issue that needs to be verified by future research is whether the effective teaching and learning strategies found in this research are really effective. These strategies include the ones detected from the research and the ones recommended based on the principles concluded from the research. In the research, the effectiveness of these strategies was based on the interview and the documentary analysis, but it was not evidenced by empirical studies. In other words, effective learning and teaching strategies not only should be guided by experience and theories, but also need to be tested by empirical studies. For example, based on the findings of this research, it is postulated that pushed output activities can facilitate FAV learning. However, whether the postulation is correct and how much pushed output will be adequate to promote FAV growth need to be testified by empirical studies. If these pushed output activities are confirmed to be effective by empirical studies, they can then be adopted more frequently in FAV teaching and learning, and the threshold problem will be more effectively tackled in this way. Therefore, it is suggested that more empirical research be conducted to verify the effectiveness of these strategies. It is believed that with quantitative-evidence support, the conclusion will be more convincing, and more instructive to FAV learning.

Empirical studies will help answer a significant question raised by Laufer (1998) as well. The question is whether the threshold phenomenon occurring in FAV development reflects the nature of FAV learning, or whether it is just the consequence of certain types of teaching and learning. In other words, whether FAV stagnation will occur irrespective of the load and style of teaching and learning, or whether it is a result of them. The question seems to be significant, but it has not been satisfactorily answered yet until now. Longer longitudinal studies and studies testifying teaching and learning strategies will help answer the question.

It is also expected that the limitations of the present study can be overcome in future research. Due to time constraints, the present research only measured the breadth of FAV. The development pattern of the depth of FAV was not touched upon. Therefore, it is unknown yet whether the threshold phenomenon only occurs in the breadth of FAV, or in both the breadth and depth of it. In addition, due to the limited research conditions, the sample sizes in this research are comparatively small. As it is known, the sample size is one of the factors that influence the robustness of quantitative empirical studies. Therefore, it is expected that in future studies bigger sample sizes can be obtained.

Lastly, the word association approach adopted in the study can only be applied to observe the network structure of the target words in learners' mental lexicon. More detailed information, such as the density of the lexical network, the strength and length of connections the target words have with other nodes in the network, cannot be measured by word association tests. Other tools, such as Event-related Potentials (ERP), eye-movement tests, and response-time tests, may need to be applied to obtain the information in future research.

Chapter 10   Extended Research

10. 1   Introduction

With the development of the research, two sub-studies were conducted to further explore the FAV threshold phenomenon. The first one was a 36-month longitudinal study, and the second one was a documentary analysis. This chapter introduces these two sub-studies, compares their results with previous sub-studies, and makes conclusions.

10. 2   The Longitudinal Sub-study

The 36-month longitudinal sub-study was conducted to further explore the development pattern of FAV. The participants of the sub-study shared all the demographic characteristics of the participants in the 12-month longitudinal study, except that they were at the end of Year One when they participated in the study. Therefore, their ages were 18 to 19 at the beginning of the sub-study, and 21 to 22 at the end of it.

Forty randomly selected students participated in the sub-study. In the first month, the twelfth month, the twenty-fourth month, and the thirty-sixth month, tests were conducted to measure the participants' PV, CAV and FAV size. The test instruments adopted were: (1) Receptive Vocabulary Levels Test (PVLT); (2) Controlled Active (or Controlled Productive) Vocabulary Levels Test (CAVLT or CPVLT); (3) Lex30 test. All the instruments have been introduced in Chapter 4. The sub-study adopted the same versions of the three tests as the 12-month longitudinal sub-study did. However, unlike the 12-month longitudinal sub-study, the writing tasks were excluded in the 36-month longitudinal sub-study. This was to keep the working load at a reasonable level to maintain the participants' patience, as the participants would do the tests for four times in the sub-study. Therefore, only Lex30 was conducted to measure FAV.

After all the datas were collected, the valid data was selected for analysis. Since the sub-study was longitudinal, test papers done by the testees who failed to participate in all the four rounds of tests were removed. Only the data done by subjects who participated in the first month, the twelfth month, the twenty-fourth month, and the thirty-sixth month tests were kept for further examination. Data with handwritings that were difficult to be read were removed. In total, 13 participants' datas were removed. After the screening, 27 participants' test papers were determined as valid data for the final analysis.

The scoring methods were the same as those in the 12-month longitudinal sub-study. Statistical Package for Social Science (SPSS) of version 20.0 was used to conduct data analysis. All the scores of PVLT, CAVLT and Lex30 were entered into SPSS for statistical processing. The purpose of this sub-study was to obtain a more comprehensive picture of FAV development. The statistical test adopted in this sub-study was One-Way Within-Subject AVOVA. It was used to compare passive vocabulary size, controlled active vocabulary size and free active vocabulary size respectively. Results again showed that the development patterns of PV, CAV and FAV were different. Generally, PV and CAV were found to keep growing in the 36 months. The repeated measures AVOVA indicated that PV and CAV size was significantly different across the time points, with PV's results being $F(1.68, 43.80) = 106.178, p < 0.05$, and CAV's results being $F(1.80, 46.82) = 86.63, p < 0.05$. In addition, the estimated marginal means of PA and CAV scores through time showed that both PV and CAV consistently increased in the 36 months. In terms of FAV, the scores in the 12th month were significantly higher than those at the beginning of the study ($MD = 12.37$). There was not a significant difference in FAV scores between the 12th month and the 24th month, and between the 24th month and the 36th month. In other words, although the participants' PV and CAV grew significantly from the end of Year Three to the end of Year Four, their FAV failed to grow during that period of time. Therefore the 36-month longitudinal sub-study confirmed the Threshold Hypothesis of Laufer (1991). This result is consistent with the result of the 12-month longitudinal sub-study.

In addition to revealing results that were consistent with the 12-month longitudinal sub-study, the 36-month longitudinal sub-study provided a more comprehensive picture on the FAV development. It showed that FAV was growing from the end of Year One to the end of Year Two; starting from the end of Year Two, i.e., the 12th month, FAV failed to grow until the end of Year Four. This result seemed to reveal another feature of the threshold phenomenon: the threshold tends to occur early. As early as the end of Year Two, the FAV stopped increasing. In addition, the results confirm other features detected from the

12-month longitudinal study; the threshold phenomenon tends to be long-lasting and "stubborn", as it persisted until the end of the sub-study, and was not promoted by the improvement of students' L2 proficiency, PV and CAV.

10. 3   The Documentary Analysis

In this sub-study, the course structures in the period of the 36-month longitudinal sub-study were collected and investigated. It was found that in the first 12 months, there were 540 academic hours' input-focused units, and 108 academic hours' output-focused units; in the second 12 months, there were 504 academic hours' input-focused units, and 72 academic hours' output-focused units; in the third 12 months, there were 108 academic hours' input-focused units, and 144 academic hours' output-focused units. Although the amount of input-focused and output-focused units cannot represent students' entire input and output practice and training in L2 study, school instruction is the major source from which English-major students obtain L2 training and practice. Additionally, most of them would spend a great deal of time and effort in studying the units out of class in order to pass the final examinations. The units, therefore, were expected to shed light on the possible effect of input and output on FAV acquisition.

The result of this sub-study seems to be interesting. The data in the third year indicate that a large amount of input in school instruction may not necessarily mean a growth of FAV. The data in Year Two, Year Three and Year Four also indicate that the change of the amount of output training and practice in school may not be correlated with the change of FAV either. These results have led to more questions: can input and output promote FAV development, as is always expected? If so, can all types of input and output do so, or can only specific types of input and output do so? In other words, what are the key factors in input and output that would affect FAV acquisition? It is hoped that answers to all these questions can be found in future research.

10. 4　Conclusion

This chapter has introduced the longer longitudinal sub-study and documentary analysis sub-study. The two sub-studies provided robust support for the findings in the previous sub-studies. In addition, they resulted in more information on the FAV threshold phenomenon. It is expected that in the future, more research in this area can be conducted so that findings of this research can be tested, and more substantial findings can be obtained.

References

[1]Aitchison,J. (1994). *Words in the Mind : An Introduction to the Mental Lexicon* . Oxford : Blackwell.

[2]Albrechtsen,D. , Haastrup, K. & Henriksen, B. (2008). *Vocabulary and writing in a first and second language : Processes and development* . New York : Springer.

[3]Arash, A. (2016). Effects of non-negotiated pre-modified input, negotiation of input without output, and negotiation of input plus pushed output on EFL learners' vocabulary learning. *Journal of Language Teaching and Research* ,7(4) : 773-779.

[4]Astika, G. G. (1993). Analytical assessments of foreign students' writing. *RELC Journal : A Journal of Language Teaching and Research in Southeast Asia* ,24(1) : 61-72.

[5]Bachoud-Lévi, A. C. , Dupoux, E. , Cohen, L. & Mehler, J. (1998). Where is the length effect? A cross-linguistic study of speech production. *Journal of Memory and Language* , 39 (3) : 331-346.

[6]Barcroft, J. (2004). Effects of sentence writing in second language lexical acquisition. *Second Language Research* , 20 (4) : 303-334.

[7]Barcroft, J. (2006). Can writing a new word detract from learning it? More negative effects of forced output during vocabulary learning. *Second Language Research* ,22(4) : 487-497.

[8]Bayazidi, A. & Saeb, F. (2017). Assessing reliability of

two versions of vocabulary levels tests in Iranian context. *Advances in Language and Literary Studies*,8(1):30-43.

[9]Binder,J. R.,Westbury,C. F.,McKiernan,K. A.,Possing,E. T.& Medler,D. A.(2005). Distinct brain systems for processing concrete and abstract concepts. *Journal of Cognitive Neuroscience*,17(6):905-917.

[10]Bock,K.& Levelt,W.(1994). Language production: Grammatical encoding. In M. A. Gernbascher(Ed.). *Handbook of psycholinguistics*(pp.945-984). Sandiego,CA:Academic Press.

[11]Caramazza,A.,Laudanna,A.& Romani,C.(1988). Lexical access and inflectional morphology. *Cognition*,28(3): 297-332.

[12]Carolyn,Y.,Ping,H.,Gutchess,A. H.,Hedden,T., Hiu-Ying Mary,C.,Qicheng,J.& Yao,C.(2004). Category norms as a function of culture and age:Comparisons of item responses to 105 categories by American and Chinese Adults. *Psychology and Aging*,(3):379.

[13]Carroll,D. W.(1986). *Psychology of Language*. Pacific Grove,California:Brooks/Cole Pub. Co.

[14]Channell,M.(1990). Vocabulary acquisition and the mental lexicon. In J. Tomaszczyk,B. Lewandowska-Tomaszczyk & R. Burchfield(Eds.). *Meaning and Lexicography*(pp. 21-30). Amsterdam:Benjamins.

[15]Charmaz,K.(2006). *Constructing Grounded Theory: A Practical Guide Through Qualitative Analysis*. London:Thousand Oaks:SAGE.

[16]Chen,S.(2006). Semantic representations of bilingual mental lexicon. *Foreign Language and Literature Studies*,23(1): 6-11.

[17]Chen, S.,Peng, J.,Yang, H.,Hou, L.& Fang, H.

(2011). A study on the familiarity effects in representing English words in English-Chinese mental lexicon. *English Education in China*, 32(2):1-16.

[18]Chen,X.& Zhang,J. (2008). Comparison of the cognitive factors in Chinese verbs and Chinese nouns. *Journal of Huanan Normal University (Social Science Edition)*,(4):119-123.

[19]Chow,I. H. S. ,Inn,A.& Szalay,L. B. (1987). Empirical study of the subjective meanings of culture between American and Chinese. *Asia Pacific Journal of Management*,4(3):144-151.

[20]Clark,E. (1995). *The Lexicon in Acquisition*. Cambridge: Cambridge University Press.

[21] Coady, J. , Magoto, J. , Hubbard, P. , Graney, J. & Mokhtari,K. (1993). High frequency vocabulary and reading proficiency in ESL readers. In T. Huckin,M. Haynes & J. Coady (Eds.). *Second Language Reading and Vocabulary Learning* (pp. 217-228). Norwood,NJ:Ablex.

[22] Cobb, T. (2003). Analyzing late interlanguage with learner corpora:Quebec replications of three European studies. *Canadian Modern Language Review*,59(3):393-424.

[23]Collins,A. M.& Loftus,E. F. (1975). A spreading-acti-vation theory of semantic processing. *Psychological Review*, 82 (6):407-428.

[24]Collins,A. M.& Quillian,M. R. (1969). Retrieval time from semantic memory. *Journal of Verbal Learning and Verbal Behavior*,8(2):240-247.

[25]Collins,A. M.& Quillian,M. R. (1972). How to make a language user. In E. Tulving & W. Donaldson (Eds.). *Organisa-tion of Memory*. New York:Academic Press.

[26]Costa,A. (2005). Lexical access in bilingual production. In J. F. Kroll & A. M. B. De Groot (Eds.). *Handbook of Bilingualism*:

Psycholinguistic Approaches（pp. 308-325）. Oxford：Oxford University Press.

［27］Costa，A.，Miozzo，M.& Caramazza，A.（1999）. Lexical selection in bilinguals：Do words in the bilingual's two lexicons compete for selection? *Journal of Memory and Language*，41（3）：365-397.

［28］Costa，A.& Santesteban，M.（2004）. Lexical access in bilingual speech production：Evidence from language switching in highly proficient bilinguals and L2 learners. *Journal of Memory and Language*，（50）：491-511.

［29］Coxhead，A.（2000）. A new academic word list. *TESOL Quarterly*，34（2）：213-238.

［30］Craik，F. I. M.& Lockhart，R. S.（1972）. Levels of processing：A framework for memory research. *Journal of Verbal Learning and Verbal Behavior*，11（6）：671-684.

［31］Cramer，P.（1968）. *Word Association*. New York：Academic Press.

［32］Crutch，S. J.& Warrington，E. K.（2005）. Gradients of semantic relatedness and their contrasting explanations in refractory access and storage semantic impairments. *Cognitive Neuropsychology*，22（7）：851-876.

［33］Cui，Y.（2006）. *An Exploration into the Development of Lexical Competence of Chinese Tertiary English Majors*. Doctoral dissertation，Shanghai Jiaotong University，Shanghai，China.

［34］Cui，Y.（2010）. Word association tests and second language vocabulary acquisition：A Re-examination. *Contemporary Foreign Languages Studies*，（7）：55-59.

［35］Cui，Y.& Wang，T.（2006）. The development pattern and correlation of receptive vocabulary，productive vocabulary and depth of knowledge. *Modern Foreign Languages*，29（4）：392-400.

[36]Dale,E.(1965). Vocabulary measurement: Techniques and major findings. *Elementary English*,(42):895-901.

[37]de Groot,A.M.B.(1989). Representational aspects of word image ability and word frequency as assessed through word association. *Journal of Experimental Psychology: Learning, Memory, and Cognition*,15(5):824-845.

[38] de Groot, A. M. B. (1992). Determinants of word translation. *Journal of Experimental Psychology: Learning, Memory, and Cognition*,18(5):1001-1018.

[39]de Groot,A.M.B.(1993). Word-type effects in bilingual processing tasks. In R.Schreuder & B.Weltens (Eds.). *The Bilingual Lexicon* (pp.27-51). Amsterdam:John Benjamins.

[40]Deese,J.(1962). Form class and the determinants of association. *Journal of Verbal Learning and Verbal Behavior*, (1):79-84.

[41]Deese,J.(1966). *The Structure of Associations in Language and Thought*. Baltimore:Johns Hopkins Press.

[42]Dong,L.& Zhang,P.(2011). The non-semantisation of mental lexicon. *Journal of Southeast University (Philosophy and Social Science)*,13(Supplement):101-104.

[43]Duan, S.& Yan, C. (2004). Effects of multiple-choice annotation on ESL incidental vocabulary acquisition. *Foreign Language Teaching and Research*,36(3):213-218.

[44]EAT. (2015). *Edinburgh Association Thesaurus*. Retrieved from http://www.eat.rl.ac.uk/

[45] Education, C. M. O. (2000). *The Syllabus of English Courses for College English Majors*. Beijing: Foreign Language Teaching and Research Press.

[46]Ellis,R.& He,X. (1999). The roles of modified input and output in the incidental acquisition of word meanings. *Studies in*

Second Language Acquisition ,21(2):285-301.

[47]Engber,C. A. (1995). The relationship of lexical proficiency to the quality of ESL compositions. *Journal of Second Language Writing* ,4(2):139-155.

[48]Entwisle,D. R. (1966). *Word Associations of Young Children* . Baltimore:Johns Hopkins Press.

[49]Ervin,S. M. (1961). Changes with age in the verbal determinants of word-association. *The American Journal of Psychology* ,74 (3):361-372.

[50]Fan,M. (2000). How big is the gap and how to narrow it? An investigation into the active and passive vocabulary knowledge of L2 learners. *RELC Journal* ,31(2):105-119.

[51]Ferré,P.& Sánchez-Casas,R. (2014). Affective priming in a lexical decision task:Is there an effect of words' concreteness? *Psicológica* ,35(1):117-138.

[52] File, K. A. & Adams, R. (2010). Should vocabulary instruction be integrated or isolated? *TESOL Quarterly* ,44(2): 222-249.

[53]Fitzpatrick, T. (2006). Habits and rabbits:Word associations and the L2 lexicon. *EUROSLA Yearbook* ,(6):121.

[54]Fitzpatrick, T. (2007). Word association patterns:Unpacking the assumptions. *Vocabulary and Language Teaching* ,17(3): 319-331.

[55]Fitzpatrick, T. & Clenton, J. (2010). The challenge of validation:Assessing the performance of a test of productive vocabulary. *Language Testing* ,27(4):537-554.

[56]Fitzpatrick, T.& Izura, C. (2011). Word association in L1 and L2:An exploratory study of response types, response times, and interlingual mediation. *Studies in Second Language Acquisition* ,33(3):373-398.

[57]Fitzpatrick, T. & Meara, P. (2004). Exploring the validity of a test of productive vocabulary. *VIAL: Vigo International Journal of Applied Linguistics*, (1):55-73.

[58]Fitzpatrick, T., Wray, A., Playfoot, D. & Wright, M. J. (2015). Establishing the reliability of word association data for investigating individual and group differences. *Applied Linguistics*, 36(1):23-50.

[59] Fontana, A. & Frey, J. (2000). The interview: From structured questions to negotiated text. In N. K. Denzin & Y. S. Lincoln (Eds.). *Handbook of Qualitative Research* (2nd ed., Vol. 2, pp. 645-672). Thousand Oaks: SAGE.

[60] Forster, K. (1976). Accessing the mental lexicon. In R. J. Wales & E. Walker (Eds.). *New Approaches to Language Mechanisms* (pp. 257-287). Amsterdam: North-Holland.

[61] French, R. M. & Jacquet, M. (2004). Understanding bilingual memory: Models and data. *Trends in Cognitive Sciences*, 8(2):87-93.

[62]Fu, Y., Cui, Y. & Chen, H. (2009). A longitudinal study of the developmental pattern of SL mental lexicon. *Foreign Language and Literature Studies*, 26(1):16-23.

[63]Fuente, D. L. & José, M. (2002). Negotiation and oral acquisition of L2 vocabulary: The roles of input and output in the receptive and productive acquisition of words. *Studies in Second Language Acquisition*, 24(1):81-112.

[64] Gina, N., Jennifer, L., Jill, C., Marco, A. & Guy, T. (2011). Examining multiple dimensions of word knowledge for content vocabulary understanding. *The Journal of Education*, 192(2/3):49-61.

[65]Gong, R. (2008). The optinization of cognitive factors affecting the semantic netwok of L2 mental lexicon of college

English learners. *Journal of PLA University of Foreign Languages*, 31(3):56-62.

[66]Green, D. W. (1998). Mental control of the bilingual lexico-semantic system. *Bilingualism: Language and Cognition*, 1 (2):67-81.

[67]Gu, Q. & Li, X. (2013). Study on productive vocabulary size of non-English major students. *Journal of Tonghua Normal University*, 34(3):80-83.

[68]Hazrat, M. & Hessamy, G. (2013). The impact of two types of vocabulary preparation on listening comprehension, vocabulary learning, and vocabulary learning strategy use. *Theory and Practice in Language Studies*, 3(8):1453-1461.

[69]Heatley, A., Nation, P. & Coxhead, A. (2002). *Range* [Computer software]. Retrieved from www. victoria. ac. nz/ lals/staff/paul-nation/nation. aspx

[70]Henriksen, B. (1999). Three dimensions of vocabulary development. *Studies in Second Language Acquisition*, 21(2): 303-317.

[71]Henriksen, B. (2008). Declarative lexical knowledge. In D. Albrechtsen, K. Haastrup & B. Henriksen (Eds.). *Vocabulary and Writing in a First and Second Language* (pp. 22-66). New York:Springer.

[72]Hu, A. & Liu, S. (2013). Model of memory processing system in the retrieval of translated words. *Foreign Languages and Their Teaching*, 273(6):49-52.

[73]Hu, Y. (2013). Effects of English and Chinese words' cultural difference on English reading comprehension. *Journal of Inner Mongolia Normal University*(*Educational Science*), 26 (11):102-104.

[74]Huang, S. (2012). An evaluation of productive vocabulary

capacity of English major students. *Journal of Beijing Second Foreign Langue University*, 212(12):75-78.

[75]Jared, D. & Kroll, J. F. (2001). Do bilinguals activate phonological representations in one or both of their languages when naming words? *Journal of Memory and Language*, 44(1): 2-31.

[76]Johnson, B. & Christensen, L. B. (2014). *Educational Research: Quantitative, Qualitative, and Mixed Approaches* (5th ed.). Thousand Oaks, California: SAGE.

[77]Jullian, P. (2000). Creating word-meaning awareness. *ELT Journal*, 54(1):37-46.

[78]Källkvist, M. (1999). *Form-class and Task-type Effects in Learner English: A Study of Advanced Swedish Learners*. Lund: Lund University Press.

[79]Khazaeenezhad, B. & Alibabaee, A. (2013). Investigating the role of L2 language proficiency in word association behavior of L2 learners: A case of Iranian EFL learners. *Theory and Practice in Language Studies*, 3(1):108-115.

[80]Kittay, E. F. & Lehrer, A. (1992). Introduction. In A. Lehrer & E. F. Kittay (Eds.). *Frames, Fields and Contrasts* (pp. 1-20). Hillsdale, NJ: Lawrence Erlbaum.

[81]Kolers, P. A. (1963). Interlingual word associations. *Journal of Verbal Learning and Verbal Behavior*, 2(4):291-300.

[82]Krashen, S. (1981). *Second Language Acquisition and Second Language Learning*. Oxford: Pergamon Press.

[83]Krashen, S. (1982). *Principles and Practice in Second Language Acquisition*. Oxford: Pergamon.

[84]Krashen, S. (1989). We acquire vocabulary and spelling by reading: Additional evidence for the input hypothesis. *The Modern Language Journal*, 73(4):440-464.

［85］Krashen, S. (1998). Comprehensible output? *System*, 26(2):175-182.

［86］Kvale, S. & Brinkmann, S. (2015). *Interviews: Learning the Craft of Qualitative Research Interviewing* (3rd ed.). Los Angeles: Sage Publications.

［87］La, H. (2005). Selection processes in monolingual and bilingual lexical access. In J. F. Kroll, A. M. B. & D. Groot (Eds.). *Handbook of Bilingualism: Psycholinguistic Approaches* (pp. 289-307). Oxford: Oxford University Press.

［88］Lambert, W. E. & Tucker, G. R. (1972). *Bilingual Education of Children: the St. Lambert Experiment*. Rowley, Mass: Newbury House Publishers.

［89］Laufer, B. (1989). A factor of difficulty in vocabulary learning: Deceptive transparency. *AILA Review*, (6):10-20.

［90］Laufer, B. (1991). The development of L2 lexis in the expression of the advanced learner. *The Modern Language Journal*, 75(4):440-448.

［91］Laufer, B. (1994). The lexical profile of second language writing: Does it change over time? *RELC Journal*, 25(2): 21-33.

［92］Laufer, B. (1998). The development of passive and active vocabulary in a second language: Same or different? *Applied Linguistics*, 19(2):255-271.

［93］Laufer, B. & Goldstein, Z. (2004). Testing vocabulary knowledge: Size, strength, and computer adaptiveness. *Language Learning*, 54(3):399-436.

［94］Laufer, B. & Hulstijn, J. (2001). Incidental vocabulary acquisition in a second language: The construct of task-induced involvement. *Applied Linguistics*, 22(1):1-26.

［95］Laufer, B. & Nation, P. (1995). Vocabulary size and

use: Lexical richness in L2 written production. *Applied Linguistics*, 16(3):307-322.

[96] Laufer, B. & Nation, P. (1999). A vocabulary-size test of controlled productive ability. *Language Testing*, 16(1):33-51.

[97] Laufer, B. & Paribakht, T. S. (1998). The relationship between passive and active vocabularies: Effects of language learning context. *Language Learning*, 48(3):365-389.

[98] Leech, G. (1974). *Semantics*. London: Penguin Books Ltd.

[99] Leech, G. (1983). *Principles of Pragmatics*. London: Longman.

[100] Leedy, P. D. & Ormrod, J. E. (2005). *Practical Research: Planning and Design* (8th ed.). Upper Saddle River, New Jersey: Merrill Prentice Hall.

[101] Lei, L., Wei, Y., Ye, L. & Zhang, M. (2007). A study of incidental vocabulary acquisition through writing by Chinese EFL learners. *Journal of PLA University of Foreign Languages*, 30(1):53-56.

[102] Lextutor. (2017). *The Scoring Program for Controlled Active Vocabulary Levels Test*. Retrieved from http://www.lextutor.ca/tests/levels/productive/

[103] Li, Q. (2008). A study on the associative meaning and its embodiment in the color words of English and Chinese. *Journal of Southwest Agricultural University (Social Science Edition)*, 6(3):133-135.

[104] Li, R. (2003). Associative meaning in social and cultral perspective. *Journal of Xiangfan University*, 24(6):76-78.

[105] Li, S. (2004). Cultural association of English words on colors. *Research of Administration Science*, 18(3):110-111.

[106] Liu, S. (2001). Exploring word knowledge and its acquisition patterns: An experimental study of word meaning and

affix. *Foreign Language Teaching and Research*,33(6):436-441.

[107]Liu,S.,Fu,B.& Hu,A.(2012).Mental lexicon representation with L2 learners of different levels as shown in syntagmatic and paradigmatic semantic responses. *Journal of PLA University of Foreign Languages*,35(2):57-70.

[108]Lognostics.(2017). *The Lex30 Test Online*. Retrieved from http://www.lognostics.co.uk/tools/Lex30/index.htm

[109]Lotto,L.& de Groot,A.M.B.(1998).Effects of learning method and word type on acquiring vocabulary in an unfamiliar language. *Language Learning*,48(1):31-69.

[110]Lovatt,P.,Avons,S.E.& Masterson,J.(2000).The word-length effect and disyllabic words. *The Quarterly Journal of Experimental Psychology:Section A*,53(1):1-22.

[111]Lu,M.(2008).A study of productive vocabulary's development in breadth of knowledge. *Foreign Language Learning Theory and Practice*,(2):10-15.

[112]Maréchal,C.(1995). *The Bilingual Lexicon:Study of French and English Word Association Responses of Advanced Learners of French*. Master's thesis,University of Dublin,Dublin,Ireland.

[113]McCarthy,M.(1990). *Vocabulary*. Oxford:Oxford University Press.

[114]McNeill,D.(1966).A study of word association. *Journal of Verbal Learning and Verbal Behavior*,5(6):548-557.

[115]Meara,P.(1983).Word associations in a foreign language. *Nottingham Linguistics Circular*,11(2):29-38.

[116]Meara,P.(1984).The study of lexis in interlanguage. In A.David,A.Howart & C.Criper (Eds.). *Interlanguage* (pp. 225-235).Edinburgh:Edinburgh University Press.

[117]Meara,P.(1990).A note on passive vocabulary. *Second Language Research*,6(2):150-154.

[118]Meara,P.& Alcoy,J. C. O. (2010). Words as species: An alternative approach to estimating productive vocabulary size. *Reading in a Foreign Language*,22(1):222-236.

[119]Meara,P.& Buxton,B. (1987). An alternative to multiple choice vocabulary tests. *Language Testing*,4(2):142-154.

[120]Meara,P.& Fitzpatrick,T. (2000). Lex30: An improved method of assessing productive vocabulary in an L2. *System*, 28 (1):19-30.

[121]Meuter,R. F. I.& Allport,A. (1999). Bilingual language switching in naming: Asymmetrical costs of language selection. *Journal of Memory and Language*,(40):25-40.

[122]Namei, S. (2004). Bilingual lexical development: A Persian-Swedish word association study. *International Journal of Applied Linguistics*,14(3):363-388.

[123]Nation,P. (1983). Testing and teaching vocabulary. *Guidelines*,5(1):12-25.

[124]Nation,P. (1984). *Vocabulary Lists: Words, Affixes, and Stems*. Wellington:English Language Institute,Victoria University of Wellington.

[125]Nation,P. (1990). *Teaching and Learning Vocabulary*. New York:Heinle & Heinle Publishers.

[126]Nation,P. (2001). *Learning Vocabulary in Another Language*.Cambridge:Cambridge University Press.

[127]Nation, P. & Beglar, D. (2007). A vocabulary size test. *The Language Teacher*,31(7):9-13.

[128]Nation, P.& Heatley, A. (1994). *Range: A Program for the Analysis of Vocabulary in Texts* [Computer software]. Retrieved from http://www. victoria. ac. nz/lals/staff/paul-nation/nation. aspx

[129]Navracsics,J. (2007). Word classes and the bilingual

mental lexicon. In Z. Lengyel & J. Navracsics (Eds.). *Lexical Processes: Applied Linguistics Perspective. Clevedon: Multilingual Matters* (pp.17-35). Toronto: Multilingual Matters Limited.

[130]Neath, I., Bireta, T. J. & Surprenant, A. M. (2003). The time-based word length effect and stimulus set specificity. *Psychonomic Bulletin & Review*, 10(2):430-434.

[131]Nelson, D. L. & Schreiber, T. A. (1992). Word concreteness and word structure as independent determinants of recall. *Journal of Memory and Language*, 31(2):237-260.

[132] Nelson, K. (1977). The syntagmatic-paradigmatic shift revisited: A review of research and theory. *Psychological Bulletin*, 84(1):93-116.

[133]Neuman, W. L. (2004a). *Basics of Social Research: Qualitative and Quantitative Approaches*. Boston: Pearson Education.

[134]Neuman, W. L. (2004b). *Social Research Methods: Qualitative and Quantitative Approaches*. Boston: Pearson Education.

[135] New, B., Ludovic, F., Christophe, P. & Marc, B. (2006). Reexamining the word length effect in visual word recognition: New evidence from the English lexicon project. *Psychonomic Bulletin & Review*, 13(1):45-52.

[136]Nissen, H. B. & Henriksen, B. (2006). Word class influence on word association test results. *International Journal of Applied Linguistics*, 16(3):389-407.

[137]O'gorman, E. (1996). An investigation of the mental lexicon of second language learners. *Teanga: The Irish Yearbook of Applied Linguistics*, (16):15-31.

[138]Palermo, D. S. (1971). Characteristics of word association responses obtained from children in grades one through four. *Developmental Psychology*, 5(1):118-123.

[139]Pietila, P. & Merikivi, R. (2014). The impact of free-time

reading on foreign language vocabulary development. *Journal of Language Teaching and Research*,5(1):28-29.

[140]Piper, T. H.& Leicester, P. F. (1980). *Word Association Behavior as an Indicator of English Language Proficiency*. Vancouver,BC:The University of British Columbia.

[141]Postman, L. J.& Keppel, G. (1970). *Norms of Word Association*. New York:Academic Press.

[142]Qian,D. (1999). Assessing the roles of depth and breadth of vocabulary knowledge in reading comprehension. *Canadian Modern Language Review*,56(2):282-308.

[143]Read,J. (1988). Measuring the vocabulary knowledge of second language learners. *RELC Journal*,19(2):12-25.

[144]Read,J. (1993). The development of a new measure of L2 vocabulary knowledge. *Language Testing*,10(3):355-371.

[145] Read, J. (2000). *Assessing Vocabulary*. New York: Cambridge University Press.

[146]Read,J. (2004). Plumbing the depths:How should the construct of vocabulary knowledge be defined? In P. Bogaards & B. Laufer (Eds.). *Vocabulary in a Second Language*:Selection, *Acquisition, and Testing* (pp. 209-227). Amsterdam, Netherlands:Benjamins.

[147]Renmin University of China. (2017). *Report on the Passing Rate of TEM*4. Retrieved from http://sfl. ruc. edu. cn/ displaynews. php? id=1741

[148]Richards,J. C. (1976). The role of vocabulary teaching. *TESOL Quarterly*,10(1):77-89.

[149] Richards, J. C. (2001). *The Context of Language Teaching*. Beijing:Foreign Language Teaching and Research Press.

[150] Riegel, K. F.& Zivian, I. W. M. (1972). Study of inter- and intralingual associations in English and German. *Language*

Learning,22(1):51-63.

[151]Roelofs,A. (1998). Lemma selection without inhibition of languages in bilingual speakers. *Bilingualism: Language and Cognition*,1(2):94-95.

[152]Romani,C.,McAlpine,S. & Martin,R. C. (2008). Concreteness effects in different tasks:Implications for models of short-term memory. *The Quarterly Journal of Experimental Psychology*,61(2):292-323.

[153]Schmitt,N. (1998). Quantifying word association responses:What is native-like? *System*,26(3):389-401.

[154]Schmitt,N.& Meara,P. (1997). Researching vocabulary through a word knowledge framework:Word associations and verbal suffixes. *Studies in Second Language Acquisition*,19(1):17-36.

[155]Schmitt,N.,Schmitt,D. & Clapham,C. (2001). Developing and exploring the behaviour of two new versions of the Vocabulary Levels Test. *Language Testing*,18(1):55-88.

[156]Schwanenflugel,P. (1991). Why are abstract concepts hard to understand? In P. Schwanenflugel (Ed.). *The Psychology of Word Meaning* (pp.223-250). Mahwah,NJ:Erlbaum.

[157]Seidman,I. (1998). *Interviewing as qualitative research: A Guide for Researchs in Education and Social Sciences* (2nd ed.). New York:Teachers College Press.

[158]Singleton,D. (1999). *Exploring the Second Language Mental Lexicon*. Cambridge:Cambridge University Press.

[159]Siok,H. L.& James,M. (2006). From receptive to productive:Improving ESL learners' use of vocabulary in a postreading composition task. *TESOL Quarterly*,40(2):295.

[160]Söderman,T. (1993). Word associations of foreign language learners and native speakers:The phenomenon of a

shift in response type and its relevance for lexical development. In H. Ringom & T. Björkfors (Eds.). *Near-native Proficiency in English* (pp. 91-182). Turku, Finland: bo Akademi University.

[161]Sökmen, A. (1993). Word association results: A window to the lexicons of ESL students. *JALT Journal* 15(2): 135-150.

[162]Soleimani, H. & Mahmoudabadi, Z. (2014). The Impact of interactive output tasks on developing vocabulary knowledge of Iranian EFL learners. *Iranian Journal of Applied Linguistics*, 17(2): 93-113.

[163]Son, J.-S., Do, V. B., Kim, K.-O., Cho, M. S., Su-wonsichon, T. & Valentin, D. (2014). Understanding the effect of culture on food representations using word associations: The case of "rice" and "good rice". *Food Quality and Preference*, (31): 38-48.

[164]Steyvers, M. & Tenenbaum, J. B. (2005). The large-scale structure of semantic networks: Statistical analyses and a model of semantic growth. *Cognitive Science*, 29(1): 41-78.

[165]Stolz, W. S. & Tiffany, J. (1972). The production of "child-like" word associations by adults to unfamiliar adjectives. *Journal of Verbal Learning and Verbal Behavior*, 11(1): 38-46.

[166]Swain, M. (1985). Communicative competence: Some roles of comprehensible input and comprehensible output in its development. In S. M. Gass & C. G. Madden (Eds.). *Input in Second Language Acquisition* (pp. 235-253). Rowley, MA: Newbury.

[167]Swain, M. (1995). Three function of output in second language learning: Principles and practice in applied linguistics. Oxford: Oxford University Press.

[168]Swain, M. (2000). The output hypothesis and beyond: Mediating acquisition through collaborative dialogue. In J. P. Lantolf (Ed.). *Sociocultural Theory and Second Language Learning*

(pp. 97-114). Oxford: Oxford University Press.

[169]Tallerman, M. A. (2015). *Understanding syntax*. London: Routledge.

[170]Tan, X. (2006). A study of Chinese English learners' productive vocabulary development. *Foreign Language Teaching and Research*, 38(3): 202-207.

[171]Tan, X. (2007). A study of English learners' development of In-depth knowledge on productive vocabulary. *Foreign Language Education*, 28(2): 52-56.

[172]Tashakkori, A. & Teddlie, C. (1998). *Mixed Methodology: Combining Qualitative and Quantitative Approaches*. United States: SAGE.

[173] Teijlingen, V. , Edwin & Hundley, V. (2002). The importance of pilot studies. *Nursing Standard*, 16(40): 33-36.

[174]Teng, F. (2015). The effectiveness of extensive reading on EFL learners' vocabulary learning: Incidental versus intentional learning. *Brazilian English Language Teaching Journal*, 6(1): 82-96.

[175] Theanalysisfactor. (2017). *How to Use Chi-square Test*. Retrieved from http://www. theanalysisfactor. com/observed-values-less-than-5-in-a-chi-square-test-no-biggie/

[176]Thoughtco. (2017). *Function Word（Grammar）*. Retrieved from http://www. thoughtco. com/function-word-grammar-1690876

[177]Tong, S. (2009). An empirical study on the development of English major's oral productive vocabulary. *Foreign Language Research*, 150(5): 161-164.

[178]Tongji University of China. (2017). *Report on the Passing Rate of TEM*8. Retrieved from http://sfl. tongji. edu. cn/content. dep? m=news&id=14648273962813872

[179]Treisman, A. M. (1960). Contextual cues in selective listening. *Quarterly Journal of Experimental Psychology*, 12(4):

242-248.

[180]van Hell,J.& de Groot,A. M. B. (1998). Conceptual representation in bilingual memory:Effects of concreteness and cognate status in word association. *Bilingualism : Language and Cognition*,1(3):193-211.

[181] van Hell, J. & Tanner, D. (2012). Second language proficiency and cross language lexical activation. *Language Learning*, 62(s2):148-171.

[182] Von, H. & Mani, N. (2012). Language nonselective lexical access in bilingual toddlers. *Journal of Experimental Child Psychology*,113(4):569-586.

[183] Walters,J. (2012). Aspects of validity of a test of productive vocabulary:Lex30. *Language Assessment Quarterly*,9 (2):172-185.

[184]Webb,S.(2005). Receptive and productive vocabulary learning:The effects of reading and writing on word knowledge. *Studies in Second Language Acquisition*,27(01):33-52.

[185]Webb,S.(2007). The effects of repetition on vocabulary knowledge. *Applied Linguistics*,28(1):46-65.

[186]Webb,S.(2008). Receptive and productive vocabulary sizes of L2 learners. *Studies in Second Language Acquisition*,30 (1):79-95.

[187]Webb,S.(2009). The effects of receptive and productive learning of word pairs on vocabulary knowledge. *RELC Journal*,40(3):360-376.

[188]Wen,Q.(2006). A longitudinal study on the changes in speaking vocabulary by English majors in China. *Foreign Language Teaching and Research*,38(3):185-195.

[189]Wen,Q.,Wang,L.& Liang,M. (2009). *Spoken and Written English Corpus of Chinese Learners* (2.0). Beijing:For-

eign Language Teaching and Research Press.

[190] Wesche, M. & Paribakht, T. S. (1996). Assessing second language vocabulary knowledge: Depth versus breadth. *Canadian Modern Language Review*, 53(1): 13-40.

[191] West, M. (1953). *A General Service List of English Words*. London: Longmans, Green.

[192] Wilks, C. & Meara, P. (2002). Untangling word webs: Graph theory and the notion of density in second language word association networks. *Second Language Research*, 18(4): 303-324.

[193] Wolter, B. (2001). Comparing the L1 and L2 mental lexicon: A depth of individual word knowledge model. *Studies in Second Language Acquisition*, 23(1): 41-69.

[194] Wolter, B. (2002). Assessing proficiency through word associations: Is there still hope? *System*, 30(3): 315-329.

[195] Wu, J., Lang, J. & Dang, Q. (2007). Incidental vocabulary acquisition and Task-induced Involvement. *Foreign Language Teaching and Research*, 39(5): 360-365.

[196] Wu, X. & Chen, X. (2000). Development of lexical competence in the EFL classroom setting. *Modern Foreign Languages*, 23(4): 349-360.

[197] Xue, G. Y. & Nation, P. (1984). A university word-list. *Language Learning and Communication*, 3(2): 215-229.

[198] Yamamoto, Y. (2011). Bridging the gap between receptive and productive vocabulary size through extensive reading. *Reading Matrix: An International Online Journal*, 11(3): 226-242.

[199] Yang, S. (2007). The development of productive vocabulary in Chinese EFL learners. *Foreign Language and Literature*, 94(4): 254-259.

[200] Yu, W. (2011). Vocabulary problems and solutions in ESL writing. *Shandong Foreign Language Teaching Journal*, 140

(1):61-66.

[201]Yue,Y.(2006). "Acquiring" or "learning" English? *Foreign Language Teaching and Research in Basic Education*,66 (8):21-23.

[202]Yue,Y.(2008). Research on L2 incidental vocabulary acquisition in China: Review and inspiration. *Journal of Taiyuan Normal University (Social Science Edition)*,7(2):165-167.

[203]Yue,Y.,Dai,J.& Zhang,H.(2012). Effects of form and semantic processing on incidental vocabulary acquisition. *Journal of PLA University of Foreign Languages*,35(2):61-65.

[204]Yue,Y.,& Fan,S.(2019). Response Categorization in Word Association:Problems and Solutions. *Studies in philosophy of Science and Technology*,36(5),62-67.

[205]Yue,Y.,& Wang,X.(2019). Breaking through the Threshold in Middle School L2 Free Active Vocabulary Acquisition. *Teaching and Administration*,27(9),86-88.

[206]Zareva,A.(2007). Structure of the second language mental lexicon:How does it compare to native speakers' lexical organisation? *Second Language Research*,23(2):123-153.

[207]Zareva,A.& Brent,W.(2012). The "promise" of three methods of word association analysis to L2 lexical research. *Second Language Research*,28(1):41-67.

[208] Zareva, A., Schwanenflugel, P. & Nikolova, Y. (2005). Relationship between lexical competence and language proficiency: Variable sensitivity. *Studies in Second Language Acquisition*,27(4):567-595.

[209]Zhang,B.(2008). Different types of word links in the mental lexicon. *College Student Journal*,42(2):431-439.

[210]Zhang,G.,Han,S.& Zhu,M.(2005). Development of L2 passive and active vocabularies: A comparative study on

English and non-English majors. *Modern Foreign Languages*, 28 (4):374-382.

[211]Zhang, P. (2009). Word association and mental lexicon: A review of lexical network structure research. *Foreign Language Teaching and Research*, (3):71-82.

[212]Zhang, P. (2010a). Choice of prompt words and classification of responses in word association tests. *Journal of PLA University of Foreign Languages*, 33(1):41-45.

[213]Zhang, P. (2010b). A comparative study of word association patterns in Chinese EFL learners' mental lexicon. *Foreign Language Teaching and Research*, 42(1):9-16.

[214]Zhang, P. (2011). A comparative study of concreteness effect in the word associations of English and Chinese mental lexicon. *Foreign Language Learning Theory and Practice* (3):54-62.

[215]Zhang, P. & Wang, Q. (2012). Effects of familiarity and frequency: Dynamic L2 mental lexicon. *Education Forum* (5):106-107.

[216]Zhang, S. (2003). Study on vocabulary acquisition from the response type perspective. *Foreign Language Teaching and Research*, 35(4):275-281.

[217]Zhang, S. (2004). Restructuring the L2 mental lexicon. *Journal of Sichuan International Studies University*, 20(2):66-75.

[218]Zhang, S. (2005). Investigating connections in L2 mental lexicon with word association tests. *Journal of PLA University of Foreign Languages*, 28(2):52-55.

[219]Zhang, S. (2006). Exploring the English L2 mental lexicon via word associations. *Modern Foreign Languages*, 29 (2):164-171.

[220]Zhang, S. (2008). The developmental course of the

L2 mental lexicon: A longitudinal study. *Journal of Sichuan International Studies University*, 24(6):120-124.

[221]Zhang, W.& Zhang, Q. (2007). Word retrieval mechanism and mental lexicon representation by advanced bilinguals. *Foreign Language Education*, 28(6):50-53.

[222]Zhang, Y.& Zhang, J. (2014). Effects of word length on Chinese language production. *Journal of Psychology*, 46(9): 1232-1241.

[223]Zhao, P. (2013). Review and future directions of L2 mental lexicon research. *Journal of Chongqing University of Technology (Social Science)*, 27(6):81-85.

[224]Zhao, Y. (2011). Fossilization in the output of high-frequency words from the "noticing" perspective. *Foreign Language Research*, 160(3):100-102.

[225]Zhuang, J.& Zhou, X. (2001). Effects of time span on language production. *Journal of Psychology*, 33(3).

Appendix A
The Passive Vocabulary Levels Test

右边竖行的解释适合左边竖行的哪个词？请在空格处填上相应的数字。请不要翻查字典，此成绩不会影响你的任何期末成绩。做题方法：每组先看右边竖行带空格的那三个词义，然后再从左面竖行的六个词中选择符合词义的词。不认识的词不要猜，空下即可。

Part A

1 copy
2 event
3 motor   _____ end or highest point
4 pity   _____ this moves a car
5 profit   _____ thing made to be like
6 tip   another

1 accident
2 debt   _____ loud deep sound
3 fortune   _____ something you must pay
4 pride   _____ having a high opinion of
5 roar   yourself
6 thread

1 coffee
2 disease   _____ money for work
3 justice   _____ a piece of clothing
4 skirt   _____ using the law in the right
5 stage   way
6 wage

1 clerk
2 frame   _____ a drink
3 noise   _____ office worker
4 respect   _____ unwanted sound
5 theater
6 wine

1 dozen
2 empire   _____ chance
3 gift   _____ twelve
4 opportunity   _____ money paid to the
5 relief   government
6 tax

1 admire
2 complain   _____ make wider or longer
3 fix   _____ bring in for the first
4 hire   time
5 introduce   _____ have a high opinion
6 stretch   on someone

1 arrange
2 develop   _____ grow
3 lean   _____ put in order
4 owe   _____ like more than
5 prefer   something else
6 seize

1 blame
2 elect   _____ make
3 jump   _____ choose by voting
4 manufacture   _____ become like water
5 melt
6 threaten

1 ancient
2 curious   _____ not easy
3 difficult   _____ very old
4 entire   _____ related to God
5 holy
6 social

1 bitter
2 independent   _____ beautiful
3 lovely   _____ small
4 merry   _____ liked by many people
5 popular
6 slight

Part B

1 bull
2 champion   _____ formal and serious manner
3 dignity   _____ winner of a sporting event
4 hell   _____ building where valuable
5 museum   objects are shown
6 solution

1 abandon
2 dwell   _____ live in a place
3 oblige   _____ follow in order to catch
4 pursue   _____ leave something
5 quote   permanently
6 resolve

1 blanket
2 contest   _____ holiday
3 generation   _____ good quality
4 merit   _____ wool covering used on
5 plot   beds
6 vacation

1 assemble
2 attach   _____ look closely
3 peer   _____ stop doing something
4 quit   _____ cry out loudly in fear
5 scream
6 toss

1 comment
2 gown   _____ long formal dress
3 import   _____ goods from a foreign
4 nerve   country
5 pasture   _____ part of the body which
6 tradition   carries feeling

1 drift
2 endure   _____ suffer patiently
3 grasp   _____ join wool threads together
4 knit   _____ hold firmly with your hands
5 register
6 tumble

1 administration
2 angel   _____ group of animals
3 frost   _____ spirit who serves God
4 herd   _____ managing business and
5 fort   affairs
6 pond

1 brilliant
2 distinct   _____ thin
3 magic   _____ steady
4 naked   _____ without clothes
5 slender
6 stable

1 atmosphere
2 counsel   _____ advice
3 factor   _____ a place covered with grass
4 hen   _____ female chicken
5 lawn
6 muscle

1 aware
2 blank   _____ usual
3 desperate   _____ best or most important
4 normal   _____ knowing what is happening
5 striking
6 supreme

Part C

1 analysis
2 curb
3 gravel _____ eagerness
4 mortgage _____ loan to buy a house
5 scar _____ small stones mixed with
6 zeal sand

1 cavalry
2 eve _____ small hill
3 ham _____ day or night before a
4 mound holiday
5 steak _____ soldiers who fight from
6 switch horses

1 circus
2 jungle _____ musical instrument
3 nomination _____ seat without a back or
4 sermon arms
5 stool _____ speech given by a priest in
6 trumpet a church

1 artillery
2 creed _____ a kind of tree
3 hydrogen _____ system of belief
4 maple _____ large gun on wheels
5 pork
6 streak

1 chart
2 forge _____ map
3 mansion _____ large beautiful house
4 outfit _____ place where metals are
5 sample made and shaped
6 volunteer

1 contemplate
2 extract _____ think about deeply
3 gamble _____ bring back to health
4 launch _____ make someone angry
5 provoke
6 revive

1 demonstrate
2 embarrass _____ have a rest
3 heave _____ break suddenly into small
4 obscure pieces
5 relax _____ make someone feel shy or
6 shatter nervous

1 correspond
2 embroider _____ exchange letters
3 lurk _____ hide and wait for someone
4 penetrate _____ feel angry about something
5 prescribe
6 resent

1 decent
2 frail _____ weak
3 harsh _____ concerning a city
4 incredible _____ difficult to believe
5 municipal
6 specific

1 adequate
2 internal _____ enough
3 mature _____ fully grown
4 profound _____ alone away from other
5 solitary things
6 tragic

Part D

1 alabaster
2 chandelier   _____ small barrel
3 dogma   _____ soft white stone
4 keg   _____ tool for shaping wood
5 rasp
6 tentacle

1 dissipate
2 flaunt   _____ steal
3 impede   _____ scatter or vanish
4 loot   _____ twist the body about
5 squirm   uncomfortably
6 vie

1 benevolence
2 convoy   _____ kindness
3 lien   _____ set of musical notes
4 octave   _____ speed control for an
5 stint   engine
6 throttle

1 contaminate
2 cringe   _____ write carelessly
3 immerse   _____ move back because of fear
4 peek   _____ put something under water
5 relay
6 scrawl

1 bourgeois
2 brocade   _____ middle class people
3 consonant   _____ row or level of something
4 prelude   _____ cloth with a pattern or gold
5 stupor   or silver threads
6 tier

1 blurt
2 dabble   _____ walk in a proud way
3 dent   _____ kill by squeezing someone's
4 pacify   throat
5 strangle   _____ say suddenly without
6 swagger   thinking

1 alcove
2 impetus   _____ priest
3 maggot   _____ release from prison early
4 parole   _____ medicine to put on wounds
5 salve
6 vicar

1 illicit
2 lewd   _____ immense
3 mammoth   _____ against the law
4 slick   _____ wanting revenge
5 temporal
6 vindictive

1 alkali
2 banter   _____ light joking talk
3 coop   _____ a rank of British nobility
4 mosaic   _____ picture made of small pieces
5 stealth   of glass or stone
6 viscount

1 indolent
2 nocturnal   _____ lazy
3 obsolete   _____ no longer used
4 torrid   _____ clever and tricky
5 translucent
6 wily

Part E

1 area
2 contract   _____ written agreement
3 definition   _____ way of doing something
4 evidence   _____ reason for believing
5 method   something is or is not true
6 role

1 alter
2 coincide   _____ change
3 deny   _____ say something is
                  not true
4 devote   _____ describe clearly
and exactly
5 release
6 specify

1 debate
2 exposure   _____ plan
3 integration   _____ choice
4 option   _____ joining something into a
5 scheme   whole
6 stability

1 correspond
2 diminish   _____ keep
3 emerge   _____ match or be in
                agreement with
4 highlight
5 invoke   _____ give special
attention to something
6 retain

1 access
2 gender   _____ male or female
3 implementation   _____ study of the mind
4 license   _____ entrance or way in
5 orientation
6 psychology

1 bond
2 channel   _____ make smaller
3 estimate   _____ guess the number
or size of something
4 identify
5 mediate   _____ recognizing and
naming a person or thing
6 minimize

1 accumulation
2 edition   _____ collecting things over time
3 guarantee   _____ promise to repair a broken
4 media   product
5 motivation   _____ feeling a strong reason or
6 phenomenon   need to do something

1 explicit
2 final   _____ last
3 negative   _____ stiff
4 professional _____ meaning "no" or
"not"
5 rigid
6 sole

1 adult
2 exploitation _____ end
3 infrastructure _____ machine used to move
4 schedule   people or goods
5 termination _____ list of things to do at
6 vehicle   certain times

1 abstract
2 adjacent   _____ next to
3 controversial _____ added to
4 global   _____ concerning the
whole world
5 neutral
6 supplementary

Appendix B
The Controlled Active
Vocabulary Levels Test

填写词汇（每个词的前几个字母已给出），请注意时态、人称、数量等语法规则。为了避免对结论造成误导，请不要翻查字典。不认识的词请不要猜，空下即可。

Part A

1. I'm glad we had this opp _____（机会）to talk.

2. There are a doz _____（一打）eggs in the basket.

3. Every working person must pay income t _____（税）.

4. The pirates buried the trea _____（财宝）on a desert island.

5. Her beauty and ch _____（魅力）had a powerful effect on men.

6. La _____（缺乏）of rain led to a shortage of water in the city.

7. He takes cr _____（奶油）and sugar in his coffee.

8. The rich man died and left all his we _____（财富）to his son.

9. Pup _____（小学生们）must hand in their papers by the end of the week.

10. This sweater is too tight. It needs to be stret _____（撑大）.

11. Ann intro _____（介绍）her boyfriend to her mother.

12. Teenagers often adm _____（尊敬,崇拜）and worship pop singers.

13. If you blow up that balloon any more it will bu _____ （破裂）.

14. In order to be accepted into the university, he had to impr _____（改善）his grades.

15. The telegram was deli _____（传递,投递）two hours after it had been sent.

16. The differences were so sl _____（轻微）that they went unnoticed.

17. The dress you're wearing is lov _____（可爱）.

18. He wasn't very popu _____（受欢迎的）when he was a teenager, but he has many friends now.

Part B

1. He has a successful car _____（职业,事业）as a lawyer.

2. The thieves threw ac _____（酸性物质）in his face and made him blind.

3. To improve the country's economy, the government decided on economic ref _____（改革）.

4. She wore a beautiful green go _____（晚礼服,裙子）to the ball.

5. The government tried to protect the country's industry by reducing the imp _____（进口）of cheap goods.

6. The children's games were amusing at first, but finally got on the parents' ner _____（神经）.

7. The lawyer gave some wise coun _____（忠告,劝告）to his client.

8. Many people in England mow the la _____（草坪）of their houses on Sunday morning.

9. The farmer sells the eggs that his he _____（母鸡）lays.

10. Sudden noises at night sca _____（使……害怕）me a lot.

11. France was proc _____（宣布）a republic in the 18th century.

12. Many people are inj _____（受伤）in road accidents every year.

13. Suddenly he was thru _____（用力推）into the dark room.

14. He perc _____（感觉到,看到）a light at the end of the tunnel.

15. Children are not independent. They are att _____（黏着,紧挨）to their parents.

16. She showed off her sle _____（细长的,苗条的）figure in a long narrow dress.

17. She has been changing partners often because she cannot have a sta _____（稳定的）relationship with one person.

18. You must wear a bathing suit on a public beach. You're not allowed to bath na _____（裸体的,不穿衣服的）.

Part C

1. Soldiers usually swear an oa _____（誓言）of loyalty to their country.

2. The voter placed the ball _____（投票）in the box.

3. They keep their valuables in a vau _____（金库）at the bank.

4. A bird perched at the window led _____（架,突出物,窗台）.

5. The kitten is playing with a ball of ya _____（纱,线,毛线）.

6. The thieves have forced an ent _____（入口）into the building.

7. The small hill was really a burial mou _____（小丘,沙堆,墓冢）.

8. We decided to celebrate New Year's E _____ (除夕夜) together.

9. The soldier was asked to choose between infantry (步兵队) and cav _____ (骑兵队).

10. This is a complex problem that is difficult to compr _____ (理解).

11. The angry crowd sho _____ (用力推,推开,推挤) the prisoner as he was leaving the court.

12. Don't pay attention to this rude remark. Just ig _____ (忽视,不理) it.

13. The management held a secret meeting. The issues discussed were not disc _____ (揭露,泄露,显露) to the workers.

14. We could hear the sergeant (陆军中士) bel _____ (吼) commands(命令) to the troops.

15. The boss got angry with the secretary and it took a lot of tact (机智) to soo _____ (使……震惊,使……缓和) him.

16. We do not have adeq _____ (足够的) information to make a decision.

17. She is not a child, but a mat _____ (成熟的) woman. She can make her own decisions.

18. The prisoner was put in soli _____ (独自的,一人的) confinement (关押).

Part D

1. There has been a recent tr _____ (倾向,趋势) among prosperous families toward a smaller number of children.

2. The ar _____ (区域,面积) of his office is 25 square meters.

3. Phil _____ (哲学) examines the meaning of life.

4. According to the communist doc _____ (信条,教义), workers should rule the world.

5. Spending many years together deepened their inti _____ (亲密,亲近).

6. He usually read the sports sec _____ (部分)of the newspaper first.

7. Because of the doctors' strike,the cli _____ (诊所)is closed today.

8. There are several misprints on each page of this te _____ (课文).

9. The suspect(嫌犯)had both opportunity and mot _____ (动机)to commit the murder.

10. They insp _____ (检查,视察) all products before sending them out to stores.

11. A considerable amount of evidence was accum _____ (积累)during the investigation.

12. The victim's shirt was satu _____ (浸透)with blood.

13. He is irresponsible. You cannot re _____ (依靠)on him for help.

14. It's impossible to eva _____ (评价)these results without knowing about the research methods that were used.

15. He finally att _____ (达到,获得)a position of power in the company.

16. The story tells about a crime and subs _____ (随后的,作为结果的)punishment.

17. In a hom _____ (相同种类的,同性质的) class all students are of a similar proficiency(水平).

18. The urge to survive is inh _____ (天生的,先天的)in all creatures.

Part E

1. The baby is wet. Her dia _____ (尿片)needs changing.

2. The prisoner was released on par _____ (假释).

3. Second year university students in the US are called soph _____（大二学生）.

4. Her favourite flowers were or _____（兰花）.

5. The insect causes damage to plants by its toxic（有毒的）sec _____（分泌物）.

6. The evacu _____（撤离，疏散）of the building saved many lives.

7. For many people, wealth is a prospect of unimaginable felic _____（幸福）.

8. She found herself in a pred _____（困境）without any hope for a solution.

9. The deac _____（执事，信徒代表）helped with the care of the poor of the parish（新区居民）.

10. The hurricane whi _____（鞭打，席卷）along the coast.

11. Some coal was still smol _____（闷烧）among the ashes.

12. The dead bodies were mutil _____（把……切断）beyond recognition.

13. She was sitting on a balcony and bas _____（晒太阳）in the sun.

14. For years waves of invaders pill _____（掠夺）towns along the coast.

15. The rescue（营救）attempt could not proceed quickly. It was imp _____（妨碍）by bad weather.

16. I wouldn't hire him. He is unmotivated and indo _____（懒惰的）.

17. Computers have made typewriters old-fashioned and obs _____（赶不上时代的）.

18. Watch out for his wil _____（诡计多端的，狡猾的）tricks.

Appendix C
The Lex30 Test

请写出你从该词所能联想到的任何词（任何词都可以，没有限制）。请不要翻查字典。

例如：**feel**　　**sense**　　**numb**　　**smooth**　　**peel**

attack　　_____　_____　_____　_____

board　　_____　_____　_____　_____

close　　_____　_____　_____　_____

cloth　　_____　_____　_____　_____

dig　　_____　_____　_____　_____

dirty　　_____　_____　_____　_____

disease　　_____　_____　_____　_____

experience _____　_____　_____　_____

frui　　_____　_____　_____　_____

furniture　　_____　_____　_____　_____

habit　　_____　_____　_____　_____

hold　　_____　_____　_____　_____

hope　　_____　_____　_____　_____

kick　　_____　_____　_____　_____

map　　_____　_____　_____　_____

obey　　_____　_____　_____　_____

pot　　_____　_____　_____　_____

potato　　_____　_____　_____　_____

real　　_____　_____　_____　_____

rest   ———————— ———————— ———————— ————————

rice   ———————— ———————— ———————— ————————

science   ———————— ———————— ———————— ————————

seat   ———————— ———————— ———————— ————————

spell   ———————— ———————— ———————— ————————

substance   ———————— ———————— ———————— ————————

stupid   ———————— ———————— ———————— ————————

television   ———————— ———————— ———————— ————————

tooth   ———————— ———————— ———————— ————————

trade   ———————— ———————— ———————— ————————

window   ———————— ———————— ———————— ————————

Appendix D
Writing Task One

Please write a composition of no less than 200 words according to the topic below.（请不要翻查字典。）

经济发展往往是衡量一个国家成功与否的标准之一。但是也有人认为其他因素也很重要。你认为还有哪些因素？哪个因素是最重要的？

Appendix E
Writing Task Two

Please write a composition of no less than 200 words according to the topic below.（请不要翻查字典。）

好的性格是帮助人们取得成功的因素之一。但是一些人认为其他因素也很重要。你认为还有哪些因素？哪个因素是最重要的？

Appendix F
Word Association Test One

一、请写出你从该词所能联想到的任何词。（没有任何限制，任何词均可，请快速地写下自己的第一反应，在三分钟左右完成。）请不要翻查字典。

educate（*v.*）　_____　_____　_____

afraid（*adj.*）　_____　_____　_____

damage（*v.*）　_____　_____　_____

quickly（*adv.*）_____　_____　_____

especial（*adj.*）_____　_____　_____

shout（*n.*）　_____　_____　_____

happy（*adj.*）　_____　_____　_____

二、下列词符合哪一个选项，请选出。（如果选的是Ⅲ，Ⅳ，或Ⅴ，请在后面的横线上按该选项的要求填空）。请不要翻查字典。

Ⅰ. I don't remember having seen this word before.

Ⅱ. I have seen this word before but I don't know what it means.

Ⅲ. I have seen this word before and I think it means _____.（近义词或翻译）

Ⅳ. I know this word. It means _____.（近义词或翻译）

Ⅴ. I can use this word in a sentence, e.g. : _____.（请造句）

例如：apple   <u>V</u>   This apple tastes sweet and sour.

educate（*v.*） _____ _____

afraid（*adj.*） _____ _____

damage（*v.*） _____ _____

quickly（*adv.*） _____ _____

especial（*adj.*） _____ _____

shout（*n.*） _____ _____

happy（*adj.*） _____ _____

Appendix G
Word Association Test Two

一、请写出你从该词所能联想到的任何词。（没有任何限制，任何词均可，请快速地写下自己的第一反应，在三分钟左右完成。）请不要翻查字典。

civilize（v.）　　　_____　　　_____　　　_____

cowardly（adj.）　_____　　　_____　　　_____

wreck（v.）　　　　_____　　　_____　　　_____

amused（adj.）　　_____　　　_____　　　_____

hastily（adv.）　　_____　　　_____　　　_____

peculiar（adj.）　　_____　　　_____　　　_____

roar（n.）　　　　　_____　　　_____　　　_____

二、下列词符合哪一个选项，请选出。（如果选的是Ⅲ，Ⅳ，或Ⅴ，请在后面的横线上按该选项的要求填空）。不要翻查字典。

Ⅰ. I don't remember having seen this word before.

Ⅱ. I have seen this word before but I don't know what it means.

Ⅲ. I have seen this word before and I think it means _____.（近义词或翻译）

Ⅳ. I know this word. It means _____.（近义词或翻译）

Ⅴ. I can use this word in a sentence，e. g. :_____.（请造句）

例如：apple   __V__ This apple tastes sweet and sour.

civilize（*v.*） _____ _____

cowardly（*adj.*）_____ _____

wreck（*v.*） _____ _____

amused（*adj.*） _____ _____

hastily（*adv.*） _____ _____

peculiar（*adj.*）_____ _____

roar（*n.*）   _____ _____

Closing Remarks

Free active vocabulary is an important aspect in ESL learning. However, the threshold phenomenon seems to be a big obstacle in FAV development. This research project aims to have a deeper and more comprehensive investigation into the phenomenon. It is expected that the research could help ESL teachers and learners obtain a better understanding of the threshold's occurrence, features, and inner mechanism. It is also expected that the research can provide some guidance in teaching and learning to tackle the threshold problem. Although the proposed questions have been well answered, the research has led to new queries that need to be explored and answered in future studies. Therefore, this research is not an end, but rather a commencement opening up more possibilities for future research.